Corporate Tribalism

Corporate Tribalism

*White Men/White Women
and Cultural Diversity at Work*

THOMAS KOCHMAN AND
JEAN MAVRELIS

THE UNIVERSITY OF CHICAGO PRESS   CHICAGO AND LONDON

THOMAS KOCHMAN and JEAN MAVRELIS founded Kochman Mavrelis Associates in 1986 as a merger of Kochman Communication Consultants and Jean Mavrelis Associates. Thomas Kochman is the author of *Black and White Styles in Conflict,* published in 1981 by the University of Chicago Press. Jean Mavrelis is the author of numerous articles on gender, culture, and leadership.

The University of Chicago Press, Chicago 60637
The University of Chicago Press, Ltd., London
© 2009 by The University of Chicago
All rights reserved. Published 2009
Printed in the United States of America

17 16 15 14 13 12 11 10 09   1 2 3 4 5

ISBN-13: 978-0-226-44957-9 (cloth)

ISBN-10: 0-226-44957-2 (cloth)

Library of Congress Cataloging-in-Publication Data

Kochman, Thomas.
    Corporate tribalism : white men/white women and cultural diversity at work / Thomas Kochman and Jean Mavrelis.
        p. cm.
    Includes bibliographical references and index.
    ISBN-13: 978-0-226-44957-9 (cloth: alk. paper)
    ISBN-10: 0-226-44957-2 (cloth: alk. paper)
    1. Diversity in the workplace. 2. Intercultural communication. 3. Cultural awareness.
4. Whites—Attitudes. I. Mavrelis, Jean. II. Title.
    HF5549.5.M5K63 2009
    331.11'43—dc22   2008031033

♾ The paper used in this publication meets the minimum requirements of the American National Standard for Information Sciences—Permanence of Paper for Printed Library Materials, ANSI Z39.48-1992.

FOR BILL MAVRELIS, SHEP MAVRELIS, ALLEN HARRIS, SANDOR LOEVY, TAALIB-DIN MAHDI AND ILYA ADLER — BROTHERS WHO WENT BEFORE.

Contents

Preface

This book owes much to many: most of all to the KMA (Kochman Mavrelis Associates, Inc.) team of diversity trainers whose voices resonate throughout this book. They are Kenneth Addison, Ilya Adler, Leah Arndt, Margaret Brigham, Cynthia Bryant Pitts, Adrian Chan, Tatyana Fertelmeyster, Gudy Grewal, Barry Mar, Robin Payne, Lan Nguyen Roberts, and Wageh Saad. Many will find in the book the things they say in course of the training. For reasons of style, we don't cite them as often as we use their words or ideas. We are also indebted to others who have shared their perspectives and life experiences with us: Denise Ajeto, Aloria Ashley, Brigette Blair, Bobbie Bowman, Ellen Boyer, Carole Carmichael, Shelly De Jesus, Maggie Finch, Susan Goldberg, Rose Hampton, Faye Belson Hardin, Lisa Holt, Ramona Hopkins, Adrienne Kochman, Wanda Lloyd, Sandor Loevy, Taalib Din Mahdi, Jacqui Love Marshall, Cristina Mavrelis, Sandy Meade, Mae Killebrew Mosley, Maria Nicholson, Sharon Rosenhause, Doris Salomón, Yuri Shishido, Louise Stone, Geri Tucker, Joyce Tucker, Yvonne Vargas, Cynthia Velasco, David Yarnold, Steven Zuckerman, and the women of the Society of Women Engineers, Mujeres Latinos in Acción, and Amigas Latinas. We also want to especially thank Adrian Chan for his valuable feedback during the writing process and our editor, David Brent—and lifelong thanks to Mary Doheny and David Gross.

There are also the voices of those diverse groups that have gone through KMA training. The report of their individual and collective experiences, issues, and concerns at work have added greatly to the information we present here and generated many of the quotes that are used parenthetically throughout the book. Their testimony also serves to illustrate and document our social and cultural understanding of what is going on for them and other groups in today's corporate workplace. Endnotes of matters of record and case examples are also provided, respectively, as documentation and support for the patterns of difference discussed in the book.

Introduction

What this book offers is a greater understanding than exists to date of the social and cultural conflicts that happen when different groups interact with each other within corporate America and within the U.S. society at large. Drawing on extensive research conducted with many different groups, we are able to pinpoint areas of disagreement and suggest better strategies for working intergroup conflict than are in place now. We also enable readers to look at the relative comfort/fit that members of different groups experience at work owing to differences between their culture and the dominant U.S. mainstream ("Anglo") corporate culture. At another level—because both of us are advocating, as social change agents, greater parity and social inclusion for different groups—we also advocate looking for multicultural (rather than assimilationist) solutions to social adjustment issues.

For example, multicultural solutions work both sides of the fence—the accommodation process is reciprocal—toward outcomes based on what is culturally at stake for the parties involved. Assimilationist solutions work one side of the fence—the accommodation process is unilateral—favoring the culture of the dominant group. At best, assimilationist solutions work to build a bridge between the subordinate culture (that of newcomers or outsiders) and the host culture, such as might happen with immigrants in the United States in an ESL (English as a Second Language) class. More often than not, assimilationist "solutions" simply thrust outsiders and newcomers into new host cultural settings and let them muddle through as best they can.

How Each Part of the Book Is Different

The first part of the book—written by Kochman—is about U.S. corporate white men (hereafter CWM) and understanding what is going on between CWM and others in the U.S. workplace. The second part of the book—written by Mavrelis—is about U.S. corporate white women (hereafter CWW) and not only what is going on between them and members of other groups in the U.S. workplace but also what is going on within and among CWW themselves. The starting point for each group, their relative influence within U.S. companies, their social and cultural agendas and issues, and the growth work that each group needs to do to create social parity and develop multicultural flexibility are quite different. Consequently, because CWM and CWW stand alone as well as together, they should be treated as such when they do: at times sharing the same platform, at times not. In that respect, the two parts of the book demonstrate, as well as argue for, the principle that multicultural solutions need to respect and understand what is at stake for all parties involved.

Following the same path, the book reflects the different individual/cultural styles of the two authors. The Kochman part on CWM is written in the third person and moves forward in linear fashion, reflecting what Deborah Tannen has referred to as "competitive, alternating speaker listener [CWM] 'report' talk." The Mavrelis part on CWW is written in the first person and moves forward in a more circular fashion, often as part of a contextual narrative reflecting what Tannen calls "cooperative, consensus building [CWW] 'rapport' talk."[1] In respect of these differences—having both cultural styles represented—the book also enables each author to communicate in ways that allow them to be authentically who they are.

Methodology and Approach

The research perspective and approach used in both parts has its roots in the social sciences, specifically, anthropology and sociolinguistics. That means, as participant/observers and researchers, we do not just look at what people do—their patterns of behavior—but also try to figure out what values, principles, or rules shape and drive that behavior. We also know that these are different for different groups of people. The other thing that we know is that people do not have an upfront awareness of what shapes their attitudes or worldview or the rules that drive or govern their behavior. For example, if you asked people what they do that they consider "work" and what they do that they consider "play," they could probably give you a list pretty quickly. But if you asked them what makes work "work" and what makes play "play"—attitudes, values, or cultural features that underlie and define each category for them—that would require a deeper level of probing, reflection, and analysis.

Our job as researchers is to work with members of different groups and to make explicit what for them is culturally implicit. Our discussions with them are interactive and facilitative: we talk to people to find out how they see things. We also pay close attention to how they talk about what they see and how they behave. We then take what we have heard and observed and formulate a cultural understanding of what we think is going on for them. We then reflect that understanding back to them. This process is called ethnographic. Their participant role in the research is to accept or reject our formulations and make suggestions on what they think needs to change. Validation comes when they acknowledge and affirm that what we have theorized about what is going on for them matches up with what they think is going on for them. Social scientists call this construct validity. Further validation comes when our theoretical formulation is confirmed by members of that group throughout the United States and from other researchers doing similar work with the same groups.

Training Sessions

The training sessions that we have conducted in U.S. companies have been mainly at the management level. The racial, ethnic, gender makeup of these groups has been preponderantly CWM, followed by (in descending numerical order) CWW; African Americans; East, Southeast, and South Asians; and Hispanics. In any single training session, in a group of thirty or more, the total number of African American, Hispanic, and Asian managers together rarely exceeds six. Many times members of one or another of these groups are absent altogether. In laying down a foundation for the research findings offered here, the presentations and participant feedback that we receive at company training sessions have allowed us to augment and refine our theoretical formulations. They have also given us an opportunity to test for cultural consistency with members of the same race, ethnic, and gender groups in different parts of the United States. They have also been a gathering place for new information. One of the assignments that we give in our program—we call it social mapping—breaks people into different groups along lines of race, ethnicity, and gender—more recently, also, transgender and sexual orientation—and asks them what it is like to be them as a member of their group working within the company. The focus here is on experiences, issues, and concerns. At times, we have also asked them to list their pet peeves of members of other groups, as well as their own, to say not only what bothers them, but also why. We have also asked people at different times to talk about what they value about themselves that they leave at the door when they come into work, what they would like members of other groups to know about them that they think others do not know or do not know well enough, and why it is important to their group that others know this about them.

The information that has come from these groups over the past twenty or more years has been remarkably consistent for the same race, gender, and ethnic groups—and in the last five years, for LGBT (lesbian, gay, bisexual, and transgender) groups as well—within different U.S. companies, both in establishing reliability for the culturally based patterns of difference that our research has developed as well as in identifying issues around comfort/fit with the culture of the company within which they work. As might be expected the workplace agendas of members of each racial, ethnic, gender, or LGBT group—while consistent within their own group—are quite different from each other. Part of this has to do with the different experiences that each group has at work as it relates to comfort/fit. Part of it also has to do with the different social experiences and cultural influences that members of these groups bring into the workplace. At the same time, the amount of research that we have been able to do with these groups has been uneven. Consequently, the amount of coverage that different groups get in the book—in direct proportion to the research that we have been able to do with them—is not the same. But rather than wait until we have been able to equalize things, we thought that we would present what we know here, even as we recognize that there is yet much more work to do.

We expect the audience for this book to be similar to those that attend our workshops—with similar misgivings over generalizations that are being made about people in groups. The initial (knee-jerk) response to generalizations is to see them as stereotypes and, as such, socially inadmissible. Also, because mainstream people within the United States hear generalizations as applying to all members of a group, they often dismiss them out of hand, based on the supposition that no generalization is likely to be true for every member of a group. The generalizations we make about groups of people are not stereotypes, of course, yet the predisposition of the general U.S. public to see them that way introduces an element of resistance that, if not addressed at the outset, will negatively affect how the information will be received. As in a court of law, questions over the admissibility of evidence need to be addressed before the evidence itself can be considered.

The way we deal with the resistant attitude toward generalizations in training is to start by asking the group the question: "How many people in this room are suspicious about generalizations made about people in groups?" The group agreement with that statement, through a show of hands, is almost total. We then ask, "Would it be a good generalization to say that people in this room are suspicious of generalizations made about people in groups?" People laugh and concede the point that not all generalizations about people in groups must automatically or necessarily be wrong. We then ask the group to examine more closely what it is about stereotyping that they find objectionable. Typically, it is the accusatory tone behind the characterization and that it is leveled at all members of a group by someone outside the group, as in men saying to women, "Ah! You women are all too emotional." We then ask them if the group characterization would be more acceptable if the accusatory tone were taken out of it, as in "Maybe women *are* more in touch with their feelings than men," or if we allow that there are those who identify themselves as members of a particular group but, at the individual level, do not feel that any particular group characterization applies, as in Eric Liu's example, "There was plenty about Dad, after all, that didn't fit anybody's stereotype of 'Chinese character.'"[2] Finally, we ask the group not to allow their understanding of cultural differences to be sidetracked by questions of their applicability—how many members of one or another group own or embrace these patterns. To that end we say things like "That the patterns of difference may not be true for *all* members a group, doesn't make them less true for those who *do* feel represented by them" and "Not talking about differences doesn't make them go away." We then introduce the term and concept "cultural archetype" to describe patterns of difference that ethnic group insiders would agree are true, authentic, and representative of the culture of the group and show in the following list how archetyping is different from stereotyping:

Archetypes	Stereotypes
Scientifically generated through the "ethnographic" process.	Nonscientific characterizations.
A shared value, pattern, or attitude that insiders would accept as representative of a significant number of members of their group.	An outsider's view of another group's behavior.
A descriptive generalization that is applicable to many members of a group: one that represents learned values, beliefs, and assumptions.	An abusive generalization applied to all members of that group: often assumed to reflect innate characteristics.
Strategic goal behind archetyping promotes social inclusion, right/left thinking, and more open communication.	Strategic goal behind stereotyping promotes social exclusion, right/wrong thinking, and closed or restrictive communication.
Behavior: Insiders look at the behavior of members of their group and can say with greater authority what that behavior probably means based on greater knowledge of (and access to) other members of that group.	Behavior: Outsiders look at the behavior of another group and can only speculate on what that other group's behavior means because they have only their own cultural standard to draw on as reference.

We have also found that a good way to deal with the question of cultural representation within any particular group—anthropologists often use the term "salience"—is to show a bell-shaped curve (fig. 1) and talk about which group members might find themselves in the middle of the curve and which members, because of their different socialization, might be considered outliers. We make the case that those in the middle of the bell-shaped curve—not the outliers—would represent the cultural view of that group often drawing on surveys to document the point.

Among the things we discuss are that the bell shape of the curve would be greater (fewer outliers) for first-generation immigrants and ethnic minorities living in relatively segregated areas than for second-, third-, and

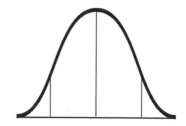

FIGURE 1. The bell-shaped curve

fourth-generation immigrants and ethnic minorities who are more assimilated to the U.S. mainstream culture. We also note that there might even be outliers among natives from within their own country with respect to the dominant cultural patterns of the group. For example, in one survey, the response of Anglos to the statement, "When the day comes for a young man to take a job, he should stay near his parents, even if it means losing a good opportunity" was 97 percent disagreement, 3 percent agreement.[3] The percentage of agreement of Mexican-Americans was 24 percent. We also cite a survey that asked the question, "Do you expect to rely on your children for financial support in your old age?" to Japanese and Anglo (U.S.) parents and produced the following pattern of agreement. In Japan, 90 percent of those surveyed said yes. In the United States, 90 percent of Anglos surveyed said no. While we have not been able to find the source for this particular survey, Sussman and Romeis found that "three-fourths of Japan's elderly, 65 years of age and older, live with their children.... These compare to 25 percent for the U.S."[4] While these percentages do not match the level of response in the survey, they show the power of culture to shape reality within the two societies. In both surveys the respective 97 percent and 90 percent Anglo level of response falls within the center of the bell curve. The weight of their representation within each of the groups qualifies them as "cultural." The 3 percent and 10 percent responses would fall among the outliers. They do not have sufficient representation within the group to qualify as "cultural."

While making this point, we also ask the participants in the U.S. training session parenthetically how many of them expect (or plan) to rely on their children for financial support in their old age. In over twenty years of training we have only had one U.S. participant, a CWM newspaper city editor, say that he planned to rely on his children for financial support. However, he reconsidered his position after checking with his children that night. Following our presentation of the results of the survey we also ask what the participants believe is, culturally speaking, driving the level of agreement/disagreement. In that regard, U.S. participants sometimes say that aging parents, because of circumstances, may have to rely on their children for financial support in their old age. We then explain, however, that the reality of *having to* rely on children is different from *expecting* and *planning to* rely on children for financial support in old age regardless of circumstances. Likewise, family circumstances in East Asian families may be such that children are not able to support or have their parents live with them, but that doesn't necessarily change their expectation or that of their parents that children should.

A good marker of the cultural difference and a way to introduce the power of culture is who would experience shame/guilt in the two situations. In the U.S. setting, it would be parents who would be the ones to feel shame or guilt at having to rely on their children insofar as that repudiates the U.S. mainstream cultural values of independence and self-reliance. In East Asian societies, it would be the children who would experience shame/guilt at not being able to support their parents in their old age insofar as it repudiates the cultural value of filial piety—as Doi says with respect to Japan: "The tradition of repaying one's *on,* that is, one's spiritual debts . . . to one's parents."[5] Consistent with the views expressed here, an AARP survey showed Asian Americans expressing the most guilt (72 percent) for not having done more for their aging parents, followed by Hispanics (65 percent), African Americans (54 percent), and non-Hispanic whites (44 percent).[6] In the Chandler survey, the Mexican American agreement with the statement, "When the day comes for a young man to take a job, he should stay near his parents, even if it means losing a good opportunity" was 24 percent. This level of agreement, while significantly different from the Anglo 3 percent agreement with this question is lower than we might expect given the importance of family—and family cohesiveness—within Mexican and Mexican American culture. In explaining the 24 percent agreement (or 76 percent disagreement), we might cite the influence of Anglo U.S. mainstream culture or economic circumstances that force people to move away. Again, the level of shame/guilt that individuals experience when circumstances force them to act in one or another way is a good indicator of their cultural position. Another is the way people rationalize things that happen. One Mexican American woman told us—she was one of two that left her community to graduate from college—that the other person to leave had an accident at college and died. The community reaction to the news was that "if he didn't leave the community, that wouldn't have happened."

Another social criterion for determining the cultural currency or salience of any particular position is who would have to explain or defend their position to their coworkers or friends. In the first example, the 3 percent of Anglos who agreed to "stay near their parents even if it meant losing a good opportunity" would probably have to defend their position. The 97 percent would not because their responses fall into the category of "received wisdom" or "common sense." Likewise, Mexican Americans who left their family to move away when economic circumstance did not require it would probably have to explain or justify that decision to their more traditional coworkers or friends. In the second example, Japanese parents who were not planning to rely on their children for financial support would probably need to explain themselves. In the United States, it would be those parents who *were* planning to rely on their children for support in old age.

Having addressed in this introduction the resistance factor found within the training group—and perhaps also within readers of this book—we consider in detail cultural differences along race, ethnic, and gender lines in what follows.

PART I

CWM and the New Social Order
Players in Search of a Role

This section of the book is about CWM at work and others who want to understand them better than they do. It is also about understanding conflicts between CWM, CWW, and others in the workplace owing to different cultural styles and social experiences. Finally, it is about creating a socially inclusive workforce at all levels of the organization and about becoming better cross-cultural managers, strategists, marketers, and communicators.

CHAPTER ONE

CWM and Corporate Diversity Initiatives

CWM in the United States often feel that corporate diversity initiatives do not include them—that "diversity is about everyone else but them" or that "they are the ones who now have to understand others, but others don't have to understand them." At face value, neither of these statements is true. CWM are key players in any organization, and the success of diversity initiatives needs their creative involvement just as it does the creative involvement of others. Moreover, members of other groups have spent decades leaving their different culture at the doorstep of the U.S. mainstream workplace to try to adopt or adapt to a cultural style that mainly fits and serves CWM. CWM miss the extent to which others have had to change their ways to accommodate them, so it seems now that the onus of having to change falls only on them. CWM, looking for others to ante up, fail to notice that the money of others is already in the pot.

But to argue the truth of what is being said, in many ways, is beside the point. The real issue is the distress that CWM feel over the idea that the world is changing, and to keep pace, CWM have to change in ways that they haven't had to before, when the "name of the game" was, in most respects, doing it *their* way. CWM don't see things as having been their way because, as with anyone, they are not aware of what they *didn't* have to change about themselves in order to fit into the U.S. corporate culture. They have been aware of things that they *did* have to change about themselves as individuals, however, and feel that this is on a par with everyone else. They may, down the road, ultimately find out that this is not the case—that others have had to struggle much more than they to achieve a sense of comfort/fit within the U.S. workplace. But right now CWM are where they are, and where they are is to see themselves as having to bear the principal brunt of change. The following statement of anguish essentially captures this view. It is titled "The White Male Tale of Woe." Hardy Freeman suggested that "woe" also works as an acronym for "Was Once Entitled." "Owe" (Once Was Entitled) probably works at some level, too.

The White Male Tale of Woe

Ok. What used to be the way it was is no longer the way it is. And it looks like it's not going to go back to the way it was for us. Not ever. Ouch!

Not that the "way it was" was ever that great. It was just easier to accept when it wasn't, because that's the way it was (or wasn't) for everyone—you know, like the Great Depression.

But now it looks like it's not going to be there for us when that's not the same for everyone else. And that's what really hurts.

Not only are others getting stuff that used to be ours, they're getting it when we aren't.

And it's basically other white guys that are the ones doing it to us. You know— senior-level guys who are there to make sure that everyone is getting part of the action. Except that it's not their action that they're giving away. It's ours. They've already got theirs.

And another thing, Try getting some sympathy for how you feel. When you happen to get to talk about this stuff—which you generally don't—all those other folks say, "Hey, you don't like it! Tough! Welcome to the club! What do you think it's been like for us all these years while you were hogging it all for yourselves. The problem is that you white guys think that you deserve all that you used to get then, and don't deserve what you're getting now, even though you're still getting more than anyone else. I mean, get real!"

You see. Not only isn't there any sympathy for what you're going through, you can't even get consideration. Also, I don't know who they're talking about when they talk about "You white guys." I know they're not talking about me and what I'm getting. I'm not living high on the hog and no one ever handed me anything on a silver platter. Also, what I got, I earned!

And what they're complaining about in the past—I wasn't the one that did that to them. I wasn't even born then. And what about the "sins of the fathers not being visited on the sons."

I mean, give me a break.

But all they can think about now is themselves, what *they* had and still have to go through and how it's now *their* turn.

Ok. I've said my piece. This is the new reality. This is what I have to take and live with. Just don't tell me I need to take it easy.

So the worm is turning, and white men are squirming. Where do we go from here? CWM do have a point about being misunderstood and misrepresented. Other groups do not understand them well or as well as they need to. And CWM hardly know or understand members of other groups at all. So maybe we can start there: everyone needing to know more about each other than they presently do to try to find better ways to create comfort/fit working together.

Understanding CWM

The sentiments expressed in the "White Male Tale of Woe" reflect the pressures that CWM feel trying to reconcile individual and family self-interest with company-wide diversity initiatives. As one senior executive said, "You want to do what's right for the company. But you also don't want it to be you personally that has to take the hit." This statement and the tension that develops from it is at the heart of the matter at work and in the larger society. There are other issues as well. CWM, accustomed to competition from other CWM, are now also being challenged by CWW and people of color for positions that previously fell within their domain. At the interpersonal level, CWM have to cope with the general view of them from other groups, as "racist, sexist, till they prove they're not" or as privileged members of the "good old boy network." There are also pressures to become more attuned and effective dealing with people issues. At the personal level, they may have to come to grips with the discomfort that comes with the realization that there is a social advantage to being a CWM relative to other groups that undermines the image they have of themselves as "sharing" and "wanting to be fair" and as being basically "decent, good guys." CWM are also accustomed to being praised and admired and have a strong wish to be liked that often gets in the way of having to make decisions on hiring and promotion where the person who didn't get what they wanted or expected hates them. The unhappy choice for CWM today is whom they would rather have hating them, CWW and people of color or other CWM.

Historically, they have endured, and in many cases, become inured to, the hatred and anger of white women and people of color. Actively pushing and promoting diversity, however, in effect, now asks CWM to also endure the anger and hatred of other CWM. For CWM, this is a much harder pill to swallow, especially if it puts their social standing with other CWM at risk. As one CWM said, "It's not much of a group, but it's the only group I have." Apart from matters relating to their own individual self-interest, the personal willingness or reluctance of CWM to endure the anger and hatred of others of their own group is key to the ultimate success or failure of diversity initiatives. Our colleague Ken Addison said, "There is one set of issues when you're falling from a height and another set of issues when you're crawling out of a hole." With regard to the latter situation, Paulette Brown, a member of the American Bar Association said, on women of color leaving law firms, "We're not even talking about trying to get up through a glass ceiling; we're trying to stay above ground."[1] The social/cultural story here is about CWM on a height peering over a precipice. It is also about trying to weigh and balance their issues and interests against diverse others in an increasingly competitive world and workplace.

African Americans, Hispanics, and Asian Americans typically see CWM at work as members of a group much the same way they see themselves: as having a strong communal identity and personal ties to other members of their group. None of that is true of CWM. A place of gathering of CWM at work is not so much an oasis, as it is for members of other groups, as it is a parking place—organized more around separation and individuation than reciprocal loyalty and connection. Social etiquette manifests itself there as "I do for me and you do for you," not "I do for you and you do for me" or the more tribal and familial "one for all and all for one." Consideration of other CWM in that context is reflected by showing courtesy, to be sure, but more pointedly, not intruding on each other's time and space. By way of contrast, the standard cultural protocol for CWW shows consideration of others through caretaking: active involvement and concern with the emotional state and well-being of others. The view that others have of CWM misses that the group that CWM might individually identify with—to the extent that they do—is outside of work: typically one or another immigrant ethnic group (residues from the U.S. "melting pot"—Jewish, German, Irish, Italian, Polish, etc.) or regional group (e.g., southerners). At work, CWM relate to each other as a collection of individuals, not as members of a white male group.

The general litmus test for determining whether you have a member of group identity is whether you, as an individual, feel implicated by what other members of your group do. In that regard, each CWM feels, by and large, responsible only for what he does or has done as an individual, not for what other white men have done. This is in stark contrast to the more ethnic/tribal view of members of other groups who do feel implicated by what other members of their group do. Compare the different group responses to Milwaukee serial killer Jeffrey Dahmer (white) and the Washington DC sniper shooters, John Allen Muhammad (African American) and Lee Boyd Malvo (Jamaican). No U.S. white man thought that he was personally implicated by what Dahmer had done. Likewise, no white man in the United States felt personally implicated by the actions of Timothy McVeigh in Oklahoma City. To white men in the United States, the fact that Dahmer and McVeigh also happened to be white men was irrelevant. White men said, "That was Dahmer and McVeigh. That wasn't me!" However, in the African American and Jamaican communities, the talk was filled with consternation and astonishment on the discovery that the snipers were, respectively, African American and Jamaican. African Americans and Jamaicans said, "Why did it have to be one of *us.*" African Americans added, "We never do serial killing. That's a white thing!" Likewise the Korean community response to the Virginia Tech shooter, Cho Seung-Hui, was "When Yung Yang, a South Korean–born secretary in Annandale, heard the first rumors that the man who had slaughtered 32 people at Virginia Tech University was Asian, she said a fervent prayer: 'Please don't let him turn out to be Korean.'"[2] Other Koreans responded in similar fashion, most notably, South Korea's ambassador to Washington, Lee Tae Shik, who said, "The Korean American community needed to 'repent' . . . to prove that Koreans were a 'worthwhile ethnic minority in America.'"[3]

Within the workplace, each CWM is primarily out for himself. In the broader social context, white men can be out for themselves without shame or guilt (or without being labeled "selfish" by other CWM). By way of contrast, when our colleague Ilya Adler asked his class of Mexican college students whom they thought Anglos referred to when they spoke of "looking out for number one," their responses ranged from "family" to "boss," to "mother" and were shocked when told that each U.S. CWM meant himself when "looking out for number one."

Despite their representation in high-level positions, CWM do not attribute their success to having been members of a white male group, but, rather, to individual qualities and forms of preparation that enabled them to take advantage of opportunities at different times in their life. Given the disproportionate representation of CWM in high-level positions as compared with other groups, a question might be why they don't see their own race and gender as having been more instrumental in enabling them to reach those positions. Part of the answer stems from the social contexts in which CWM customarily operate.

Self/Group Awareness

Self/group awareness for CWM, as for others, is context sensitive. It is within the United States that CWM imagine themselves to be a collection of individuals and not members of group. When traveling outside the United States or when finding themselves to be in the minority in a social context within the United States, this self/group awareness changes. Abroad, the group that CWM identify themselves as a member of is "American," and in that context CWM do feel implicated by what other "Americans" do. As one CWM said who spent time abroad, "I was in a café when a very loud and boisterous couple came into the café in stereotypically 'Ugly American' fashion." I said to my wife, 'I hope they don't sit down next to us.'" Inside the United States, CWM primarily become aware of their own race/gender when those features distinguish themselves from surrounding others—especially if they feel targeted or at risk, as when making the proverbial "wrong turn" on the freeway and ending up in a black neighborhood. We refer to this event in our training as "driving while white." They may also be aware of their gender when they are the only man among a group of women. The CWM race/gender aspect of self/group awareness is ephemeral, however. It ends when CWM leave the nonmainstream group or neighborhood and return to customary and familiar mainstream social surrounds.

Sometimes race/gender self/awareness is more permanently etched on the CWM psyche. In training sessions when I ask CWM if they see themselves as a tribe or ethnic group or as a collection of individuals, their typical response is to see themselves as a collection of individuals. In one session, however, one CWM saw himself as a "member of a [white male] group." Since his response was atypical, I asked him where he grew up. He said South Africa. Within the South African context, notwithstanding the dominant social position of whites, he was very much aware of himself as a targeted "other." Like CWM in the United States, he had a subjective sense of self, but he also had internalized an objective sense of himself as a member of a group—as others saw him—not just how he saw himself. In another session, a Dutchman gave an example of having been in Mozambique during the South African elections when the white candidate opposing Nelson Mandela was ahead in the voting. He said a young white man came into the room, all excited, and said, "The white *tribe* is winning!" CWM in the United States don't typically think of themselves that way, operating as they do within dominant social contexts where CWM race/gender—add also culture—is normative. When those contexts change, so does CWM awareness of their own race, gender and culture—accentuated when CWM feel targeted or at risk.

Luke Visconti, one of the founders of the *DiversityInc* online newsletter, represents himself objectively as a member of a white male group in the title of his special features column: "Ask the White Guy." But his choice of that title, as he put it, "is meant to be ironic," which suggests an element of choice and detachment not available to those whose socially programmed objective sense of self is often a matter of survival.[4] I was again reminded of the different social risk that I experience compared to my African American friend when I told him that I would leave an envelope that he wanted in my mailbox for him to pick up. He balked at the suggestion, saying, "How is it going to look: a black man going through someone else's mailbox in a predominantly white neighborhood? I don't think so."

While CWM see themselves in the United States as a collection of individuals, they see everyone else as members of a group before they ever see them as individuals. Seeing a white woman, CWM mark only for gender—white being the dominant and socially normative category—but they will also mark for race and ethnicity if the woman is African American, Asian, or Hispanic. Seeing men, CWM mark African Americans, Asians, and Hispanics only for race and ethnicity, not gender. This view of others as members of a group along race/ethnic/gender lines has implications for a more collective CWM race/gender self/member group awareness. If there is awareness of *them,* there must also be awareness at some level of (not) *us.* But this awareness is different from the more upfront objective sense of race and gender that CWM experience and exhibit when they are the minority. In contexts where CWM are the dominant majority group, as in the corporate workplace, their view of others as *them,* accompanied by a subjective sense of self and group as a collection of individuals, blocks or clouds CWM self/group race/gender awareness. Thus, if you showed

CWM a picture of a corporate boardroom consisting only of CWM and asked, "What's wrong with this picture?" they typically would not say that "the group consists only of CWM." Or when CWM complain about having to take race and gender into account when hiring or promoting individuals to new positions, the race and gender that they have in mind is that of white women and people of color, not their own.

There are times when the CWM implicit sense of self/group race and gender surfaces. But here again it is framed in terms of *them*—the *us,* to the extent that it exists, is masked. For example, in one training session a CWM reported that, of his seven-person work group, the last four people he hired were African American women. In reporting this he made it clear, however, that he did not hire them because they were African American but because they were the "best qualified" for the job. After he hired the fourth African American woman, however, another CWM came to him and said that he was taking the company diversity initiative "too seriously." Since it was not his intent to hire on the basis of race or gender, he was taken aback at the suggestion that they were "diversity hires." His attempt to hire people regardless of race, ethnicity, and gender was seen by the other CWM—and this is the archetypical CWM position—as hiring on the basis of race, ethnicity, and gender. This inescapable, more general, CWM view of others as *them* implicates a subtle, but nonetheless real, CWM self/group race/gender awareness of (not) *us.* Apart from what that example says about CWM self/group race/gender awareness, it also speaks to the personal struggle that CWM individually face when promoting diversity within the company. Questions arise: What will the CWM who hired the four African American women do the next time a position opens? Will he still hire the "best qualified" without regard to race, ethnicity, and gender, or now that he is more cognizant of how that will look to other CWM will he give in to their implicit request and find a way to make sure that his next hire is a CWM? And if he doesn't, what will his social standing be within that group?

The above example also illustrates the way the social exclusion of members of other groups happens. Extending Heidi Hartman's definition of patriarchy,[5] the solidarity of white men is achieved in opposition to (or against) other race/ethnic/gender groups—Hartman was talking about male solidarity against women—rather than as loyalty to or preference for members of their own race/ethnic/gender group. This distinction is important insofar as it establishes that the criteria that qualify people for social exclusion—race, ethnicity, and gender—are not, at least on the surface, the criteria that qualify people for social inclusion. For example, if everyone who walks through the door is a CWM, then race and gender become nonissues and, as such, disappear from the radar screen. What begins to matter then is everything but race, ethnicity, and gender. That is why CWM can say that it wasn't their race and gender that got them hired and promoted, but rather, individual qualities, good preparation, and being in the right place at the right time. What CWM do not connect or equate is the race/gender disqualification of others with race/gender preferential consideration for themselves. Reitman calls this lack of racial awareness or color blindness a form of whitewashing. However, in the high tech environment she studied, color blindness seems to have been applicable to everyone. As she put it, "The nonracist model of colorblindness encouraged employees to ignore the racial identities of their colleagues as well as their own." This orientation belies what is going on culturally for CWM in the United States, which is to be color blind with respect to their own race/ethnicity/gender but not that of others. In this regard Reitman's comment that "Bill's whiteness allowed his race to disappear behind his individualism, while John's Asianness became the center of caricatured attention" is—except in her use of the verb "allowed"—more reflective of CWM cultural reality.[6] Similarly, Dyer writes, "[Whites] will speak of . . . the blackness or Chineseness of friends, neighbors, colleagues, customers or clients . . . but we don't mention the whiteness of the white people we know."[7]

Even when CWM acknowledge that the disqualification of others ultimately leaves only CWM in the "hunt" (as one CWM put it), since CWM relate to these matters as individuals, they contend that they were still in a competitive situation even if the pool consisted only of other CWM. As such, it did not guarantee that they *individually* would benefit from the exclusion of members of other groups from the candidate pool. Moreover, because they were in a competitive situation CWM argue that, as individuals, each of them still "earned what they got."

This framing of the situation enables CWM not only to think of themselves as having gotten promoted or rewarded (or promoting or rewarding other white men) entirely on the basis of individual merit. It also accounts for why they resent and resist the charge leveled at them by other groups of being "privileged." To the charge that "90 percent of corporate boardrooms consist of CWM," CWM respond, "Yeah, but that's not me!" But while this way of framing the situation may give CWM a temporary respite from and protection against the charge of "privilege" leveled at them, it is

not satisfying—not at all to members of other groups who look at CWM
in a state of disbelief at their not making the connection between the exclusion of non-CWM on the basis of race, ethnicity, and gender and CWM
inclusion on the basis of their race and gender. But it is also not really that
satisfying to CWM themselves. For example, in those situations where the
CWM are confronted by others with the charge of being privileged, they
often respond angrily, even belligerently, saying, "I work twelve hours a
day" and "No one ever handed me anything on a silver platter." By using
"working hard" as a justification of entitlement and framing "privilege" as
somebody "handing them something on a silver platter," CWM hope to
avoid having to acknowledge that because of their race and gender, the
road they personally went down had fewer obstacles in its path than that
of other groups. The level of anger and defensiveness that CWM exhibit
in playing down the idea that their race and gender gave them a social
advantage, however, suggests a chord within them has been struck.

Maybe at some level they wonder whether their individual success
would have been what it was if the game had not been rigged in their favor. At another level, they may wonder how it would play out with other
groups if they did concede that their race and gender gave them a social
advantage. Their resistance indicates that they think that that concession
would increase their vulnerability—in effect constituting an admission of
guilt or culpability and opening the door for further attack. What they
often discover, however, is just the opposite. On those occasions when
a CWM acknowledges a privilege ("privilege" here even by CWM standards)—"I was hired without an interview" or "I was hired without having filed an application," members of other groups (African Americans
especially) look at them more favorably: as potential allies in the general
struggle to create greater social parity within the organization. They view
those CWM who don't acknowledge—even extreme—privilege or make
the connection between the race/gender disqualification of others with
race/gender preferential consideration for themselves as caught up in denial. When CWM begin to acknowledge that they have also benefited as
individuals, not just as a group, from the exclusion of other groups from
the candidate pool or from high-profile assignments that qualify people
for that pool, they may also start feeling empathy for what members of
other groups have gone through (whether they actively contributed to
creating the problem or not). They also begin to think differently about
their relative privilege when they have had a chance to see the obstacles
that members of other groups have had to face and overcome that they

didn't.[8] They also start feeling accountable in ways that they didn't before and see what they can do personally to address the problem. Going down this path, however, CWM also discover that the newly acquired social conscience and accountability has a price tag attached to it: most notably, taking action that might antagonize other CWM that will lead to their social isolation and ultimate ostracism from other CWM at work.

CWM Language and Culture

When other groups talk about CWM as a group, each CWM feels that they are also talking about him personally. One reason for that is that individual CWMs can and do identify themselves as part of a race/gender group when called on do so. But another reason that CWM hear general statements about CWM as a group as applying to them personally has to do with linguistics. For example, a grammatical rule within mainstream U.S. English treats generalizations of a group categorically: as applying to *all* members of a class or group. That is why CWM, and CWW also, qualify the generalizations they make when they do not intend the generalization to apply to everyone present by saying, "Present company excepted." In similar fashion, CWM and CWW hear generalizations about them and others as all inclusive as well. Occasionally, this implicit understanding becomes explicit as in the following letter to the editor by Robert Aterman, from Toronto. In response to a Spike Lee interview that appeared a week earlier,[9] Aterman said, "I take issue with Lee's comment that 'white males have problems with black men's sexuality. It's as plain and simple as that. They think we've got a hold on their women.' No, Spike, it isn't as simple as that. There may well be *some* white males who have such problems, but to say that *all* do is bigotry and stereotyping." Note that Spike Lee's statement about "white males" did not say "all"; rather, that is how Robert Aterman and the *Newsweek* editors who printed his letter heard it. In this regard, they reflect the linguistic pattern and perspective of Anglos in the United States (and probably Anglos elsewhere, as well). This CWM and CWW interpretation of general characterizations conflicts with that of African Americans, for example, who, when making generalizations don't view them as categorical ("We don't mean 'all'"). Perhaps because they don't, blacks also don't feel the need to qualify them when talking about "white folks" or "white men." Rather they expect that those hearing it will decide on the validity of what is being said ("If the shoe fits, wear it") and invoke the individual exclusion rule if they feel the characterization does not apply to them specifically ("I know you're not talking to me.").[10] The reason for bringing this pattern of difference to the forefront here is that in the course of our training, CWM and CWW hear generalizations categorically: as implicating everyone who fits the category or classification and consequently either dismissing them as overgeneralizations—as they do stereotypes—or reacting to them with indignation as having been personally and, to their mind, falsely accused. Consequently, it becomes necessary, to repeat more than once during the training that when African Americans talk about "white folks" they do not necessarily mean all white folks, just those for whom the "shoe fits."

CWM individualism is also manifest in the way CWM respond to general statements about them as a group. So even if a CWM thought that a characterization of white men was true of most white men, he would still challenge it to the extent that it was not personally true of him. In one training session, in response to some of the issues and problems that members of other groups were presenting, a CWM said (protesting the categorical view of white men that he saw being presented), "I'm not like that." As facilitators, we framed his comment as expressing a general wish of CWM to have others see them as individuals, and, for himself, to be seen by others as an individual who is basically a "good person." He agreed. However, another CWM demurred, saying, that what he was about was trying to find ways to "fix the problem," not about showing himself to be a "good" person. Both CWM responses illustrate the resistance and personal exception that CWM take when generalizations about them as a group are made.

Remedies

There are two ways to remedy the situation to create a more inclusive workforce at all levels of the company. One way is for CWM to enlarge the pool of people that they both work and network with to include CWW and people of color, with the hope that they can also see the latter as individuals as they do other CWM and not only, or overwhelmingly, as members of other groups. Much preparation has to be done to achieve this because CWM are concerned over being labeled "racist/sexist" and the zero tolerance policy that exists in their company around doing or saying something that others might find offensive. This concern, in conjunction with the absence of any established behavioral guidelines to steer them in the right (risk-free) direction, feeds their uncertainty, lack of social control, and personal insecurity. CWM characterize this as a "guilty as charged," "walking on eggshells" work climate. To counter this, diverse groups of people need to be brought together to work through these problems and issues that, in part, arise from them not really knowing each other that well or well enough to effectively navigate the new multicultural internal and global work/marketplace. This has to be done in a training context that emphasizes learning over performance, at least during the time when people are wondering about and working on how to get things right. We consider one immediate measure of success of our training: can members of different groups have different kinds of conversations with each other than they could have had before?

Another way to create greater diversity is simply to mandate that qualified women and people of color will be included in the pool from which candidates are drawn. The problem with this strategy is that CWM view such mandates as due to affirmative action, which they see as part of a "quota" and self-righteously resist. The reason their resistance has a self-righteous ring to it is because the mythology of the U.S. workplace that serves CWM as a group at the expense of other groups—CWM seeking to claim the moral high ground for themselves—is that when they get promoted it is because they were "qualified," whereas when members of other groups are promoted it was because of "affirmative action," implying a less-than-qualified or less-qualified person. This attitude occurs in part because CWM see themselves as individuals and others as members of a group. That is also why no CWM in U.S. corporate culture ever said, "We had a white man in this position before and it didn't work out." But they have often said it of members of other groups to the general detriment of individuals from those groups. This attitude is often fed and sustained by CWM bosses telling CWM subordinates they didn't get the particular job that they wanted and applied for because it was "wired," even when the actual reason that they got beat out by the CWW or person of color was because the latter was better qualified. CWM minimize or deny to others what they claim for themselves—being better qualified— and minimize or deny for themselves what they impute to others: a race/ gender workplace advantage. This CWM way of framing the situation is reminiscent of historical attitudes of white superiority. As Albert Murray writes, "The folklore of white supremacy is built upon a fakelore of black pathology."[11] This mis- or disinformation disserves CWM and workplace morale in several ways. For one, it exacerbates intergroup conflict in the workplace. In addition, CWM get reinforced what they would like to believe anyway: that the job would have been theirs, except for the presence of, and preferential consideration given to, members of other groups. Social entitlements also are a factor here. CWM social programming and expectations—one CWW executive reported her CWM counterparts saying, "They're taking away *our* jobs"—take precedence over issues of social parity or equity owing to past discrimination. Herbert Hill writes, "It is . . . *the removal of the preferential treatment traditionally enjoyed by white workers at the expense of blacks as a class* that is at issue in the affirmative action controversy."[12] That myth disserves CWW and people of color since their members constantly have to prove themselves to be considered qualified. It also backfires later on CWM, since, when CWW and people of color are added to their workgroup, they find themselves working harder than they did before so as not to be outdone by members of these other groups. The net effect may be greater effort in the workforce from everyone having to prove themselves both against and in support of the mythology around affirmative action, but at a cost of increased levels of stress all around.

Hiring and Promotions

The respective individual and collective mindsets of CWM and people of color clash within the workplace when it comes to hiring and promotion. For example, the highest ranking African American in one organization, a vice president, retired. Other African Americans felt that that position should be filled by an African American, especially since there were no other African Americans at that level in the organization and the organization claimed to be committed to diversity. In searching for a replacement, the CEO of that company—he was of Lebanese origin—created a candidate pool for the position consisting of only white men. The person chosen was one whom the CEO considered most qualified for the position. When African Americans brought up the issue of the race and gender of the person chosen to replace the retiring African American vice president, the CEO dismissed it as immaterial and irrelevant. He saw himself as selecting an individual, not a member of a group. He also did not see having a member of a diverse group reporting to him as adding value to how people think about and do their job. Since he also did not make any special effort to find an equally or better-qualified woman or person of color for the position, the morale of African Americans in the company sunk to a new low. They saw their group as having lost a key player in the organization. They also viewed the CEO as insincere in his efforts to promote diversity in the organization. By way of contrast, one newly appointed CWM head of operations, in his opening statement to his group of direct reports, made a distinction between *most* qualified and *best* qualified. Most qualified for him was someone who brought something more "but with basically the same strengths and weaknesses." "Best qualified" were those who also brought something "different." The message behind this distinction was to let the other CWM managers in the room know to expect greater diversity in future hiring and promotions.

Means and Ends

Behind the different attitudes that CWM and African Americans have on hiring and promotion are different views on what constitutes a fair process to create greater diversity in the workplace. CWM consider a process "fair" if the opportunity to participate is open to everyone—that is, nondiscriminatory—even if a person of color or a woman is not selected. Fairness is giving people an equal chance to participate, not steering the process toward a predetermined outcome. CWM call that playing favorites. African Americans and members of other disenfranchised groups believe that a fair process is one that remedies the situation for which the process was created. Selecting people who are underrepresented in the workplace to create greater overall parity is perfectly justified even if it means, for a time, that only members of these groups are chosen. These different views of fairness—process oriented versus outcome oriented—collide regularly, not only in the workplace, but within the society at large.

For example, in the recent Supreme Court ruling on discrimination in the case *Parents Involved in Community Schools v. Seattle School District No.1*, the statement by Chief Justice Roberts—"The way to stop discriminating on the basis of race is to stop discriminating on the basis of race"—is a process-oriented view of fair (nondiscriminatory) behavior, in contrast with the more outcome-oriented "integrationist" view represented by the Seattle School District that consciously tried to achieve racial integration by assigning students to particular schools.[13] Note also the parallel between the views expressed by African Americans in the workplace and those of Lani Guinier.[14] Arguing for more proportional representation, Guinier said in an interview with Brian Lamb, "The fact that some of us may think the rules are fair doesn't mean that the *effect* of those rules on all of the participants is fair or legitimate."[15] Assessing processes with regard to outcomes—the African American cultural position and the one also taken by Guinier—was also discussed by Mark Tushnet in a review of Guinier's book. He characterized Guinier's position as a result-based theory of fairness in opposition to the U.S. mainstream (and CWM) process-based winner take all view of fairness that is currently in place.[16] Guinier has said, "We're basically saying in this democracy that some of the people can rule all of the time and other of the people don't get any power, ever."[17] Viewing processes with respect to outcomes is also something we consider in our training. We distinguish between double standard 1—treating people differently when you should be treating them the same—and double standard 2—treating people the same when you should be treating them differently (such as when treating everyone the same produces unequal results). As Kenneth Blanchard writes, "Nothing is so unequal as giving equal treatment to unequals."[18]

These different views of fairness—process versus outcome—have a direct impact on recruitment: especially how hard an organization works to ensure that everyone applies, since not all groups believe that their chances are really equal. CWM will see an organization as having acted properly once a policy of equal opportunity is established. However, because CWM operate from the more process-oriented view of fairness and see the taking advantage of opportunities as culturally rooted in self-reliance and individual initiative—in effect distinguishing between creating equal opportunity and equal outcome—they don't see themselves as having any responsibility beyond establishing a process-oriented policy of fairness to reach out to ensure that diverse groups of people actually apply. As one CWM said, "You give people the right to vote, but they are the ones who need to assume responsibility in exercise of that right." African Americans, given their notion of what constitutes fairness, will recruit in ways that ensure that goals and outcomes are achieved. In that regard, they will also be aware of where the company is doing the recruiting. One company that said they wanted to be more diverse recruited incoming engineers primarily from a local university that had mostly white students. The one African American vice president they had in the company (out of fifty-seven vice presidents) characterized that as "looking for love in all the wrong places."

The different white and black notions of fairness also contain different concepts of social justice. The one that CWM use is "two wrongs don't make a right" and is the basis of suits of "reverse discrimination" that

CWM have filed and won in many companies.[19] The other social justice concept is "turn about is fair play," which, in qualified form, African Americans, Hispanics, and other disenfranchised groups use as the rationale and justification for affirmative action to reach a "level playing field."

CWM also resist affirmative action because their culturally influenced sense of social justice is framed around what they did personally within their own lifetime. The CWM cultural position on social accountability is "I am responsible for what I did, and could reasonably have prevented or controlled. I am not responsible for what happened." Note the contrast between this position and the one taken by a member of the Church of England, the Reverend Simon Bessant, who said, with respect to the slave trade, "We were directly responsible for what happened. In the sense of inheriting our history, we can say that we owned slaves, we branded slaves; that is why I believe that we must actually recognize our history and offer an apology."[20] Similarly, filmmaker Katrina Browne said, "A lot of white people think they know everything there is to know about slavery—we all agree it was wrong and that's enough. But this was the foundation of our country, not some Southern anomaly. We all inherit responsibility."[21] Because the CWM sense of social liability is rooted in the present along with a sense of disconnect with what other white men have done—even members of their own family—CWM feel they are being asked to pay the price for something that others did, not something that they did. Even though the social price they are being asked to pay is not close to what others have paid, CWM consider any price as unfair and unjust.[22] The following example, albeit framed within an argument against affirmative action, reflects this position, too. The Boston University College Republicans offered a "$250 Caucasian Achievement Recognition Scholarship" as a statement of opposition to scholarships set aside for candidates of color. In explaining this award, they wrote, "Did we do this to give a scholarship to white kids? Of course not. Did we do it to trigger a discussion on what we believe to be the morally wrong practice of basing decisions in our schools and our jobs on racial preferences rather than merit? Absolutely!"[23]

CWM who state that they feel no responsibility for things that have happened in the past, occasionally also invoke the past in trying to establish their innocence ("I didn't own any slaves!"). But this statement is not so much a contradiction of their cultural position of feeling socially and morally responsible only for the things that have done in the present as a responsible adult as it is a way to avoid embracing things that have happened in the past, such as slavery and the genocide of American Indians, that cause shame and guilt and are inconsistent with the image that they have of themselves as good people. Other psychological and cultural matters also factor into taking responsibility for things that have happened in the past. Albert Memmi identified a psychological phenomenon he called the "Nero complex" after the Roman emperor Nero, who, after killing Britannicus, the rightful heir to the throne, also killed Britannicus's family and destroyed everything that would remind him that he was a usurper. Memmi sees this as the basis of colonial guilt and an explanation for the horrific acts committed against indigenous people. He writes, "[The colonizer] endeavors to falsify history; he rewrites laws; he would extinguish memories. Anything to succeed in transforming his usurpation into legitimacy."[24]

Within that framework, the resistance of CWM and others in U.S. mainstream to examine the past and take responsibility for it constitutes a form of denial. Denial may also apply to Marshall McLuhan's statement that "what the English can never remember, the Irish can never forget."[25] While the purpose behind McLuhan's statement was to describe the different effects of orality and literacy on what people remember, his statement also has a bearing on issues of colonial denial and who was and wasn't the victim of social oppression. In contemporary terms, the Nero complex—expressed as fear of retaliation by African Americans for slavery, lynchings, and racial oppression in general—may also explain the level of official vigilance, profiling, and overreactive police action directed against African American men, as in the case of Sean Bell "who died in a burst of 50 police bullets outside a Queens strip club" or Amadou Diallo "an unarmed African street peddler who was felled by 19 of 41 police officers' bullets fired at him in 1999"[26]—and especially so, if they offer any resistance, as in the case of Rodney King.[27] In U.S. mainstream companies, it may also manifest itself as sensitivity to African American men getting together as a group. In one organization, when African Americans got together after hours to discuss strategies for dealing with racism at work, they were seen by CWM as conspiring to quit. Culturally, the lack of accountability for things that have happened in the U.S. past is also grounded in a society that is future oriented and focused on opportunity, reflected in such expressions as "this is the first day of the rest of your life" and "the next big thing!." The United States is also a country of settlers and immigrants who come wanting its future but not its past. Their past was socially somewhere else.

CWM also resist the idea of affirmative action because they think that it gives members of other groups a competitive advantage even if most of the top level positions in a company still go to white men. This latter fact is no consolation to them, however. Indeed, CWM are quite unsettled by the idea that other groups should have a leg up in the overall competition even if that edge is only theoretical. At the same time, CWM also say they would not trade their chances for getting ahead in the organization with a member of a group that, within the framework of affirmative action, theoretically should have an advantage over them (e.g., African American women). That being the case suggests that CWM know the difference between having an edge "on paper" and actually winning the game on the field of play. So why, knowing this, are CWM so unsettled?

Part of CWM unsettledness stems from having to face an uncertain future. For example, in response to U.S. labor department projections on the ratio of white men to white women and people of color in the U.S. workforce and population as a whole that come out every two years, CWM saw themselves as an "endangered species." Interestingly, at the same group session, African American men, also had "endangered species" on their list. As might be expected, the meaning of that term was quite different for the two groups. CWM were concerned about where their opportunities were going to come from. African American men were concerned about their physical survival as a group. Looking at the level of representation of them in the group, they asked rhetorically, "Where are we?" African Americans are often surprised that CWM are so unsettled: in part, because they see CWM as the power group in the company and in the society at large and, in part, too, because dealing with an uncertain future and "going through changes" has been the "name of the game" for African Americans in the United States generally.

What they miss about CWM is that what African Americans have experienced and dealt with historically, CWM are now experiencing and dealing with for the first time. CWM grew up with an idea of the future that had an aura of social predictability, which is precisely what they feel is now being taken away from them. CWM still express their wish for greater predictability from time to time. Some of them say, "Just tell me what the rules are!" The problem of course is that rules for the multicultural workplace do not presently exist. They are in the stage of being developed. Out of their comfort zone, CWM hope for a time of greater social stability and certainty, such as existed in the not too distant past when "one size fit all" and the rules that existed applied to everyone across the board. As applied to CWM, that size, by and large, fit OK. To the extent that it didn't fit so well, they at least knew what to expect.

There are also other factors that enter into the current CWM unsettled state and African American surprise over that. It has to do with what members of each group see as a threat. What constitutes a threat to CWM is when someone says they are going to do something to you. African Americans consider a threat real when someone actually "makes a move on you." Until then, it's only "talk." Numbers also play a role. CWM feel that the workplace, like a neighborhood, is "integrated" when the first woman or person of color moves in. Blacks and members of others groups see that as tokenism. For members of these groups, integration happens when the proportion of whites and members of other groups is, if not equal, then at least proportionate with respect to the larger population. Back home, what blacks call "integrated," whites call a "changing neighborhood." When the neighborhood changes for CWM at work, the question becomes, "Do they leave or stay?" or, within the context of the workplace, "Withdraw or engage?" Part I of the book is written for CWM who stay engaged.

CHAPTER TWO

Americanization

The social management of pluralism in the United States from the late nineteenth and early twentieth century up to and through the 1960s followed a path popularly known as the "melting pot," the goal of which was to create unity from diversity—or, as engraved on the U.S. penny, *e pluribus unum* ("one out of many"). As part of a broader concept of "Americanization," melting pot thinking set qualifying terms and conditions for the integration of newly arrived European immigrants into the larger society, which also led to the segregation of ethnic minorities. Some key elements of this attitude are exemplified in a letter Theodore Roosevelt wrote to the president of the American Defense Society on January 3, 1919, three days before his death:[1]

> If the immigrant who comes here in good faith becomes an American and assimilates himself to us he shall be treated on an exact equality with everyone else ... but this [equality] is predicated on the man's becoming in very fact an American, and nothing but an American.... There can be no divided allegiance here. Any man who says he is an American but something else also, isn't an American at all.... We have room for but one language here, and that is the English language, for we want to see that the crucible turns our people out as Americans, of American nationality, and not as dwellers in a polyglot boarding house.

Woodrow Wilson, expressed a similar view around the same time when he said, "A man who thinks of himself as belonging to a particular national group in America has not yet become an American."[2]

Social accommodation within the melting pot was presented as a trade-off. European immigrants and (ostensibly) nonwhite groups, too, would adapt to the white Anglo-Saxon Protestant way of thinking and behaving (the "us" in Roosevelt's proclamation). In return, the dominant group would grant social opportunities that, over time, would allow members of immigrant groups to achieve the "exact equality with everyone else" that Roosevelt spoke of. The idea of "equality"—social equity or parity—that Roosevelt proposed, however, and which federal and state governments regulate, is restricted to U.S. society-wide public institutions. Social equality or equity does not extend to the private sector, nor did assimilation (as a social construct) within the melting pot aim for total social absorption by members of the dominant group. Dominant groups maintain their dominance or privilege by perpetuating race, ethnic, and gender distinctions and boundaries, not by obliterating them.[3] While Roosevelt and other mainstream Anglos promoted assimilation, or perhaps, more accurately, detribalization, its realization by immigrant and ethnic minority groups was different. Members of European immigrant groups, from the first "sacrifice" generation on ("I will suffer and work hard, so my children won't have to"), embraced the proposition that detribalization and assimilation were keys to full social equality. Because they were white, they were able to achieve the trade-off that Roosevelt proposed: loss of ethnic group identification and affiliation in exchange for individual social opportunity.

No matter how far they might try to distance themselves from their original group, members of ethnic minority groups could not lose the caste identifier that marked them as a member of that "other" group. As Eric Liu said, "America ... finds itself ever more in flux: between a white self image and a colored face."[4] Unable to blend into the white American mainstream, ethnic minorities were classified and treated as "unassimilable." It was a term that labor leader Sam Gompers used in a conversation with Leonora O'Reilly ("It's OK to discriminate against unassimilables. Women are unassimilable, so it's OK to discriminate against them.") in response to a complaint by O'Reilly about the restricted access that white women had to white male unions. I have been unable to find the source for this quote. However, following Degler, it does mirror the view that Gompers had toward the restrictive role that white women could play in the labor union movement.[5]

The true meaning of "Americanization" is manifest in the terms and conditions that are set for the integration of immigrants into mainstream society. These are to relinquish the primacy of ethnic group identification and become, instead, an individual whose allegiance, first and foremost, is to the laws set forth by U.S. mainstream social and political institutions. In practical terms, since the workplace was the first avenue of social access for ethnic white men, the transfer of loyalty (and gratitude) also got extended to U.S. mainstream corporations. When asked the question, "What do you see when you look at yourself in the mirror in the morning?" CWM either say "I see myself!"—that is, their name—or "I see a manager" or "I see an engineer"—that is, their workplace role or occupation. Insofar as members of European immigrant groups were able to move up socially through collective unionization and the labor movement, they curtailed their involvement in ethnic politics in exchange for social opportunities. White ethnic group affiliation today, to the extent that it has survived, has taken on a decidedly social (rather than political) character. This process of Americanization was instrumental in shaping and promoting individualism among CWM.

The dominant group attitude and strategy toward ethnic minority groups was not to disperse them but to keep them collectively in place by force, law, and social covenants.[6] Because of the way these groups achieved social access—suddenly and politically, through social action and legislation, rather than, as CWM did, through a form of gradual social and cultural change over two to three generations—ethnic minority groups entered the U.S. mainstream workplace different from their white male counterparts in at least five respects. These were a basic distrust of U.S. institutions, a readiness to engage in social activism to overcome institutional inequities, a collectivistic (as opposed to individualistic) reference group orientation,[7] a greater sense of cultural distinctiveness, and an insistence on social and cultural reciprocity from members of the dominant group.

Social distrust expressed itself in the deal that members of these groups struck with U.S. institutions. First, they rejected the trade-off that white ethnic men accepted and achieved: loss of national/ethnic group identification and allegiance in exchange for individual opportunity. Instead, ethnic minority groups saw that proposition as part of a "divide and conquer" strategy, the aim of which was to undermine the collective will that fed and sustained the civil rights movement. As Alba and Nee write, the "old conception of assimilation has become passé . . . done in by many forces and events, but perhaps above all . . . by the broad impact of the civil rights movement and the identity politics it spawned."[8] Building on the identity politics of the 1960s, ethnic minorities did not buy into the proposition that they should regard themselves as individuals who just happened to be American Indian, African American, Hispanic, or white female. They saw that as tantamount to social and political suicide: both as a group and as an individual from that group.

Moreover, because ethnic minorities were grouped in socially segregated ethnic enclaves, they emerged in the 1960s with a sense of group cohesion and cultural distinctiveness intact. They also emerged with a different attitude regarding the repudiation of their different and distinctive culture. Resisting a key prerequisite to melting pot assimilation—detribalization—members of these groups openly challenged the value of repudiating their racial and ethnic group identification and affiliation that made them authentically who they were. Among the things they publicly debated were less what they would gain by disconnecting from their racial/ethnic group than what they would lose. It is along these lines that ethnic minority resistance to assimilation occurs: not so much as not wanting to acquire the language and culture of CWM, but, rather, not wanting to relinquish those aspects of their culture that identify who they are as a member of their own group. As Eric Liu said, "I do not want to be white. I only want to be integrated."[9] Liu's statement highlights that the civil rights movement for ethnic minorities and white women was not a separatist movement. Religious groups may occasionally push for separation from the U.S. mainstream. But, with the exception of American Indians, whose primary issue with the U.S. government is around tribal/national sovereignty, ethnic minority groups still want social integration into the larger society. However, they want it on different terms (e.g., with Hispanics, "English *plus*" rather than "English *only*"). The strength of this new proposition has set into motion a new social dynamic with different terms and conditions for integration into the society as a whole and for social interaction in the workplace in particular. What was a process of unilateral accommodation to the dominant social group has become a multilateral one. In that regard, it is no longer only a question of how well CWW and people of color can accommodate and relate to the cultural style of CWM. It is also a question of how well CWM can accommodate and relate to the cultural styles of CWW and people of color.

CHAPTER THREE

Social and Cultural Conflicts in the Workplace

·

The different social history of CWM, CWW, and people of color in the United States has led to a collision over whether someone can be loyal to two entities (e.g., ethnic group and company or ethnic group and country) at the same time. These different views (either/or vs. both/and) have materialized in the workplace with the development of affinity groups (e.g. African American, Hispanic, Asian, or CWW). At issue for CWM is divided allegiance. Operating from the premise that individuals can only serve one master at a time, CWM worry that the interests of the group will be served before those of the company should the interests of the group and those of the company collide. Consequently, their first reaction to the formation of these groups has been one of distrust: suspecting them of ulterior motives and wishing, that they, like labor unions, would go away. Members of affinity groups come from a both/and mentality. They feel that the interests of their group and the company can be served simultaneously. Their view is, "Why would we want to sink the ship that keeps us all afloat?"

The same either/or versus both/and collision occurs when race, ethnicity, and gender are brought into consideration when filling a slot for a particular position. CWM view race, ethnicity, and gender as contaminating the process of selecting who is "most" or "best" qualified for a particular position. The theory here is that diversity issues or concerns will get in the way of making pragmatic ("best practice") decisions. Members of minority groups not only feel that diversity and pragmatic issues and concerns can be addressed simultaneously—that race, ethnicity, and gender can be taken into consideration when identifying qualified people for a position—they also feel that diversity adds value insofar as it allows for a richer mix of ideas and perspectives than can come from any one cultural group. By keeping diversity and bottom line considerations separate, CWM imply that, to the extent that race, ethnicity, and gender concerns are addressed, standards are lowered, and white men are quick to notice any time a criteria for a position is changed to accommodate CWW and people of color.[1,2] CWW and people of color are equally alert to criteria being changed to accommodate CWM, in support of their views that CWM look out for each other and the "good old boy" system is alive and well. For example, when Elizabeth Vargas, the Latina coanchor of ABC's *World News Tonight,* said that she was walking away from her job in preparation for giving birth to her second child, *DiversityInc* reported, "She is being replaced by Charles Gibson, *a white man.*"[3]

CWW and people of color find the implication that standards are lowered when taking race, ethnicity, and gender into account repugnant and unsupported in fact. Their contrary view is that, because their qualifications are suspect, they have to work harder to prove themselves qualified in the positions they hold. They feel that they are being held accountable to a higher standard, saying, as one African American woman, did, "How come I need to have an advanced degree for the position, when the white guy before me didn't?" A Mexican American woman said, "When I left, they had to hire three people to do my job!" Another common complaint has to do with the greater level of support that CWM receive when given a supervisory or management position. One Hispanic man said that he was responsible for managing over two hundred people in his work sector. He was not only angry at having been replaced by a CWM, but at subsequent levels of support that the CWM got that he did not get in that position.

Race Relations

CWM got messages growing up that the world is either benign or indifferent and the only obstacles that stood in the way of their becoming successful were those that they, as individuals, put in front of themselves. As one CWM said, "The only person who can hold you back is you." For ethnic minorities—African Americans, Hispanics, and Asian Americans—the world outside their family, friends, and community was a place in which you had to be careful. CWW also acknowledge that to a lesser extent. But for CWW being careful was related to situations where they might be sexually vulnerable. For members of ethnic minority groups, it was more generally being in the wrong place at the wrong time. Our colleague Kenneth Addison, growing up in Boston's Roxbury section, for example, heard from his mother (with respect to the Irish on one side and Italians on the other), "Don't go over there, they'll get you. Don't go over there, they'll kill you." When entering the workplace, the messages people of color got were "You've got to work twice as hard to get half as far." The prevailing view there was that there were real obstacles out there, not just those that you put in front of yourself. Arthur Ashe, when he first started to play professional tennis, is reputed to have been taught to hit all the balls that were slightly out, preparing for the possibility (or likelihood) that he would not get the benefit of a close call.

Trust

The different worldviews and collateral experiences of CWM and people of color impact the issue of trust. For CWM, within their own race/gender circle, trust is not an issue until it becomes an issue. A corollary of this view is "I am (and want to be considered) trustworthy till I prove I'm not." Outside of their race/gender circle the CWM expectation that they should still be considered trustworthy remains. The extent to which they see others as equally trustworthy depends on the person and circumstances. Our African American colleague Ken Addison said he does not sense that CWM consider him trustworthy on meeting him for the first time. Of course, Ken Addison, like other African Americans, Hispanics, Asians, and white ethnics (Italian, Greeks, etc.), comes from a place where trust initially is an issue until it becomes a nonissue. The rule there is, "Those outside my immediate circle of family and friends are not trusted or considered trustworthy till they prove that they are." One group, predominantly, CWM but also CWW, see trust as a given, members of ethnic minority groups and some white ethnic groups, predominantly see trust as something that has to be earned. So when a CWM is recruiting an African American man for a position within a company, the CWM often feels that he is being "checked out" or kept "at arms' length." He thinks, "I haven't done anything to this person, why doesn't he trust me?" The black man thinks, "You haven't done anything to make me think that I could trust you. Besides, the last person who did me in looked just like you." What is relevant about this encounter is not only the underlying issue of trust, but the way each man initially views the other person and himself. The CWM sees the African American man subjectively and objectively but himself only subjectively—as an individual. The black man sees himself and the CWM as individuals, but also objectively, as respective members of an African American and CWM group. Consequently, he may also wonder what the CWM can tell him about what it is like to be a black man working within that company.

Race Awareness

When white men and women experience different qualities of service in stores that they usually shop in, they don't think that race had anything to do with the way they were treated. African Americans do. Race awareness and the vigilance that attends it are indelibly imprinted on the African American psyche, just as they are absent in the psyche of whites. So if a white couple is told by a real estate agent that an "offer had just been made" on the house they were interested in buying, they would accept it at face value, or they might think, as one CWM did, that they were trying to "jack up the price." One African American couple having been told that an offer had been made wondered not about price but about race: had an offer really been made on that house or was this something that materialized only after the real estate broker saw that she and her husband were black? Similarly, when I asked the undergraduate students in my class how they explain the attentive service that they get from sales clerks at the boutiques on Michigan Avenue, the white women in the class said, "That's simply the service you get at better stores." The African American and Hispanic women in the class said they were "being watched because they think we're going to steal something." These different views of behavior and situations are rooted in the different social experiences that whites and people of color have in the United States. For example, one young black woman from an inner city area said that when police drive through her neighborhood and talk to her and her group of friends they don't say, "How you doin'" but "Whatcha doin'?" Blacks, Hispanics, and Asians as a group are suspect and profiled: African Americans and Hispanics of theft and other criminal activity, Asians, as "perpetual foreigners" of possible disloyalty to the United States, Arab Americans as "terrorists," and so forth. None of this suspicion and profiling attaches to whites.

Workplace Conflicts

Conflicts abound in the workplace around the issue of race especially in situations where the meaning of what happened is open to interpretation. Whites start from the premise that race is not a factor until you prove that it is. African Americans start from the premise that race is a factor until you prove that it is not. Each group puts the burden on the other to prove that something different is going on from how they see it. While each group is reluctant to concede to the other group's view of the situation, the meaning and level of resistance for members of each group is different. White men and women resist the view that African Americans face more obstacles getting their needs met than they do, because to agree that things really are different would mean that they would either have to feel guilt or do something about the problem, neither of which they really want—this, despite the fact that the evidence of different treatment is overwhelming.[4] African Americans resist the view that race might not have been a factor in situations where they got into trouble because they would otherwise feel personal shame. For example, Latrell Sprewell's 1997 accusation that the National Basketball Association was racist stemming from having been given a one-year suspension for threatening and choking Warrior head coach P. J. Carlesimo would have carried more weight and gotten more support from other blacks—the punishment was seen as excessive and inconsistent with what had been done in the past—if they didn't also feel that Sprewell deserved *some* punishment for what he did.[5]

While resistance operates on both sides of the divide, there are also key differences. For African Americans, race and racism are part of everyday reality, grounded in concrete experience. As such, the African American view that race is a factor is specific to the situation in which it happens and operates as much as a question as it does a conclusion. For example, an African American journalist recalls an incident that happened when she was a new reporter having been taken to task by her white woman editor in her first three-month review—there was no initial discussion on how she should do her job—for things that she as yet did not know she was supposed to be doing. Her recollection of that experience twenty-five years later was still a question: was her editor a "racist" or simply a "bad manager"? While that question never got answered for her—the impact was painful regardless—the question sometimes can, within the context of what happened, be clarified and sometimes disproved.

For example, the African American woman who reported being told that an offer had been made on the house that she and her husband were interested in later reported having gotten a call from that same broker with the message that the offer she spoke of earlier fell through, and if she and her husband were still interested, she would show them the house whenever they were ready to see it. So what changed for the black woman? She acknowledged that her original assessment of what had happened was wrong: that the offer she had been told about was probably real rather than fabricated. However, she saw herself wrong only with respect to that specific situation. It did not change the way that she would approach that same situation in the future. She said, "That it wasn't racist that time doesn't mean it won't be racist next time." So while she and other African Americans maintain their general predisposition to see things as racist, they are still open to evidence that would prove them wrong in specific situations. In public situations, there is usually not time, opportunity, or interest to find out whether the unfriendly waitress was racist or just having a bad day. Workplace situations are different, however, given what is at stake. That is where the work of sorting things out needs to occur.

CWM and CWW talk about blacks "playing the race card" and frame it as if it's the first reaction that African Americans give to a problem situation when in reality—because of the problems that it creates for them—it is the last thing that CWM and CWW want to see brought up. This is especially frustrating for African Americans because race is often the last thing that they do bring up—also because of the problems it creates for them—having decided, from a process of elimination, that race is the only thing left to consider that would explain what happened. The reason why it is the last thing CWM and CWW want to have brought up is because, for them, race and racism operate at the abstract level of idea and principle: something that implicates their moral character or their goodness as a person. So when African Americans characterize something specific that happened or something that a white person said or did as racist, CWM and CWW don't hear it as a testable hypothesis but as a form of character assassination. They see themselves as having just been accused of being a racist—what whites do reflects on their moral character and is taken personally—and rush to defend their personal innocence or goodness.

African Americans view the focus and energy that CWM and CWW bring to the charge of racism as a sign that whites are guilty, not innocent. The African American cultural view is that for that level of focused energy to happen, a "chord had to have been struck," which, blacks believe happened because the accusation was taken as true. Note the phrasing "taken as true." Within African American culture, targeted individuals are seen to be the ones to determine whether an accusation is true or not, based on the "if the shoe fits, wear it" principle. How individuals take an accusation, therefore, is seen to be critical in determining the truth of the accusation. As blacks also say, "You throw a stone in a pack of dogs, the one that yelps is the one that got hit."[6] African Americans are correct in noting that a chord has been struck for CWM and CWW when they are accused of having done something racist, but the reason for that may have less to do with the truth of the matter, as much as it has to do with the standard of moral perfectionism within Anglo culture, which disallows any possibility of a blemish or stain on one's moral character. One Mexican American said, "You accuse an Anglo of being a 'son of a bitch,' and he doesn't care. But you accuse him of being a 'liar' and he's prepared to fight."

The move of Anglos to defend themselves as good people happens so quickly that what is lost sight of entirely is what happened that triggered the charge. The focus and issue shifts to become either the moral goodness of the person being charged or the assault that the black person just made on the white person's moral character. Both Anglos and African Americans miss something important about each other here. Blacks miss how deeply personal Anglos view and take charges of racism and what is at stake for them, generally, if they admit a prejudice. As one CWM put it, "If they are not morally perfect, they are not a good person." This is especially true if the CWM or CWW are Protestants. According to Foote and McLaren, "Relying on the authority of the Bible, the Protestant sects gave a special vitality to such doctrines as original sin . . . and heightened the awfulness of the curse of inherited guilt."[7] Blacks also miss that for Anglos, a person's prejudice works against them more than their honesty works for them. No one gets credit in Anglo culture for admitting a prejudice. Quite the opposite! Anglos fall a long way in their own eyes and those of others if they are not morally perfect and even further if they admit to not being morally perfect. Admission for Anglos is either a sign of guilt or weakness. We often ask CWM and CWW in our training sessions how far they fall in their own eyes and those of others if they have to admit a prejudice. They say "a long, long, way," which we often characterize as "being only one small step away from hell!" Jean Mavrelis says it is also because Protestantism, by eliminating purgatory, got rid of a "way station" available to Catholics that allows others to pray for sinners to reduce their afterlife sentence.

What CWM and CWW miss is that the African American charge of racism is rooted in the premise that everyone is programmed to be racist living in a racist society. The African American view is that no one is perfect, no one is immune. For Anglos, or anyone, to insist that they are not racist is, from this perspective, ludicrous. As African Americans say, "What goes around comes around!" From this perspective, therefore, the best that can happen is for people to acknowledge that about themselves and clean up their act. Anglos also miss that admitting a prejudice is treated with greater forgiveness among blacks than among members of their own group. That is because, for African Americans, a person's honesty works for them, more than their prejudice works against them, especially if they can show that they are sincerely working to correct the problem. Sometimes, the value of honesty is such in the culture that African Americans will even give people credit for honesty even if they are not working to correct the problem. For example, African Americans often say that they prefer southern racists to northern ones because white southerners are more upfront about their racial attitudes. This attitude is also expressed in the headline "Banning the 'N' Word: At Least Ann Coulter Is Upfront about Bigotry" and the statement from the article itself, "For my own purposes, I'd rather see the bigot coming at me rather than have her speech stifled and the knife aimed at my back."[8] For African Americans, admission is the first sign of hope, progress, and redemption! That's why African Americans in our training sessions see CWM who admit that they are privileged as further along than those who don't. Along these lines, what African Americans are most unforgiving of is denial. This explains the position taken by an African American equal opportunity officer when she came into one company with data that showed a clear bias against CWW and people of color. She said to the company representatives, "If you acknowledge you have a problem, I can work with you. But if you insist that you don't have a problem, then *we* have a problem."

Remedies

Since multicultural solutions work both sides of the fence, we ask what each group would have to let go of to give the other group what they want that also respects what each group values. In matters of interpretation, this means for those on the receiving end to assign a meaning to behavior that is consonant with what that behavior means to the sender and for the sender to understand how their behavior is likely to be understood by the receiver. Applying that formula to the above discussion, if Anglos understand that when African Americans say something is "racist" that is code for "there is different treatment going on here along racial lines," then the appropriate response, from the African American perspective, is to acknowledge and address the concern and make sure it doesn't happen again. For Anglos to be able to do that they would probably need to shift their focus to what actually happened that prompted the charge and not rush to protest their innocence or goodness. To enable that, it would help if they did not translate "that was racist" into "you're a racist." Also, by staying with what happened or what the concern is, Anglos may be able to turn things around. "Yeah, I did single you out, and let me tell you why?" African Americans, in turn, need to understand the power that the charge of racism has on Anglos such that when it happens, Anglos become unable to deal with the different treatment that triggered the charge. Moral character for Anglos—like respect for African Americans, *dignidad* for Latinos, face for East Asians, and honor in the Middle East—is of such importance as to be considered inviolable. Consequently, when a violation occurs, whether intended or not, it overwhelms everything else that might also be going on. So if the African American goal is really to get whites to consider that something racial was behind the treatment that they got and deal with it (and not just a "gotcha"), then it might be more productive to stay with the specifics of what happened such as, "Were you aware that the person you just waited on came in after I did? You need to look at why you did that/let that happen." Along this line our African American colleague advises training participants that a good way to distinguish a real charge from a bogus charge of racism is to ask for specifics. If the black person cannot provide any, then the truth of the charge may well be suspect. But if they can and do, then it obligates those hearing it to take it seriously.

Establishing Accountability

Cultural differences also play a role in how CWM and African Americans establish accountability. For CWM, intent or what was meant is viewed separately from what was said and done. It also serves to extenuate behavior that others might find objectionable. So when CWM say, "I didn't mean it" or "that was inadvertent," they expect to be cut some slack. The U.S. legal system also follows this pattern. Jack Kevorkian at his first trial was asked by the prosecutor if his intent was "to assist in the suicide of the woman [who died]." He said, "No! My intent was to relieve suffering!" This difference made a difference in the trial in which he was acquitted.[9] The state of mind of those accused with regard to the offense affects the type of charge that the U.S. legal system levels at them.

African American culture establishes accountability with respect to what was said and done and the impact of that on others. Intent does not extenuate behavior and ignorance only slightly: as black parents say on disciplining their children, "And you couldn't have figured that out!" What counts first and foremost is what you said and did and what happened as a result. Actions are also not treated separately from intent, as they are for Anglos—what you did versus what you meant—but rather inferred after the fact from what was said and done. The African American cultural position is, "If you didn't mean it, you wouldn't have done it." Along with the CWM position, the African American view is also sometimes taken by white women toward their husbands, as Jean Mavrelis says, holding them accountable for their actions irrespective of what they meant, not quite believing that they didn't really know the full measure of what they were doing when they said or did something that their wives found objectionable.

Views of Different Treatment

In some instances, intent and motivation alone frame and extenuate for CWM and CWW what is really going on. Not so for African Americans, especially when inconsistent treatment along racial lines is involved. The following case example illustrates these points nicely. In the 1997 C-Span program "Media and the Criminal Justice System," there was a segment dealing with the amount of media attention given to the JonBenét Ramsey case. Within this segment all of the three African American panelists discussing this matter felt that race and class were implicated in the amount of media attention being paid to this case. None of the three white panelists who were discussing this matter agreed. One white man, representing the press, called the charge made by the black panelist representing the criminal justice side "an unmentionable libel." In reply, the black man said, "No, it isn't!" and, in further support of his charge said, "How can I, as an African American man watching the 'five o'clock crime hour' not feel impacted by what I am seeing?" He charged the American press with having made "a black man the face of crime in America . . . scaring every one of black men," which, in turn, had a direct link to the number of black men in prison. The white man said in response, "I'm not telling you how you should feel. But I don't want you or anyone else to think, even for a moment, that the motivation of the American press for picking cases [like Ramsey] is racially driven." A black woman on the panel responded to that comment by saying, "Motivation is irrelevant. What is relevant is that it [the media coverage] is disproportionate, and *that* is what is relevant." Another white man on the panel said that "it is not the intention of the news media to pick cases based upon race" and that, with respect to the Ramsey case, "voyeurism is what that case is all about." The disagreement over whether race and class were implicated had to do with how each culture frames and establishes accountability.

White men on the panel argued that since there was no motivation and intent to select the case based on race or class, race and class were not present. African Americans argued that motivation was irrelevant. What mattered for them was the relative exposure given to JonBenét Ramsey as compared to the amount of media coverage given to members of other groups. As African Americans in Chicago have said in their criticism of the media, "Where is the media when the things like that happen to poor black girls in Cabrini Green [a Chicago black housing project]?" What was important to the white men was what drove the process of selection. What was important for African Americans was what happened and the impact of that on others. On this last point, note the telling exchange between the white and black man with respect to the five o'clock news. The white man, in telling the black man "I'm not telling you how you should feel" is also making a statement on the limits of his social (and interpersonal) liability. He is saying, "I'm accountable for what I meant at the time that I did it. I am not accountable for how you took it." In this regard, he is representing the cultural position of CWM and mainstream United States, generally.

From the cultural perspective of the black man, however, and African Americans generally, the white man is accountable for how the black man took it as well as the other social consequences that develop from it. If for Anglos, "things are not always what they seem," for African Americans, "things are exactly what they seem" or "How it looks is how it is!" There also may be a practical aspect to the African American view of things. To evaluate intent, as one black woman put it, "I either have to be a mind reader or know the person real well. And since I can't access what is going on in someone else's head, if the person and I don't have a track record where I have other things to go on that previously built some trust and good will, I'm going to have to deal with how it looks." In that regard, another black man said that when he initially came into the organization he thought that "eighty percent of everything that happened was 'racist.'" "Now," he said, "I think about eighteen percent of what happens is racist." I asked him what happened to change his view of the situation. He said, "I got to know these people better."

Intent versus Impact

Framing accountability around intent versus impact is not new in the legal system. The case *Griggs v. Duke Power Co.* (1971) made the case for disparate impact in which "the Court agreed that the 1964 Civil Rights Act required private employers to remove arbitrary obstacles to black advancement, even if those obstacles were not put in place with the intention to discriminate against them. However, in *Washington v. Davis* 426 U.S. 229 (1976), the court held that the Due Process Clause of the 5th Amendment (holding the Federal Government to the same equal protection standards imposed on the states by the 14th Amendment) prohibits only intentional racial discrimination and does not require the government to correct for the unintended differential racial impact of its policies."[10] But what has not been proposed until now is that there is a cultural basis—Anglo intent versus African American impact—supporting and framing the two positions. These different cultural perspectives play out time and time again in the society at large and the workplace in particular.

Inferring Motive/Intent (or State of Mind) from Result or Impact

Senator John Kerry (D-MA) dismissed as "absolutely ridiculous" the notion that his support for Iowa and New Hampshire's prominent roles in the presidential nomination process means he thinks only the votes of white people count.[11] Many Democrats complain that the two early nomination elections winnow out candidates based on votes from small states with overwhelmingly white populations. The party is considering adding, during those early weeks, one or two states in other regions to draw diverse electorates into the process. Kerry, the 2004 Democratic nominee for president, wrote a column for the *New Hampshire Sunday News* arguing that "the special role that Iowa and New Hampshire play in presidential politics has strengthened our democracy by insuring that citizens at the grass roots engage directly with candidates for the presidency." On ABC's *This Week,* Kerry bridled when told an unnamed Democratic strategist, said that, by supporting the status quo, "you're basically saying only white people's votes count in those early states." "That's so much bunk," Kerry responded. "I don't know how to describe that comment in any other way than to say that that's absolutely ridiculous. The converse of that is to suggest that the people in New Hampshire and Iowa are insensitive to those issues and don't care about them." We have no information on the race of the "unnamed Democratic strategist." The outcome-oriented cultural perspective taken, however, reflects that of African Americans.

In 1995–96 the intent versus impact distinction was also critical in characterizing the nature of a crime. When the Black Congressional Caucus asked the Federal Bureau of Investigation (FBI) why arson fires at black churches were not being classified as hate crimes, the FBI responded that it was because they have not as yet established intent. John Conyers of the Caucus is reputed to have responded, "Hey! Only Black churches are being bombed here!"[12]

Accountability Based on What You Meant versus What Happened (and What You Should Have Known)

An example of framing accountability based on intent versus outcome concerns an offensive DVD promotion of Wal-Mart's. In 2006, Wal-Mart blamed human error for its racially offensive movie suggestions.[13] Carter Cast, president of Walmart.com, the online shopping arm of Wal-Mart Stores Inc., said that the mistake resulted from a well-intentioned effort to promote a DVD about the Reverend Martin Luther King, Jr. A cross-selling system instructed those interested in buying *Charlie and the Chocolate Factory* and *Planet of the Apes* DVDs to consider black-themed DVDs such as *Introducing Dorothy Dandridge* and *Martin Luther King: I Have a Dream/Assassination of MLK.* "There was nobody here who maliciously put together that combination," said Cast. "I know the person was well-intended in trying to get the 'I Have a Dream' speech out as a cross-sell." Mona Williams, vice president of corporate communications, said in a statement that the Bentonville, Arkansas–based company was "heartsick that this happened."

Note the different cultural perspectives at work here: Carter Cast framing accountability around intent and Mona Williams framing it around what happened and the impact of that. I don't know if Mona Williams is African American—in one Web site–reported interview, "Why Wal-Mart Wants to Invade New York," she was described as having a "lilting southern accent"—but, regardless of her race, her framing of the situation in terms of "what happened," rather than "what was intended," is consistent with an African American (as opposed to Anglo) cultural position.

Another example is the city of Los Angeles, which appointed its first black chief after a black firefighter was fed dog food. "The mayor appointed the first black man to lead the city's fire department Monday after the previous chief resigned amid a furor involving a black firefighter who was fed spaghetti mixed with dog food. . . . The fire department has been plagued by complaints of discrimination and rampant hazing. 'I know that we can stop hazing and horseplay, I know that we can address the department's history of discrimination and exclusion, I know that we can build a department that looks like Los Angeles,' Barry said. Firefighter Tennie Pierce claimed that *he was fed dog food because he is black.* But other firefighters said *it was an ordinary firehouse prank with no racist intent.*"[14]

Inconsistent Treatment/Being "Singled Out"

Another aspect of accountability concerns the perception of inconsistent treatment, or being "singled out," as in the case of an African American Southwest airlines passenger: "A jury on Friday said Southwest Airlines did not racially discriminate against an overweight passenger when she was asked to buy a second seat on her flight. The jury deliberated for a little over an hour before finding against Nadine Thompson, who sued Southwest in federal court. She claimed that she was singled out because she is black and that the airline's 'customer of size' policy was unfairly applied to her after she boarded a flight at Manchester Airport in June 2003. . . . Southwest said the only mistake it made was telling Thompson that she needed to pay the extra fare for her outbound flight; since she already had boarded the plane she wasn't required to do so. The employees who addressed Thompson about the 'customer of size' policy testified *that it was their first time applying it,* and that they weren't aware of the fare provision, which was buried in the guidelines."[15] While the "first time applying the rule" statement was used by those Southwest employees as an excuse for not knowing the details surrounding the fare provision, to Thompson, and other African Americans who hear the story, it suggests that Thompson was being singled out.

Another example is Gary Sheffield's criticism of former Yankee manager Joe Torre for singling him out in team meetings and for treating black and white ball players differently: specifically for the different way that

Torre criticized black and white ballplayers—blacks, publicly and whites, privately. This again reflects the African American cultural position on what qualifies as biased treatment or racist behavior.[16]

Accountability for What You Said and Did Rather than What You Meant

An incident during an interview of Halle Berry illustrates accountability for what was said, rather than what the interviewer claims was "meant": "What [started as] a friendly chat to promote the new 'X-Men' movie turned into a frosty discussion about race on a popular morning radio program, but the British Broadcasting Corp. defended its disc jockey. Oscar-winning actress Halle Berry appeared on Chris Moyles' Radio One breakfast show Thursday and clashed with her host after he imperson-ated what he described as a 'big, fat, black guy.' 'Are we having a racist moment here?' Berry, the first black actress to win an Academy Award for a lead role, asked Moyles after she took exception to his imperson-ation. . . . Moyles made it clear on air that there was nothing racist in what he said."[17]

A similar incident concerned a national sports commentator's remarks about Tiger Woods. "On Friday, as [Kelly] Tilghman and fellow broadcaster Nick Faldo discussed Tiger Woods' dominance over the rest of golf's elites, Faldo suggested professional golf's up-and-coming players 'gang up' on Woods to beat him. Tilghman agreed and added that they 'lynch him in a back alley.' . . . Tilghman, who played college golf at Duke and works as the main play-by-play announcer during The Golf Channel's PGA Tour telecasts, [said]. 'I have known Tiger for 12 years and I have apologized di-rectly to him. I also apologize to our viewers who may have been offended by my comments.' . . . Woods has not talked publicly about the incident, but his agent, Mark Steinberg, has. 'This story is a non-issue . . . said Stein-berg in a statement he released to The Golf Channel. Regardless of the choice of words used, we know unequivocally that there was no ill *intent* in her comments."[18]

Cultural Analysis

Framing accountability along lines of intent versus impact differently shapes the way responsibility (and blame) is qualified and applied. Within Anglo culture, intent is directly connected to an individual's state of mind, with regard to what that individual knew and meant and what each individual could have reasonably been able to control or prevent (based on what they knew or reasonably be expected to have known). What is said and what is done are compartmentalized and have quasi-independent status. They are connected but dealt with separately. Individual responsibility and culpability are determined by assigning a relative weight to what that individual meant to do—his or her state of mind—and what that individual did. Blame and punishment are applied and accepted within an Anglo U.S. cultural construct of justice and fairness and are configured around these essential elements. Within African American culture, the focus is on what is said and done and the impact of that. Responsibility for impact is more global: implicating people not only with respect to what they knew but also what they should have known or could have done to have anticipated (and prevented) an unwanted result. Intent, to the extent that it matters, is inferred from what is done (e.g. "If you didn't mean it, you wouldn't have done it"). Individual responsibility and culpability are determined by assigning a relative weight to what was done or should have been done with respect to any given outcome. Blame and punishment are applied and accepted within an African American cultural construct of justice and fairness and are configured around these essential elements.

As a further point of comparison, East and Southeast Asian cultures (Chinese, Japanese, Korean, and Vietnamese) follow a similar ("I should have known") pattern. East Asians are also very self-critical. This combination (along with the need to save face) can sometimes be lethal. For example, a Japanese engineer made a presentation to a U.S. company but felt he did not do as well fielding the more speculative "what if" questions that CWM engineers often ask. He did not show up when the group looked for him the next morning in the lobby. They went to his room and found that he had hung himself.

Responsibilities of Leadership

Framing accountability along lines of (individual) intent versus (global) impact affects the way Anglo society and African Americans assign and accept personal responsibility. It also implicates how people rationalize or explain what went wrong and where fault ultimately lies. U.S. mainstream Anglo culture primarily holds individuals accountable for why bad things happen (explanations are framed with respect to that individual's state of mind—specifically, motivation or intent). African American culture also holds individuals accountable for why bad things happen, but the blame is divided between the individual who committed the act and the person or group in charge, which, either through acts of commission or omission, caused or allowed that act to happen.

Framing Accountability

Black leaders saw the church arson fires discussed above as part of a pattern and linked them, if not to an active organized group conspiracy, then, at least, to the climate of tolerance for these kinds of acts set by the administration and those in charge of the investigation, especially the U.S. Bureau of Alcohol, Tobacco and Firearms. The Reverend Jesse Jackson blamed a "cultural conspiracy—a seeping intolerance fed by white politicians' attacks on affirmative action and immigration." Bob Herbert said, "These attacks are not occurring in a vacuum. They are the work of twisted individuals who flourish in an atmosphere that is inflamed, in Mr. Conyer's words, by 'the rhetoric of hate and blame.'" National correspondent Jack E. White wrote that the church fires were most likely incited by the resentful, fear-driven rhetoric of Pat Buchanan and other conservative politicians.[19] Elsewhere, John Conyers said, "The challenge is to expose those who created the psychological environment that led sick individuals to torch the churches."[20] Congressional Black Caucus Chairman Donald Payne of New Jersey minced no words in deploring the federal government's failure to curb firebombings.[21]

White mainstream officials essentially saw these as isolated, unrelated acts committed by separate individuals with different motives: racial hatred being but one of many. For example, from the Associated Press wire service: "Amid all the frightening images of churches aflame ... amid all the fears of raging racism, a surprising truth emerges: There's little hard evidence of a sudden wave of racially motivated arsons against black churches in the South.... There is no evidence that most of the seventy-three black church fires recorded since 1995 can be blamed on a conspiracy or a general climate of racial hatred. Racism is the clear motivation in fewer than twenty cases."[22] In one newspaper account, "Pointing out that several of the fires have been ruled accidental, Judiciary Committee Chairman Henry J. Hyde (R-Ill.) said he was satisfied that the federal law enforcement agencies were doing everything they could. He said that it was premature to conclude that a racist conspiracy was at work. 'There is no way of knowing until an investigation is concluded and the perpetrators identified whether the motivation for the arson was racial hatred, personal financial profit, intra-congregational disputes or something else,' Hyde said."[23]

What is culturally relevant here for mainstream U.S. Anglos and African Americans is, respectively, the moral responsibility that accrues to an individual's state of mind versus the more global moral responsibility that connects to the U.S. collective state of mind that exists within the larger society from which individuals take their cues. These different cultural positions affect the extent to which those in leadership positions consider themselves responsible for things that happen on their watch, owing either to things they did or could have done to have kept such individual acts from happening. It also affects the way individual responsibility is qualified and framed: are individual acts primarily or solely driven by what is going on inside the head of that one individual, or are individual acts also seen to be directly affected by the moral tone or climate set by those in charge? African Americans hold those in charge to be more directly responsible (and morally accountable) for what individuals do on their watch than U.S. Anglos. They also see individual acts (especially, but not exclusively, racist acts) as more directly linked to and perhaps caused by the moral tone set by those in charge than U.S. mainstream Anglo culture does. Finally, they also assume greater direct responsibility for what happens when they are the ones in charge.

Individual versus Global Accountability

High school seniors often express anxiety when they learn that they have to pass an examination on the U.S. Constitution before they can graduate. They often blurt out when told of this requirement, "What if we don't pass?" In one such class, a white female teacher, invoking the Anglo cultural values of individual autonomy, primary individual responsibility, self-reliance, and self-determination, said to the class, "If you [as individuals] study and apply yourself, you should have no problem passing." An African American female teacher, in another such class where this happened—invoking African American cultural values of collaborative responsibility and acting as the one in charge, the one accountable for what happens and from whom the students will take their cues—said, "I won't permit that to happen!"

Parenting is also implicated here especially in the assignment of responsibility and blame if a son or daughter did not do well at school or otherwise acted inappropriately. Within U.S. Anglo culture, the actions of a son or daughter's failure reflects primarily on them as individuals. Within other cultures (African American, Hispanic, Asian, Middle Eastern, Slavic, etc.), the actions of a son or daughter strongly implicate the parents and are often seen as a direct result of their upbringing. As Wageh Saad, our Lebanese colleague, says, citing an Arab proverb, "Where would a man, whose father is an onion and his mother a garlic, get a sweet fragrance." Another example of how the actions of one individual morally implicate others—in this instance the whole family—occurs in the film *Bend It like Beckham.* An Asian Indian family broke off the engagement of their son to the other family's older daughter, because the younger daughter had been seen giving a hug to an ostensibly male friend in public—it was actually a female with short hair.

In one episode of the TV show *Law and Order,* a white woman was charged with murdering the white wife of her ex-husband (who was black but passing as white). Together, the ex-husband and wife were trying to reclaim the visibly black child that she had given birth to that they had just given up for adoption. The motive of the defendant was that she did not want it found out that the son that she had with her ex-husband was also African American—he, too was passing as white—to protect him from the racism that existed in the society at large and the ostracism that he would directly experience at the hands of his network of white friends if they knew this about him. The prosecution saw the defendant's action as motivated purely by racism and sought to prosecute the case as a hate crime. The defendant's lawyer—an African American woman—sought to bring forth witnesses from the social sciences who would argue that her client's actions were not racist but aimed at protecting her son based on a statistical assessment of the social consequences that her son would experience if it were discovered that he were black.

What applies to the cultural distinctions being made here is that the prosecution, supported by the judge, said that what was relevant was the state of mind of the defendant (not the "state of the union," as she put it), and since a direct link could not be made between the two, the information that the social scientists would supply was considered irrelevant and deemed inadmissible. African Americans, as exemplified by the African American lawyer who tried to establish a link between state of mind and state of the union, would be more likely to see the link between the two as compelling and evidentiary.

In another example, Johnny Cochran, in the O. J. Simpson trial, was successful in convincing African Americans on the jury that racism within police departments throughout the nation generally tainted the evidence that they supplied linking Simpson to the crime. Consider the headline on the CNN O. J. Simpson Web site: "The pool of prospective jurors in the O. J. Simpson civil trial split along racial lines Tuesday, with whites saying Simpson was probably guilty of murder and African-Americans saying he is innocent."

In yet another example, a recent court case, *Longmire v. Wyser-Pratte* (S.D.N.Y., No. 05-6725, September 6, 2007), ruled against a biracial African American plaintiff who was passing as white at work who had brought a "hostile work environment" claim against his employer "because his co-workers could not have been directing racist remarks specifically at him if they did not know that he was half black."[24] This ruling again shows the U.S. mainstream Anglo cultural pattern of establishing accountability with respect to intent and the underlying role that awareness plays in qualifying intent. The plaintiff case also shows how differently African Americans culturally frame and establish accountability: holding individuals accountable for what was said and done and the impact of that. The case also addresses the different cultural views on the overall responsibilities of leadership for the actions of individual employees. U.S. mainstream Anglo culture primarily holds individuals accountable for their actions, while African American culture divides the blame between those individuals who committed the act and the person or group in charge that, either through acts of commission or omission, created a climate that would allow that kind of behavior to occur.

These different cultural perspectives on intent versus impact and on leadership accountability around what happens also play out in the workplace. In one such example, African Americans asked the union steward, "How come there are only blacks are on the second shift?" The union steward said, "Seniority!" Blacks then asked, "How come whites have all the seniority?" African Americans view any inconsistent treatment along racial lines as likely to have had a racial basis or bias. Typically, CWM and CWW will react to those charges of racial bias with regard to what was meant at the time that they did it. So when blacks registered a complaint to their white supervisor that "whites got all the good vacation time," their white supervisor said that vacation times were awarded "on a first come, first serve basis." Blacks then asked, "How come whites knew to come in first?" It turned out on investigation that the reason for the racially skewed result was because the announcement to apply for vacation times was made at the first shift. Since there were only white workers on the first shift, they knew first to apply and so got the best vacation times. However, because it was not his intent to skew the distribution of vacation times to favor the white workers, the white supervisor did not see himself accountable for the outcome. Conversely, the black workers did not believe the white supervisor did not mean to direct the outcome to favor the white workers, because, for them, intent is inferred from what was said and done and, in part, because he should have known. Also, by not taking responsibility for what happened, the white supervisor lost whatever credibility he might have had with the black workers on that shift.

As it applies to the above examples, managers and supervisors need to broaden their concept of fairness to consider access and outcomes, or with respect the Supreme Court decision in *Griggs v. Duke Power,* disparate impact, not just processes that have the appearance of fairness, like, seniority or first come, first serve. As to the above workplace example, announcing that workers could start applying for vacation times at the start of the first shift created a process that, even without intentionally promoting any particular outcome, set things up for the white workers to get the best vacation times. As such, the process was tainted even by the standards for equal access that CWM consider fair, and especially so by African American standards that also take into account parity with respect to outcomes. With respect to the earlier example of press coverage of JonBenét Ramsey: broadening accountability to take into account the impact on others with respect to what is being said and done and not limiting accountability only to what was in the state of mind of the person who made the decision would also be an effective way to deal with the different U.S. mainstream and African American cultural standards of accountability described above. Looking for pragmatic ways to solve the problem of equal access and outcome for diverse groups within the U.S. workplace, or within the larger society, requires that all parties go beyond the limitations that are set by looking at things only through one (their own) cultural lens.

CHAPTER FOUR

CWM Cultural Style at Work

The standard corporate view of a "team player" is one who does what is right for the company even when—or maybe especially when— that goes against individual personal (moral or ethical) values or beliefs. It is often called "getting on board with the program." In terms of identity, and to manage the dichotomy, CWM create separate and distinct spheres of being and doing (who they are as a person from what they do at work); or they develop a "company me/we" mindset, coalescing who they imagine themselves to be with what they do for a living ("You are what you do"). This CWM being/doing dichotomy shapes their moral universe as well. The principled/moral sense that CWM have of themselves is framed by who they are—both at work and outside of work—sometimes corresponding to what they do outside of work, rarely, by what they do at work. This compartmentalized view allows CWM to see themselves as good people, regardless of what they do for a living or how they do their job. Exceptions to this rule are those CWM who are driven by strong religious convictions. For example, one engineer who was a Mennonite and had an antiwar position made sure that he worked on the commercial rather than defense side of the business. This distinction—what for him was a compromise—was not appreciated by other Mennonites in his community, however. His car mechanic, for example, refused to work on his car anymore once he found out that his employer also made "weapons of war."

Notwithstanding these exceptions, CWM, in the main, see what they do at work as promotional—moving things to one or another level of operation—driven by amoral capitalistic (bottom line) considerations—not personal, principled, ethical, or moral considerations. The motivation of companies to do ethics training is also essentially driven by the same pragmatic/opportunistic considerations. "Doing the right thing" means doing what's right for the company: not engaging in misconduct that could cost the company its license or its ability to bid on profitable federal contracts. This conflation of ethics and opportunity is epitomized in a position taken by a CEO of a company accused of ethics violations in pursuit of defense department contracts: "He wants to turn ethics into a competitive advantage for Boeing."[1] For African Americans, Hispanics, Asians, and other minority groups (e.g., LGBT people) and to a lesser degree CWW, "doing the right thing" has a moral as well as pragmatic ring to it both in the workplace and the larger society, and, as we have shown, for members of religiously minded groups, also. Unlike CWM, their moral compass does extend to what they and others do at work especially around matters relating to social inclusion and parity in the company. These differences make a difference in how these groups relate to each other at work.

CWM see the actions that they take at work for practical/pragmatic reasons as a requirement of the job, not something that they could decide not to do, for example. Others see what CWM do (or not do at work) as things that CWM could do differently, if they had a different set of priorities. One example of this is who attends conferences on diversity. It is mostly CWW, people of color, and other minorities (e.g., LGBT people). CWM managers who do attend are there by invitation; other CWM are there because they have some direct role to play in the human resources area. Members of other groups often note that in other matters—maintaining quality control or meeting production deadlines—CWM are quick to make changes in the process to ensure that results are met. Not so when the result is greater social parity of CWW and people of color in the workplace.

A CWM vice president at a steel company encouraged the development of a rating system to evaluate those managers who supported diversity within the company, those who were considered "neutral," and those who clearly opposed such efforts. These ratings were directly tied to bonuses at the end of the year and considerations for promotion. Because he was considered "diversity friendly," it came as a shock to members of diverse groups within the company when he promoted a CWM who had gotten one of the lowest ratings in support of the company's diversity initiative to a new position. The vice president's rationale for doing so was that he needed to get a "fast turn around" on the recently vacated position, and he knew that that person "could do the job." Because, the vice president felt that he had acted correctly and had already demonstrated in other ways his support of the diversity initiative within the company, he was dismayed at the reaction that he got from members of his diversity council, who saw his commitment to diversity as nothing more than lip service and not following through where it really counted.

By way of contrast, a CWW managing editor had a photo director position open at her paper. Because most of the directors at the paper were white men, as were all the internal candidates in the department who qualified for that position, and everyone in that department was either a white man or white woman, she was determined to find a person of color to fill that position. The parent company gave her a month to conduct her job search and told her that if she did not fill that position within that time, she would lose it. Through diligent effort she ultimately was able to fill the position with a person of color within that time constraint. But she said that she was also prepared to leave the position open until such time as she could find such a person even if that meant losing it. Her rationale was that positions at that level were scarce and if it were filled quickly from the available internal candidate pool of white men, it would take years for that kind of position to open up again, thus frustrating and defeating her attempt to promote greater diversity in the newsroom, especially, at the upper level. As she put it, "Nothing would change." Strategically, she also considered that by not filling that position it might open up again—the need was still there—she might still get another chance later to fill it with a diverse hire. But that option would have been foreclosed if, as she put it, she "took the easy way out" and filled the position with someone from the available white male pool just to make sure that the position would not be lost. As she put it, "The last guy who had that position was there 17 years! And you know they're not going to create another position at that level . . . the need for that just isn't there."

What Constitutes Commitment

CWM, compared to African Americans, have different views of what "commitment" to a principle or cause means. For example, in one training session, participants were asked, "How many of you think that a person should have the right to live wherever they want if they can afford it?" Almost everyone raised their hand. We then proposed the following scenario: "OK, you live in an all white neighborhood and are ready to sell your home. An African American middle-class couple comes and wants to buy your home. Your neighbors find out—many of them are your friends—and urge you not to sell. You comply and take your home off the market—to avoid a discrimination suit—and put it up again three months later and this time sell it to a white couple." Question: "Can you still, on principle, claim that you believe that a person should have the right to live wherever they want if they can afford it?" African Americans in the session say no, because your actions are inconsistent with what you said you believe. Whites are often divided. Some of the more religiously committed ones agree with the African Americans and call that inconsistency hypocritical. Others, however—and this is the position of most of the other CWM and CWW in the group—say, "Yes! I can still claim that I believe that. It's just that it's more important for me to retain the friendships that I developed with my neighbors over the past 17 years than to act on principle. Besides, I don't even know these other people." When asked if they would act on principle if it were not complicated by these other factors, some say yes. One southern white man in the group called that "situational ethics." For African Americans, this comes across as, "If it is not too expensive and not too risky, and not too inconvenient, you can count on me"—this is in stark contrast to the African American standard for sincerity: "Notwithstanding issues of cost, risk and convenience, if it is the right thing to do ('right' in a moral sense) then you need to do it." As one African American woman put it, "For blacks to consider you sincere, you have to give up at least a leg."

The U.S. mainstream pattern of qualified commitment was also shown several years ago in a survey conducted by the *Wall Street Journal* to find out if those who claimed to have environmental concerns actually made purchases that were consistent with that position. The reporter found that the decisions that members of this survey group made were heavily influenced by issues of cost or convenience. She stated that while "Americans *say* they are willing to make sacrifices for a better environment . . . what they *do* is another story. When it comes to making concrete buying decisions, many aren't the environmentalists they claim to be."[2] It comes as no surprise, therefore, that this pattern of difference—qualified versus unqualified commitment—should also manifest itself at work. For example, the National Association of Black Journalists (NABJ) conducted a survey some years ago among its members and newsroom managers. One of the questions asked was, "Does your news organization make a serious effort to recruit black journalists?" Ninety-one percent of newsroom managers—predominantly CWM—and 47 percent of NABJ members said yes. Other surveys in other organizations showed a similar discrepancy between what CWM managers and African Americans and members of other groups consider a "serious" effort.

Similarly, a bank in Chicago, concerned about the lack of African Americans in senior-level positions, set up a committee to study the problem and to find ways to remedy the situation. After more than a year there were still no African Americans found or hired. The other African Americans who worked there considered the effort being made by the committee as bogus. The CWM on the committee thought that, notwithstanding the outcome, they still should have been credited with a good faith effort. At issue here are matters related to what constitutes a fair and effective process (means and ends) that we discussed earlier. What also matters for CWM and African Americans is what qualifies someone as sincere. For CWM, their intent, or what they meant, established their sincerity or good will even if there were no immediate return on their efforts. For African Americans, what counted was the final result ("Were blacks found and hired or not?"). Also relevant is that CWM do not feel that their moral character—which houses intent, sincerity, and commitment—is implicated when decisions or outcomes are made as a result of pragmatic considerations, regardless of where the lines of cost, risk, and convenience are drawn. For members of other groups, however, moral character is implicated. Consequently, where the line is drawn is critical to their assessment of what constitutes a good faith effort.

In this regard, an African American executive editor told of one situation where she, because of budget considerations, was unable to save the summer internships at her paper that had been set aside for three African American students from a local university—it was either use the money for that or lay off a permanent employee. However, she did contact other papers to make sure that they got placed somewhere else. She also cited another time where she was able to finesse the budget situation in order to rehire an African American journalist that had left her paper a few years earlier. She did that by making an offer to the woman in anticipation that hiring a new employee would be the first thing the publisher would try to delay—that being the easy fix—to keep the budget balanced. Because an offer had already been made, however, he was unable to do that. Not so incidentally, the budget ultimately did get balanced from cutting costs elsewhere, but not at the expense of a diverse hire.

In another company, several diversity training sessions were set up for the following year in the consumer products division when the CWW in charge were told that training would have to be cancelled because the profits of the division at the end of the year were 8 percent instead of the 11 percent that had been projected. CWW felt that the company had re-neged on a commitment and felt a keen sense of betrayal as a result. CWM took the cancellations in stride. They did not believe the company had "reneged" on anything, because, in their view, nothing was promised. They also saw the cancellations as necessary given the general business climate and the accountability of the company, first and foremost, to shareholder interests and concerns.

At issue here are all of the above points of disagreement: where the lines of cost, risk, and convenience are drawn (especially around the level of sacrifice that defines being committed) and concern over fair process versus fair outcome. But there is another difference, too, with respect to what had, in fact, been proposed. CWW took what was said as a com-mitment—like a promissory note—especially since the money for the training had already been allocated. CWM never saw what was said as a promise or contract, but rather, a probability statement.[3] The basis for the view taken by CWM stems from their view of the world of work: one of constant change, which contains variables over which they often cannot control despite their best efforts. For CWM, the best that one can hope for is that things will turn out as projected. As the *Wall Street Journal* said in an editorial several years ago, even the soundest pension plans can be buffeted by stock market exigencies. The CWM felt that the 11 percent projected profit on which the budget for next year's training had been predicated was an uncertain element in the equation. Because of that, they also did not express much sympathy for the CWW's position. They saw them as having unrealistic expectations. CWW as well as Afri-can Americans and other persons of color viewed the CWM take on what happened as convenient for CWM—they were not keen on the money that had been allocated for diversity training to begin with—and brought up the issue of priorities and other things that money was being spent on that CWM supported (the golf outing) despite the smaller than expected profit.

Choices/Priorities

It would be a mistake to think that the probability position that the CWM took in the last example over having to abort best laid plans only came about because what was scrapped was diversity training. The element of uncertainty generally shapes the way CWM promote and anticipate outcomes—they engage what they want to see happen with an apprehension of things going wrong even when doing things of the highest priority: a realization captured by the phrase "Murphy's Law," which, in effect, says, "whatever can go wrong will" (to which others have added, "and at the worst possible time"). Nonetheless, the level of priority—expressed as the amount of money, time, and effort spent on a project—does affect the likelihood of its successful resolution or outcome. So the strategic challenge then becomes how to get CWM to treat things of lower priority, like diversity initiatives, with greater consideration and seriousness than they did before. One way is to manage the cost/risk factor. CWM do get behind things if you can show that the cost/risk for not getting behind a project or program is greater than for getting behind it.

For example, an African American woman, who was a senior editor at a paper, asked me what it would cost to have me address some of the cultural conflicts that blacks and whites were having in the newsroom. Her CWM boss said that the fee was too high, and so the matter ended. Two weeks later I got a call from her saying the paper wanted to bring me in. I asked her what had changed since the fee was still the same. She said that the racial conflicts she talked about earlier had been picked up by the other newspaper in town and had become a source of embarrassment to their paper. It suddenly became more expensive not to address the problem than to address it. He also found the money, leaving the African American group to wonder whether his earlier statement about not having the money was, in fact, true. It wasn't, given the literal definition of honesty that African Americans were working with. Not having the money, however, was consistent with the priorities that he had set on spending at the time. When the pragmatics of the situation changed, he found the money—perhaps in the contingency fund that he was unwilling to tap into earlier.

In like fashion, at the 1999 UNITY (journalists of color) conference, many African American journalists talked about having gotten their first job as journalists during the race riots in the 1960s, when the only person that their white editors could safely send into that situation to get the story was a journalist of color.

One CWM managing editor saw risk as a key factor in the hiring of diverse journalists by the CWM who worked for him. He said, "If we have ten AME [assistant managing editor] positions that we're hiring for, four of those might be filled with people who are diverse. If there is only one AME position available, however, we don't see any diversity." He framed that as his CWM reporters saying to themselves, "OK. With ten positions to be filled I'll take a chance and hire some diverse candidates, but if there's only one position, the risk of doing that is too great." Insofar as CWM feel that diversity hires cannot fail they create a situation where hiring diverse candidates becomes an elective rather than a requirement. This, in turn, makes it increasingly difficult to hire people who are diverse in key positions. Yet, as one African American woman journalist said, "We ought to be able to get hired and fail in these positions the same way that CWM are able to get hired and fail."

Outside the workplace, in the society at large, the way risk is managed generally impacts issues of trust, good will, and, ultimately, overall credibility. Implicit is also what level of activism is necessary to qualify someone as a good person. The CWM social standard is "do no harm." The African American social standard is to be more actively engaged in doing good. As the Vista slogan of the 1960s said, "If you're not part of the solution, you're part of the problem."

Managing Interpersonal Risk at Work

The training sessions that we run reflect the various themes that we have mentioned so far. Critical for CWM is the fear that anything they may do or say at work will come back to haunt them and ultimately jeopardize their careers. Part of the problem is that—since they do not know what they do not know—they also cannot anticipate how others might object to the things they say and do. Another part of the problem is that when CWM do find out about the effect of what they said or did had on others, they often find out about it indirectly, and, for them, even more telling, officially: someone filed a complaint with human resources or called the ethics hotline. When that happens, CWM feel blindsided and retreat to the only area at work left where they feel socially safe—that is, among other CWM. Another aspect of the problem is that the social pendulum at work and elsewhere has shifted such that the impact of what is said on others is often given greater social weight than what that individual intended or meant. The present social etiquette around cigarette smoking is a prime example of this shift in social entitlements around who is now required to accommodate whom. Years ago, smokers were free to light up whenever they wanted to, regardless of the effects of their smoking on others. The social leverage on who can smoke now—based on impact—is with non-smoking others.[4]

The impact of this societal shift on CWM is considerable, not only because of the constraints they are now generally experiencing on individual freedom—something that they cherish greatly—but also because their intentions, which implicate their moral character, are now inferred by what they said and did and its impact on others, rather than weighed or assessed separately with respect to what they meant. This new social pattern and shift in personal accountability was a key theme in Philip Roth's novel *The Human Stain*.[5] These factors contribute to the CWM present day experience of their work environment as walking on eggshells and being guilty as charged. The greater interpersonal risk that CWM feel at work—they are beginning to learn that they can no longer afford not to care—is something that CWM also now have a stake and interest in changing.

When asked what they want others to do know about them that they think others don't know or don't know well enough, CWM often say, "We're not bigots!" or "We're really not the enemy here!"—statements that reflect their sensitivity to how they are being perceived by members of other groups. CWM generally attribute this negative image to "rogue" elements within their group that give a bad name to the entire group and wish to have others see them as essentially good guys.

Cultural Style

One of the things that CWM learn within the training context is that the view that others have of them at work (e.g., selfish or uncaring) often has more to do with cultural style—how they manage themselves and others at work—than it has to do with specific things that they might say or do that others find offensive. One CWM cited, as an example, of being called to account for not greeting his subordinates when walking through their work area. He said, in explanation, that it was not "his *intent* to ignore them." He simply had other things on his mind at the time.

CWM have a view of themselves as being approachable and are surprised to learn that this view of them is not shared by members of other groups. At issue for them is that they consider the time spent problem-solving people issues—while necessary—as not really time spent on task. Consequently, despite their claim that their door is open to anyone who wants to see them, the time that they actually spend dealing with people issues is qualified by what they consider more demanding and essential bottom line considerations, such as the number of things that need to get done and the time they spend in scheduled meetings that often make them inaccessible when others want to see them. Metaphorically speaking, CWM have two signs outside their office: one says "welcome"; the other says "called to a meeting." Which sign reflects who CWM really are? CWM see the welcome sign as signaling their intent—and the basis on which their good will should be judged. They see the sign "called to a meeting" as a reflection of the pressures of the job: more something that they *have* to do than a choice. Yet for others, as discussed earlier, what CWM do, more than what they say, is the basis on which CWM are being morally judged. For example, one CWM, who was rated as not having visibly demonstrated a prodiversity stance within his company thought that he had been unfairly judged. He said when I talked to him, "They don't know what's in my heart." Another CWM, responding to the general view of CWM as racist and sexist until they prove they're not, said to non-CWM in the larger group, somewhat indignantly, "You don't know anything about me."

When CWM see how their work style implicates their moral character in the eyes of others, they become motivated to close the gap between how they are seen and wish to be seen by others. One thing that they often say at the end of training is that they think they need to make a determined effort to be more available to others than they presently are. Whether this translates to actual change in the way they manage themselves and others at work remains to be seen. Our starting position in our training is give everyone the benefit of the doubt, consequently, to deal with things as matters of ignorance—people don't know what they don't know—and to work with those who would do things differently if they had better information to work with. Our general training strategy is "pick the ripe fruit first!" This is also our approach to readers of this book.

The view that others have of CWM as uncaring also grows out of the limited personal sharing that CWM do at work. Members of other groups are more relationship driven than are CWM. However, it would be a mistake for members of other groups to think that CWM are only not sharing significant events in their personal life with them; they are also not sharing them with each other. For example, at one training session, a CWM senior-level manager asked others of his CWM group—many were those who directly reported to him—"How many of you know that I have a severely disabled son?" Most of those reporting directly to him said that they did not, even though they had worked for him for over seventeen years.

Remedies

One hoped for outcome for CWM that they express in the training context is to find ways to reduce risk. A common request of CWM of members of other groups is to tell them directly when they are doing something that offends them. This may be something that can be done as a by-product of those that have gone through the training session together. However, given the conventional, risk-averse, conflict-avoidant, absence-of-candor orientation that prevails within corporate America, it would be hard to imagine a work situation where this kind of forthright discussion between a CWM and member of another group could actually occur. Moreover, insofar as CWM are not privy to the impact that what they do (or don't do) has on others, they will also not have a sense of how they might do things differently. Until that happens, CWM will continue with business as usual: believing that how they do what they do presently is not only right, but commendable, until caught up short by a complaint about them from the ethics hotline.

Diversity councils consisting of members of each workplace group might be able to address these matters, but only after each council member goes through some form of multicultural training. This obviously applies to CWM, who often know only their own culture, but also to members of each of the other diverse groups as well. CWW, African Americans, Hispanics, Asians, and members of other ethnic groups in today's workplace have the advantage of knowing another culture—their own—in addition to knowing aspects of the mainstream U.S. work culture, but that does not necessarily make them more aware and adept in dealing with the social and cultural conflicts that they also have with each other, not just with CWM.

CHAPTER FIVE

Other Cultural Comparisons and Contrasts

CWM and American Indians

The cultural compartmentalization that CWM achieve—separating who they are as a person from what they do for a living—is very difficult for members of other cultural groups to do, such as American Indians. Margaret Brigham, our Ojibwa colleague, talks about the need for Native American people to find the true or right path ("The Red Road"), which is the one, as our Blackfoot/Blood/Metís colleague Leah Arndt says, that follows traditional teachings and ways of living. This distinction requires seeing and hearing—with the heart and mind instead of the eyes and ears—and remaining open. Margaret's test for that is, when you wake up in the morning, "if you can't say that you're 'happy to be alive,' then you're not on your true path and you need to start doing something else."

When Margaret introduced the concept of "The Red Road" in the training session, I wondered about the person's state of being when they asked themselves this question? CWM (myself included) and others who work in today's workplace gear up for the work day with a protective armor in anticipation of the stress that they are likely to experience that day. That protective gear (as well as a doing—as opposed to being—mindset and, with respect to time, a next-ness time orientation) gets in the way of being open, susceptible, and totally in the present moment, which I imagine one would need to be if one is going to get a fruitful answer to that question.

At the same time it is also, for me, a wish piece. I remember walking behind Margaret and a mentor of hers and hearing them talk about walking through the door of the longhouse at a university that her mentor had a key hand in having the university build. She asked Margaret, "Did you feel it as you walked through the door?" Margaret said yes. Later when I walked through that door I remembered that conversation. I know I really wanted to "feel it" as they did. But I also know after I walked through the door that I didn't. I think the American Indian training program has a similar pull on CWM and CWW and members of other groups, too. I know that it is always in great demand by clients even though, from a pragmatic standpoint, the ability for managers to use the information—American Indians often comprise just 1 percent of the workforce at a given company—is limited. We explain the demand for the program as having its origins elsewhere: curiosity to be sure, but also, perhaps, the need to deal with issues around colonial guilt and the hunger of people for an alternative of what their own culture offers.

CWM change jobs for material reasons or reasons that move them further along on their career path (better pay, promotion, etc.). Traditionally minded American Indians change jobs for reasons that relate to personal well-being. They also value jobs that allow them to do things for their family, community, or larger group (tribe or nation). We show this last pattern of difference in a video in which an American Indian woman, Alice, despite having a lot of individual success in her job, left because the administration was not doing enough to address the detention rate of American Indians students in the school. The importance of her personal sense of well-being along with her responsibility toward doing things to improve the situation for her people was not apprehended, let along appreciated, by either her U.S. mainstream peers or her CWM supervisor. One of her peers, trying to make sense of her leaving attributed it to "personal problems that she was having at home." They could not grasp how someone could be doing well individually, yet still leave because others of her group were not. When this video and discussion was presented at a National Association of Minority Media Executives conference, the African American participants also had a hard time relating to her decision to quit, but for different reasons. They felt that she was abdicating her "change agent" role in the organization, saying, "Who else would there be to act on behalf of your people if you leave?" What African Americans missed, and which differentiates them from American Indians, is the degree to which the latter will subject themselves to personal "wear and tear" for the sake of being a change agent for an organization in the absence of organizational support for change.

The basis for the African American position is that they do accept a lot of "wear and tear" for the sake of the group. They say, "Not only do I have to maintain a high level of productivity at work, but I also act as a change agent for the organization, and a role model within my community." They also feel that they would be letting their group down if they did otherwise, saying, "Somebody has to step up!" There is also a belief borne out of cynicism and reality that leaving to go to another place makes no sense because, in effect, the situation that you are likely to face in the new place will be no better—and may even be worse—than the one you're in at present. CWM, CWW, and members of other groups tolerate a lot of wear and tear at work trying to maintain high productivity with less and less support during times of employee cutback and low profit margins—what CWM call "doing more with less." American Indians won't accept purposeless wear and tear—"purposeless" is a key word here—and so move on to other jobs. As American Indians often say, "You don't want to make yourself sick." Also, for American Indians, the interests of the group and that of the individual are treated equally. So Margaret pointed out to the predominantly African American audience that "Alice will still be working for her people. She's just going to do it somewhere else," and she will do it in a place, as Alice says in the video, where she can also find "peace within herself."

Another reason for the different positions of American Indians and African Americans on how much wear and tear they are willing to take on behalf of their respective groups is that African Americans have a greater stake in mainstream U.S. institutions and organizations "acting right," as blacks say. Their well-being and that of their sons and daughters who will follow them into the mainstream depends on it for their livelihood and success. The social/political goal of African Americans and other ethnic minorities is still to integrate into the larger society and workplace, albeit on different terms and conditions. The social and political goal of American Indians, however, is sovereignty. The goal is to limit and protect against outside, mainly U.S. state and federal governmental, interference.

As regards the wear and tear factor, Leah Arndt makes the distinction between purposeless suffering, which leads to "imbalance," and purposeful suffering, which is "sacred." As she put it, she and other American Indians submit to a lot of wear and tear—suffering for purpose—to realize a "greater aim for ourselves and the people" during which time they also draw on traditional ways/ceremonies to help maintain harmonic balance. One critical area where many American Indians subject themselves to emotional upset is when they delve into their U.S. history to uncover the details surrounding colonial genocide. For example, when Margaret put together her multimedia presentation on this, it was initially extremely difficult for her to do that. She remembers going to her Indian instructor, Vine Deloria, saying, "I can't do this. It's too painful!" He told that she needed to do it; she needed to know about these things no matter how painful it was to go through the materials. Many American Indians still find this extremely difficult to do. One Sioux woman walked out of Margaret's presentation on this—she tolerated it for a while but then left. She said the flute music accompanying the presentation made it too hard to endure. When Margaret made the presentation to Canadian First Nations Indians, others began to weep openly—the wounds of the past were still open and raw—such that she had to stop and spend the rest of the time processing what people were feeling. Present day grabs of Indian land—as recently in Caledonia, Ontario—add to the level of pain. As Indians say, "It's still happening."[1]

American Indians are often seen as not being "team players" because they don't follow the chain of command within the organization. So their way of interacting with people in the workplace and those they come into contact with as customers and clients is to bypass those whom they consider to be simply "functionaries" and go directly to the person in charge. They say, "Otherwise it's a waste of my and other people's time." Of course, the same thing happens to them when they are the ones in charge. Margaret, as former principal of an elementary school in her American Indian community, constantly had to deal with Indian parents who bypassed those on her staff and wanted only to talk to her, even though she had delegated authority as well as responsibility to them. She said, "Twenty minutes with her counted for more than two hours with someone else" and "Everybody only wants to talk to the top dog!" Leah Arndt, likewise, told her husband, a policeman, who was complaining about someone in the department to talk to the chief. However, she added, since he works in the office of the chief and was complaining about a captain, it's "not as drastic a leap, though still a leap." Her Anglo husband, however, was still uncomfortable going over the captain's head, but, as Arndt said, "did it anyway and saw results."

U.S. mainstream organizations are risk averse, conflict avoidant, and suffer for the absence of candor. Those same characteristics describe the communication style of CWM. It also sets them at odds with other groups, like African Americans, whose communication styles are different.

CWM and African Americans

CWM and African Americans share a verbal, visible assertive mode of communication. They differ, however, when it comes to personally confronting another person around a hot topic in a direct and forthright manner. African Americans will. CWM won't. The position taken by CWM is "peace before truth" or "better an insincere peace than a sincere quarrel" in those situations that have the potential for generating conflict or push-back. The "don't ask, don't tell" conflict-avoidant protocol that the military has established for dealing with the issue of LGBT people serving in the military is another example of the U.S. mainstream position, as are caveats about discussing religion and politics in polite circles, or other matters that people are likely to have strong feelings about, such as abortion or racism. The saying, "If you can't say anything nice, don't say anything at all" has proverbial status and is often recited by CWM and, perhaps even more, by CWW, as cautionary advice about engaging in hot topics. The statement, "I can't talk to you now—you're too emotional," often said privately by white men to white women partners, also reflects CWM discomfort with volatile, high-energy, contentious discourse. The equivalent statement when things get heated at the corporate level is "put it in writing." The cultural position of African Americans is "truth before peace" or "without truth there can be no peace." Expressions that African Americans have to promote greater forthrightness are "Tell it like it is!" "Don't sugarcoat it!" and "No pain, no gain!"[2] Both CWM and African Americans see themselves as trying to promote a working relationship. The CWM strategy in that regard is "don't rock the boat!" The African American strategy is "keep it real!" Each group sees the other's approach as putting the relationship at risk. What African Americans call "truth seeking," CWM call "starting a fight." What CWM call "peace-keeping," African Americans call "going along to get along" or "not caring enough about the person or issue to want to waste the energy on it." A key issue between the two groups in the context of truth seeking is the value of struggle. CWM see such struggle as polarizing. African Americans see it as unifying. In the course of our training, we show a picture of a slide of individuals on opposite sides of a rope engaging in a tug-of-war and ask the group whether they see what's going on as "divisive" or "cooperative." We then ask those who see it as divisive, "What makes it divisive?" They say "opposition": people pulling in different directions. Their model for cooperation is people pulling in the same direction. Most of those in the group that see it as divisive are CWM. We then ask those who see the "tug of war" as cooperative, "What makes it cooperative?" Some say, "They're playing the same game." Others say, "The rope that they are using to pull in opposite directions is also holding them together." Their model for un-cooperative behavior is "letting go of the rope" or "not picking up the rope." These different views correspond to the different cultural positions of CWM and African Americans on the value of contentiousness and struggle around speaking the truth.

For example, in a *Los Angeles Sentinel* interview, Andrew Young, who at the time had a post with Working Families for Wal-Mart, was asked whether he was concerned that Wal-Mart causes smaller, mom-and-pop stores to close. "Well, I think they should; they ran the 'mom and pop' stores out of my neighborhood," the paper quoted Young as saying. "But you see those are the people who have been overcharging us, selling us stale bread and bad meat and wilted vegetables. And they sold out and moved to Florida. I think they've ripped off our communities enough. First it was Jews, then it was Koreans and now it's Arabs; very few black people own these stores."[3] Andrew Young's remarks were met with heavy criticism, ultimately causing him to resign his post with Wal-Mart. The negative reaction also seemed also to have caught him by surprise. "Things that are *matter-of-fact* in Atlanta, in the New York and Los Angeles environment tend to be *a lot more volatile,*" he said.[4] In another interview, Young defended his remarks: "I was giving a rational explanation of a historic phenomenon. . . . Can you talk about ethnicity objectively without it being demeaning or stereotypical?"[5] All of the above quotes by Young would be considered "just telling the truth" by African American cultural standards. Adding to the volatility for those who thought his remarks were inflammatory might also be the categorical way that U.S. mainstream people hear group characterizations: as implicating all members of a group, not just those "for whom the shoe fits."

With respect to these different cultural perspectives, the head of human resources of a university health center gained insight after listening to the above discussion of black and white communication style differences. She said that two of the criteria for assessing respectively negative and positive performance behavior at work were "Creates unnecessary conflict in the workplace," and, "Promotes candor in the workplace." African Americans were often evaluated by their white supervisors as "creating unnecessary conflict in the workplace." Conversely, African Americans saw themselves as "promoting candor." Accounting for the difference in interpretation are the different cultural attitudes around levels of forthrightness, passionate advocacy, and struggle.

Within the workplace an African American woman reported having had favorable evaluations on her work performance by her two previous managers, both CWM. She got a new manager, a CWW, who rated her lower on some of the performance criteria that she had been rated higher on before. Somewhat miffed, she went directly to her manager who explained to her why she got the ratings that she did. The black woman ended up agreeing with her manager's description of her work performance but commented that her previous managers had seen the same performance behavior as she had but rated her higher. The CWW said, "I have higher expectations of you." What bothered the black woman as she told the story was not so much that she was rated lower by her new manager, but that her previous managers did not tell her what she needed to know to become better at her job. We don't have any real information on why the previous manager didn't. The manager's behavior, however, is consistent with a CWM conflict avoidant-cultural orientation. Our theory is that rather than engage the African American woman in what might become a heated confrontation about a less than optimum work performance, the manager, literally, as well as figuratively, took "the path of least resistance," by rating her higher than she perhaps deserved. In support of the view that CWM often have of the cultural style of African American women, one CWM gave an example of an African American woman saying directly to the CWM present about a problem they were having, "What are you guys going to do about that?" He commented, "That kind of forthrightness, to white men, is quite intimidating."

By asking those with grievances to calm down as a prerequisite to dealing with the grievance, when what would really calm them down is doing something about the problem or situation that they are aggrieved over, CWM are again showing their discomfort dealing with emotionally charged situations. However, in matters of negotiation, the request to edit out emotions from the process has a strategic element to it also. By asking people to assume a mode of behavior before the fact—for example, suppression of anger—that would normally be possible only after the grievance has been satisfactorily resolved has the effect of creating a desired outcome without having had to give up or do anything to achieve it. The strategic aspect of this pattern can be seen in situations like the American Indian Movement (AIM) occupation of the Bureau of Indian Affairs (November 3–9, 1972). There, representatives of the U.S. federal government said that they would not negotiate with AIM as long as guns were being pointed at federal marshals. AIM spokespersons said they would lay down their arms only after a successful negotiation occurred. One wonders what would drive or compel the federal government to negotiate if they would have been able to achieve as a prerequisite to negotiations what would be (from the federal government standpoint) the object and outcome of negotiations: AIM laying down its arms.

While CWM at work may not be as aware of the strategic aspect behind asking someone to calm down as a prerequisite to talking about the problem, we might expect that professional negotiators are aware and strategize accordingly. For example, the U.S. government's condition for establishing negotiations with Iran with regard to its nuclear program was that "the Iranian regime fully and verifiably suspends its uranium enrichment and reprocessing activities." As Hersh notes, "Iran ... was being asked to concede the main point of the negotiations *before they started.*"[6] Moreover, if the strength of the grievance is grounded in emotion, for aggrieved parties to edit out emotions as a means of talking about the grievance is a catch-22 situation. If they don't edit out the emotion, then they are characterized as "irrational" or "out of control." If they do edit the emotion out, they imply that their grievance is without substance (how else would it be possible for them to be able to suppress their anger before their grievance was actually resolved?). Do those individuals also settle for less if they edit emotion out of the proceeding than if they don't? To avoid the catch-22 situation, aggrieved parties often use third-party mediators. This way they can remain true to their emotions and other, less directly affected parties can do the talking on their behalf.

CWM and Asians, Hispanics, and Middle Easterners

Individualism is a core and salient feature of white male culture. CWM place a high priority on individual freedom, autonomy, and self-determination. It is a culture within which individuals create their space. Other cultural groups emphasize the importance of the individual role within the family or larger society, which takes precedence over individual freedom, autonomy, and self-determination. Those cultures are hierarchical and role driven—constructed around individuals knowing their place. As in Confucianism, which holds that "the good society is one in which each individual occupies his proper place,"[7] individuals learn early the link between position and role and, from that, how they should behave. These different views and the cultural patterns that develop from them collide within the U.S. workplace as well as between U.S. companies and those they do business with abroad. Within the United States, they have a direct bearing on the success of company-wide diversity initiatives and the creation of an inclusive workforce.

Initiative

CWM see initiative, first and foremost, as residing within the individual. When people take or show initiative—an extension of individual self-determination—they are, in culturally appropriate CWM fashion, indicating that they see themselves as the center and starting point of creative action. In academic arenas, masters and doctoral candidates starting their thesis work are often asked by their U.S. mainstream professors, "What would you like to write on?" First-generation Asian students, who come from a master/learner educational system, respond to that question with, "Tell me what to write on." The initiating source of creative action for them is the teacher or professor. Within mainstream U.S. culture, acting on behalf of oneself is valued, promoted, and expected. It is a core value in U.S. mainstream therapy and family upbringing. Attributed to the influence of Harry Stack Sullivan, the precept, "Only do for others what they can't do for themselves. Don't do for others what they can do for themselves" is consistent with the dominant Anglo cultural values of self-reliance and individual self-determination. "Taking initiative" is also seen as a sign of self-assurance, self-confidence, self-respect, and general maturity in a person, often expressed as "standing up for what one thinks and deserves." Individuals who don't take initiative or can't (and for that reason are seen as not getting ahead at work or life) are unsympathetically characterized as having only themselves to blame. The assumption and value around self-initiative in the workplace is shown by the saying, "If you don't ask for a raise or promotion, you don't want it. If you can't ask for a raise or promotion, you don't deserve it." Initiative within traditional hierarchical cultures (Hispanic, Asian, Middle Eastern, etc.), like power and authority, appropriately belongs to and resides within the position or role that people have in a family or organization. Showing or taking initiative is a prerogative and responsibility of those in charge.

Within these cultures individuals do not ask for what they think they deserve—that is a form of self-promotion and negatively valued. Coming from cultures where work speaks for itself, asking for a raise or promotion implies that the work cannot speak for itself. On a personal level, as one Hispanic man said, "It feels like begging." The implicit contract in those cultures is that, in exchange for personal loyalty and hard work, "the boss looks out for me." Consequently, they expect those above them to know what they are doing and act appropriately on their behalf. They also assume that if they are not being recognized or rewarded by those whose role and responsibility it is to do so, then, either they are not working hard enough or the boss does not like them. They also do not feel it is their place to tell the boss what the boss is supposed to know and be doing. As our Latin American colleague said, "That's what bosses do. That's their job! If they don't know or do that, why are they the boss?" Also, because it is not only the responsibility but the prerogative of the boss to know and recognize what their employees are doing, bosses in those cultures are offended when workers ask for things or tell them what they are doing. It implies that they, the bosses, have been derelict in their duty and responsibility. Our colleague, Ilya Adler, gave the following example of someone who had spent some time in the United States asking for a raise in Mexico. He was told abruptly, "It is not your place to ask for a raise. It is my place to decide when it is time to give you a raise and it will be when I think you deserve one."

Workplace Conflict

The views that members of other cultural groups ascribe to their white male bosses for overlooking them ("He doesn't like me!") are probably not what is really going on for CWM. What is going on for CWM is that they expect others to initiate action on their own behalf much as they do themselves (as something positively sanctioned [and implicitly required] within mainstream U.S. culture). Conflicts develop in the workplace because members of other cultural groups (Asian, Hispanic, Middle Eastern, Russian, etc.) expect the person in charge to initiate action on their behalf. Communication breaks down and conflicts develop because each one is waiting for the other to make the first move. Note in the following quotes how instrumental the boss is seen to be in helping individuals with their career, especially from cultures where loyalty to the boss frames and defines the employee-to-boss relationship. "Keaton admitted that initially he was nervous about talking to his managers about the goals of his PDP (Performance Development Partnership) because they might consider his interest in moving to another area *as a sign of disloyalty.*" Kareem Muhammad said, "'If my manager didn't have interest in seeing that we attained goals, I don't see the process working.... You need a manager actively helping you in the areas where you want to improve. The manager steps in to make sure it happens, even if you go work for another group—since that would help you get to where you want to go."[8]

Solutions

There are two solutions here. One is short term, and the other is long term. The short-term solution is for CWM to know that just because their Hispanic and Asian employees are not asking for something doesn't mean they don't want it. The important thing to know is not to reward only those who ask but also those whose work speaks for itself. As one Chinese American man said when he was told by his Anglo colleague to let them know that he was interested in getting a promotion, "Don't they see how hard I have been working?" The long-term solution—long term because the change takes much longer to achieve—is for everyone to learn that, within the mainstream U.S. culture, individuals need to develop the ability to act on their own behalf, because, more often than not, others won't act on their behalf, unless and until they first act on their own behalf.

One example of this shift: a Puerto Rican manager would go to his white male boss and—consistent with his culture—respectfully ask for money that he needed to support the projects he and his team were working on. His boss regularly turned him down. After several such rejections, he asked his boss why. He was told it was because of the way he made his request: petitioning for support instead of telling him what he needed. Over time he learned to be more directly assertive with his boss—it was easier for him to do so when he told himself that he was doing it on behalf of his team, than for himself. As a result, he was much more successful getting his boss's support for his projects than before.

Another example that shows the possible adjustments that can be made to accommodate different cultural practices occurred when a CWM supervisor presented a list of those whom he regarded as deserving to be considered for salary raises and promotions to his South Asian manager. His South Asian manager asked him—something an Anglo manager, given his cultural attitude and lens, would probably not think of doing—

"Are there people who deserve to be on this list who did not ask for a raise or promotion?"

Styles of Management

One of the reasons that CWM managers don't initiate action on behalf of their employees is because the U.S. mainstream style of management, especially that of CWM, manages up and out more than down, which means that the problems that occupy their time or generally either that of their boss or those of their customers, rather than those of their employees. As managers, more than 50 percent of their time is spent in scheduled meetings,[9] which means that their knowledge of what their employees are doing is built as much or more around what their employees tell them they are doing as it is on actual observation. By delegating authority as well as responsibility to those who report to them, CWM also feel free to work on the problems of their boss and those of the company. The Hispanic and Asian management style is built around observation rather than employees telling managers what they have been doing—in those cultures work does speak for itself. Also, while responsibility is delegated downward, authority and political accountability remain with those in charge. Perhaps because of that, Hispanic and Asian managers make great efforts to know and more closely manage what their employees are doing since they are the ones that ultimately have to answer for the mistakes their employees make.

This management style of more closely monitoring often leads to conflicts between Hispanic and Asian managers and their U.S. mainstream employees who resist the shorter leash and closer oversight, accustomed as they are to having greater freedom and authority to go their own way. The essence of the culture clash is that in hierarchical cultures the boss also defines your role. There, the traffic light is red until the boss says it's green. In the U.S. mainstream CWM culture, individuals define their own role—the traffic light is green until the boss says it's red. The problem for these managers with CWM employees is that the latter do not feel the need to check with their boss to get prior approval for what they are doing. As a result, Hispanic managers, for example, see CWM as acting too much on their own and question their personal loyalty and respect for their position as a result.

Conversely, Hispanics and Asians working in U.S. mainstream companies are often looking to get approval from their boss for the work that they are doing and are reluctant to go off on their own without official authorization. This becomes a liability in those U.S. work environments where forgiveness is easier to come by than permission and where the management style is more to rein in their workers when they have over-extended themselves than to tell them what to do.

Identifying individuals for leadership positions is another area where cultural differences play a significant role. For example, CWM foreshadow the qualities and skills required for the next position in their present position. Within the mainstream U.S. workplace that is how individuals typically are identified as having leadership qualities. Individuals from hi-erarchical, role-driven cultures feel it is disrespectful to those above them to act as if they were the boss when that is not the position they hold. Their view is, "When I am the student, I don't act like the professor." Because there is not the same foreshadowing of those qualities of the next position, CWM managers assume that the person who does not show them leader-ship qualities is either not interested in being considered for the next posi-tion or not capable of doing the next job. Either way, to CWM managers, it comes across as not being leadership material.

Communication Style

Compounding the problem is communication style. Coming from a cre-ate your space culture, CWM value and prefer a more upfront, out there, verbal, visible, assertive style of leadership. By way of contrast, East Asian communication style is more modest and self-effacing—grounded in a culture that values the group more than the individual and standing in over standing out. In Japan, that view is expressed as, "The nail that stands out is hammered back down."[10] South Asians are more direct than East Asians in their communication style, but that has not made them neces-sarily more promotable. The position-sensitive, role-oriented ("know your place") cultural style of South Asians, as for East Asians and Hispanics, still falls below the radar screen of CWM managers and outside the realm of what they see and respect as leadership material.

Solutions

What needs to happen here is to broaden the way individuals are iden-tified for leadership positions. As one Asian man put it, "Just because people are not verbal, visible and assertive, or do not ask for things for

themselves, doesn't mean they won't make good managers." CWM sometimes express this last view, thinking that if individuals cannot act on behalf of themselves, they will also not be able to act well on behalf of others.
What CWM miss here is that it is easier for members of other cultural
groups to assert themselves on behalf of others than to do so on behalf of
themselves. As they say, "I can promote others. I just can't promote myself." So what needs to happen to create a pathway to leadership positions
for those individuals coming from hierarchical, role-driven cultures? The
first thing to know and note is that these individuals will display leadership skills consistent with their cultural style when they are authorized to
do so.

So before deciding that they don't have them, CWM managers need to
find out if they do by creating a quasi-leadership position for them—team
leader, for example—or observing them in an authorized leadership role
outside of work. For example, one CWM manager wanted to promote an
Asian man who worked for him but wasn't sure whether he could take
charge of a team since he presented himself in a deferential and subordinate manner when interacting with him. He attended a community function where he saw the man in an entirely different role—he was president
of his local chapter of Asian American engineers—and saw all of those
leadership qualities that he missed seeing earlier. The other thing is to
acknowledge differences in leadership style. Not everyone is comfortable
being upfront verbal, visible, and assertive. Others might be equally effective managing a group working behind the scenes and in a more self-
effacing manner.[11]

For example, a South Asian man had been told by one CWM manager that "he did not have the style that was valued within the company."
He said that he did not do well under that manager but finally got one
that recognized his ability and promoted him. He eventually ended up in
charge of an engineering division that had the reputation of delivering
products late, many of which also needed to be reengineered. He made it
his job and goal as manager to turn both things around, which he did in
two years. He said, with reference to what he had been told earlier about
his "not [sufficiently] aggressive" cultural style, "Isn't [delivering] 100 percent right, and 100 percent on time, assertive or aggressive enough?" So
what was he able to show at the back end, as our colleague Adrian Chan
often says, that some of his CWM managers did not see at the front end?
Once he had the position, he was able act in a more direct, authoritative manner and otherwise show his leadership ability. Likewise, a first-

generation Chinese American man worked for a U.S. company doing business in China. He had a strong interest becoming the one to lead that enterprise but only got picked after the company got tired of continuing to lose business to a German firm. When he finally got the position, he said to Adrian Chan, "Now I can tell my boss he was wrong."

Career Planning: Promises/Probabilities

CWM use probability statements when they do career planning with their employees. They say things like, "Before you can be considered for the next position, you have to do X, Y and Z." This does not mean, for CWM, that once an employee does X, Y, and Z that they will necessarily get the next position. It is a statement of probability: employees increase their chances for getting the next position if they have the necessary prerequisites. Whether they actually get it depends on other factors (budget, need, others in the candidate pool, etc.). Hispanics, South Asians, and others from hierarchical cultures, interpret these statements as promises or contracts. They think that once they get the prerequisites, they are a shoo-in for the next position. Their reasoning is that those in charge would not have told them this if they did not have a personal interest in promoting them or have the power to make it happen. CWM, in turn, believe they are just giving their employees information on what the next steps are to getting ahead. They are often doing this impersonally because it is part of their job or role. As such, they consider the information "free goods"—as in "no strings attached" and "no need for anyone to reciprocate." In Hispanic, Middle Eastern, South Asian, and other cultures, information is bartered, bought, sold, or otherwise traded on. It is not a free commodity. So when a Hispanic woman in the United States wanted to locate her birth certificate to find out who her real mother was—she was born in Mexico and adopted—her U.S. mainstream friend advised her to find someone who could tell her what the local institutional rules and regulations were for getting this information. The Hispanic woman thought that she would either have to befriend someone or pay someone who worked there to get that information. So when bosses share information on how to get ahead, Hispanics, Middle Easterners, South Asians, and others think that it is motivated by bosses having a personal interest in them and a stake in their career—the boss could just as well have decided not to share that information—rather than the boss simply following the rules of the organization or what they regard as their corporate role and responsibility.

Moreover, in politically driven hierarchical cultures, bosses do not propose something that they cannot make happen, since it is important to show that one is well connected, especially, in organizations and societies where who you know is essential to getting ahead. This is, after all, how they probably got to their position. So when employees learn about their promotion is when they actually get it. This is what happened to a CWM engineer who worked for a Japanese manager. His boss told him that he had promoted him to be manager. The CWM did not think that he was ready to be manager, but his boss said that it would be a great disrespect to him if he did not accept the position. He took it despite his reservations about his readiness and despite his reluctance to hand over career decisions to his boss. This reluctance comes from the CWM view that, while others can be helpful in facilitating career development, the final decision on career choice rests with the individual himself. The pattern is quite different in these other cultures. As my Sicilian barber said, talking about his son that had just started to work after having graduated with a masters degree in finance, "He got his degree, now he needs to be adopted."

Another cultural difference revolves around general assumptions and practices about who manages your career. In U.S. mainstream culture, individuals manage their own career. In hierarchical, "know your place" cultures, it is the boss who manages your career. The frustration that Hispanics and Asians experience with the individually driven "create your space" culture operating within U.S. companies is that they invest in (and expect) their boss to make things happen for their career growth. When their boss either doesn't make things happen or can't, they feel frustrated and betrayed, especially if they have shown personal loyalty to the boss or feel their work has been exemplary. They also feel helpless in not knowing what else to do. Coming from a culture where work speaks for itself and the boss is their report card, they find it extremely difficult to move to a self-validating, self-determining, individually driven culture characteristic of the U.S. workplace. This situation is exacerbated still further in companies that encourage lateral movement—learning different jobs within the company to make workers more employable—because, by transferring to a new job, workers also get a new boss. For example, one newly hired Hispanic woman had three bosses in a year and a half and, given her orientation to invest in her boss and let the boss define her role, was totally confused because each boss that she had told her something different. One boss said that she was already doing work in a different pay grade and, therefore, should either get a higher salary for the work she was doing or get a promotion to the position that corresponded to the work she was doing. Had she stayed with that boss she might have gotten those things. But she was transferred to another boss who was reluctant to move her to a different position and pay grade because of her youth and limited overall time working within the company. CWM, who primarily manage their own career, neither invest in their boss the way members of these other groups do nor expect their boss to make things happen for them the way that members of other groups do. If the boss can and does make things happen for them, fine. But if the boss doesn't, then CWM find a way to work the system and get a new boss.

Self-Initiation versus Authorized Entrée

Brainstorming serves the cultural and communication style of CWM and African Americans (verbal, visible, assertive, and self-initiating) very well. African Americans are especially adept at "getting to the hole" first, perhaps owing to the influence of jazz in the culture. If they don't speak at brainstorming meetings, it has more to do with caution and politics—the risk factor in speaking up—than ability. CWM finish a strong second in their ability to engage in the spontaneous free flow of ideas. They are first, however, when it comes to making sure their voices are heard within the meeting. The reasons for this have to do as much with entitlements and position as it does with cultural style. Other groups fall behind African Americans and CWM with regard to spontaneous self assertion. CWW who are put off by the competition for the floor and the fight for individual recognition are sometimes reluctant to enter the fray. For others the pace and structure of the meeting inhibits their active participation. The African American cultural pattern is to take the floor. CWM and CWW assume the floor is there to be taken. Asians wait to be given the floor.

In hierarchical, "know your place" cultures people don't speak until they are authorized to do so. The first person authorized to speak at work is the person in charge of the meeting who then authorizes others to speak at his or her discretion or with respect to order set by the agenda. Consequently, what inhibits the active participation of members of these cultural groups has to do with more than just developing the requisite skill set to wait for the holes and jump in. For one, there is the issue of etiquette. Asians—East Asians, especially—say, "It feels like people are criticizing and interrupting each other." There is also the importance of making sure the ideas that you propose are thought through beforehand

and right. East Asians have a "think before you speak" cultural style, not a "think as you speak," style, as CWM and other groups have. In East Asian culture, what is valued is the right opinion, not simply your own opinion. As one Japanese engineer said, "In Japan, what is written down is 100 times more important than what is said. For people to take what you say seriously it has to be officially ratified and confirmed." That is why Asians view U.S. brainstorming meetings in which ideas are simply thrown out as "shooting from the hip" or "bullshitting."

There is also the issue of hierarchy. When the boss is in the room, others speak at his or her discretion. Others may have their own opinion, but it is the boss that has the right (authorized) opinion. Because people from hierarchical cultures are often reluctant to speak when their boss is present, it often becomes a strategic move on the part of bosses to absent themselves, knowing full well the inhibiting, sometimes intimidating, effect they can have on others. Our head of operations for Latin America, Ilya Adler, suggests, "If you want to get creative input from Hispanics at a meeting, an important and effective strategic move would be to try to get the boss out of the room." Within our own training we are also alert to the inhibiting effect a boss's presence may have even within a group of CWM. Most of the time, as we watch who participates, we see almost everyone speaking up in that group. If the CWM senior-level person is doing most of the talking, we sometimes talk to him at the break and suggest that he back down and let others speak or take the lead. They generally have no problems with the request being made or complying with it. In one Hispanic male group, the highest ranking Hispanic in the company participated, despite his dominant position. He dealt with the hierarchical issue—the power distance between himself and others in the group—by taking on the role of facilitator. He used his position to make sure that the voice of each person in the group was heard and became part of the larger group agenda. Yet, when it came time for the group to report out to the larger group, the other Hispanic men, in respect of his position, stepped aside to let him represent their individual issues, despite his urging, in respect of the process, to have each group member speak for himself.

These same cultural issues impact performance evaluations in which employees are expected to offer their own opinions, even to the point of disagreeing with the boss's assessment of the situation. The cultural assumptions that CWM make are that individuals will value and present their own views of the situation, treat them on a par with everyone else, including the boss, and freely assert them throughout this process. The likelihood is slim that first- and even second-generation Hispanics, Asians, and members of other hierarchical cultures will do that. The view is "the boss is my report card."

CWM are encouraged early on—an outgrowth of self-reliance and self-determination—to see themselves as authors of their own lives and the primary source of creative thought and action. They, as parents, might say, to their children at the beach, "Hey, kids, here's a pail and shovel, go build something." And even if the first products of their kids are half-baked, they still give credit and encouragement for trying and, to the extent that it applies, for ownership and originality. For Asians, there is no such thing as partial credit for things that are less than perfect. Quite the contrary: people find flaws even in things that are very well done. For example, in the film *The Joy Luck Club,* the mother of newly crowned chess champion Waverly Jong, said to her, "How come you win by losing so many pieces?" Waverly protested, "But Mom, that's not how the game is played." Her mother replied, "Next time you win, losing fewer pieces." Because of perfectionism, there is also no public display of things that are half-baked or incomplete. For Asians, there is a right way and a wrong way, and anything less than completely right is completely wrong. Our Asian colleague gave an example of this pattern that he got from a professor/observer of a classroom in Japan. A Japanese student was making a clay horse that was perfect in every detail except the tail. His Japanese teacher crushed the entire horse and asked the student to start over from the beginning. The message being communicated was nothing less than perfect is acceptable. A U.S. mainstream teacher would have said, "So far, a great job! Now all you need to do is a little more work on the tail."

Solutions

Brainstorming, as presently conducted within U.S. mainstream companies favors the cultural style of some groups (African Americans and CWM) more than others. So what can we do to create greater parity in the workplace for groups that do not do well within this kind of process? A necessary but longer term solution would be to develop skill sets and change attitudes and values over spontaneous self-assertion that would enable everyone to participate in brainstorming on a more equal basis. A faster turnaround can be gotten by changing the pattern of the meeting to make it more accessible to groups or individuals with different cultural styles. In that regard, some organizations have started to use a "structured round robin" where individuals are given notice before the meeting what the topic is to enable them to prepare ahead of time, and, in alternating fashion, report on the topic when the time comes for them to present. This also works well with the think before you speak cultural orientation of East Asians (vs. Anglo think as you speak orientation) during brainstorming at meetings.[12] Another way would be to find ways to enable individuals to contribute outside of the meeting and treat that on a par with those contributions that occur inside the meeting. These are additive rather than mutually exclusive alternatives. For example, a second-generation Japanese American from a mixed marriage (father is Anglo and mother Japanese) was rated low in creativity in her performance evaluation because of her (nonactive) participation in brainstorming meetings. The way she did contribute to what went on at the meeting was, later on at home, organizing in detail everything that people said, adding her own thoughts, and then presenting the complete report to her boss the next day at work. It was very well received by her boss. By showing a more deliberate version of what went on at the meeting, she provided the boss with a clearer picture of what happened than he was able to recall. She was also able to create a sense of logic, sequence, and continuity that the meeting itself did not have. It also served as a blueprint for follow-up. The problem for the employee was that the company had no performance evaluation category to cover that kind of contribution. The category creativity was reserved for active participation in brainstorming meetings. Yet her contribution was also seen as valuable. What the company did was to create a new category—they called it "innovation"—that recognized her outside of meeting contribution at a level that was consistent with what others achieved through active participation in the meeting itself.

In one manufacturing site, CWM supervisors were frustrated by their (first-generation) Vietnamese factory workers saying yes repeatedly in response to the question, "Do you understand?" when their performance on the assembly line clearly showed that they really did not understand. Their view of that behavior was "why can't their yes really mean yes the way *we* use it?" That view makes the Vietnamese workers' behavior the problem. It also reflects an assimilationist view of unilateral accommodation to the host culture. There are several problems with this view from a multicultural standpoint. First, it only takes into account the reality of what is going for the supervisor, not for what is also going on for the Vietnamese worker. Second, it contains with it an expectation of change that probably can't happen until the second generation. Third, it does not consider why the Vietnamese worker is not saying, no if he does not understand. In that last regard it is important to understand the importance of harmony in Asian, especially East Asian, culture. Harmony between people is Confucianism. Harmony with nature is Taoism. Harmony within oneself is Buddhism. Following Adrian Chan: "Harmony above all!"

A key element in maintaining harmony is the avoidance of shame, or loss of face. With respect to the above situation, as our Vietnamese colleague Lan Nguyen Roberts said, "It would be shameful for the Vietnamese worker to admit, 'I do not understand.' It would also be shameful to imply, by saying, he does not understand, that maybe the instructions he was getting weren't all that clear." Thus by saying yes, he is not only saving his own face but that of his supervisor as well. In this regard, the Vietnamese worker is not only representing the Vietnamese position but one shared by other East Asian cultures as well.[13] Finally, making the other person's behavior the problem doesn't deal with the real problem from a cross-cultural standpoint, which is that the Anglo supervisor is relying on the response he gets when he asks, "Do you understand?" to give him accurate information. In situations where harmony or saving face trumps forthrightness, that reliance is misplaced. One Vietnamese supervisor found a way to get accurate information on whether her workers really understood—she also knew better than to ask them, "Do you understand?" as she would have gotten the same answer—by having all workers (not just Vietnamese) demonstrate that they understood what they needed to do directly on the factory assembly line. Also by using peer coaching—she asked those who knew to help those that needed it—she, in effect, avoided making saving face an issue.

CHAPTER SIX

Multiculturalism and Social Inclusion

How do we create greater social inclusion of women and people of color within the U.S. workplace? And what do we do about the overall cultural style of the organization? If we return to the "assimilationist" approach advocated in the not too distant past by school superintendents preparing kids for "the real world," then everyone would leave their different cultural style at doorstep of the workplace and adopt the cultural style of CWM. But the real world today is global and multicultural, not monocultural. So why promote acculturation in just one area, when the world is crying out for people with multicultural competencies and sensibilities? As Jean Mavrelis says, what is the logic behind asking someone not to speak their non-English language at home (part of detribalization within the U.S. "melting pot,"), only to ask them to learn one later on in school—when the best time for learning a second language has long since passed? What was opportunistic yesterday is not what is opportunistic today in the global marketplace where speaking more than one language and knowing more than one culture gives individuals a significant competitive advantage over those who don't.

There are also other reasons to develop other cultural competencies than just the competitive advantage it might bring in the marketplace. There is a concept in biology that "the evolutionary potential of any organism is enhanced if it has built within itself the flexibility to adapt to changing circumstances."[1] The enemy of successful adaptation is rigidity, or becoming so wedded to a "one best way" that other avenues become foreclosed as a result. People gravitate to the familiar even if they know that it won't work and resist the untried and unfamiliar because it is not part of "received wisdom" and they fear being out there all by themselves. Culture in many ways is a kind of fossilization or arrested development. It fixes a particular mode of adaptation in time and space and perpetuates itself as something sacred and familiar, as if that were the only way to do things or get things done even when those ways no longer work. Psychoanalysts call this dysfunctional fossilized mode of adaptation a "neurosis." Yet every culture leaves its adherents hungry for its alternative. CWM have developed individualism to a high degree but are hungry for community. They often wonder out loud, "How come we can't have an affinity group?" Members of ethnic or tribal cultures who can't get away from their many social obligations to family and friends have too much community and hunger for solitude.

On a practical level, a culture's greatest strength, at different times, can also become its greatest weakness. If my culture says I can only be obedient, what happens when the better choice is to be disobedient? One story along these lines concerns the investigation of an Asian airline crash that centered on the communication between the pilot and copilot in the cockpit—a key component in air safety—specifically the reluctance of the copilot to disagree with decisions made by the pilot even if he thought they were wrong. Our colleague Adrian Chan investigated the matter further and found that in Korean Airlines flight 801, which crashed in Guam in 1997, two crew members failed to take a proactive role in questioning decisions made by the captain despite having been "trained" for advocacy.[2]

In an article entitled, "Standing Out and Standing In; The Psychology of Control in America and Japan," the authors contend that all individuals seek to minimize the negative psychological impact of their environment on themselves. This can be accomplished either by changing the environment to accommodate oneself or changing oneself to accommodate the environment.[3] Optimally, the goal is to be able to do both when the situation calls for it. The extent to which individuals are restricted to a "one best way," however, gets in the way of being able to do that.

For example, CWM change the environment to accommodate themselves. Japanese men change themselves to accommodate the environment. These different orientations shape the ways CWM and Japanese position themselves toward individuals and groups. CWM expect groups to accommodate individual self-interest and self-determination. Japanese expect individuals to subordinate self-interest and self determination to the will of the group. The way members of each group choose to punish children reflects the attitudes of the two cultures. In U. S. mainstream culture, punishment takes the form of locking children in ("grounding")— thereby denying them access to the outside world and frustrating their individual need for independence and self-determination. Punishment of children in Japan takes the form of locking them out—thereby denying them full and complete in-group membership (and undermining their individual need to belong).

Standing out and standing in are closely tied to issues of control. CWM are oriented toward primary control: individuals changing the environment to accommodate themselves. This orientation is a hallmark of U.S. mainstream culture and a great cultural strength of CWM. It also impacts cultural style. So in response to a hand of cards being dealt to CWM at birth they say, "I don't like these cards, I want—and will create for myself—a new deal." In situations where individuals suffer from anxiety, CWM (and others within U.S. mainstream culture) go to therapy in the hopes of getting rid of the symptoms of anxiety. In U. S. mainstream language, this is called "stress reduction." Mainstream Japanese are oriented toward secondary control: individuals changing themselves to accommodate the environment. So, to the same hand of cards dealt to them at birth, Japanese say, "Well, this is the deal. If I'm going to get anything from it, I'd better play the hand as thoughtfully and strategically as I can." Morita therapy in Japan declares individuals to be on the right path when they begin to accept themselves as anxious persons. In Japanese, this is called "stress acceptance."[4] "Acceptance" is not surrender or resignation, but a way to get people to move beyond obsessive preoccupation with their symptoms toward more creative ways of dealing with their anxiety.[5] The Japanese would regard that ability as one of their great cultural strengths.

When Cultural Strengths Become a Weakness

The primary control orientation of CWM becomes a weakness when things don't succeed despite their best efforts. The culture of individual freedom and self-determination carries with it individual responsibility for failure as well as success. It also produces a level of optimism around what can and should be controlled. As Higman says, "Middle-class language is ... overly optimistic about the possibilities of problem solving and changing the course of the future. Middle-class persons naively suppose that, with effort, they can create happiness in marriage and raise non-neurotic children."[6] CWM become psychologically vulnerable in situations where they cannot change what they cannot accept and cannot accept what they cannot change. That is also the time where CWM start to realize the limitations of their ability to change what is wrong in their lives and contemplate suicide. Often it is their work life that is out of kilter. Where they are is likely to be where they will also end up, and that does not match where they feel they should be. CWM are also vulnerable around retirement age, especially if their identity and self-worth principally revolve around who they are and what they do at work.[7] CWM are also susceptible in other areas. They do not feel that they are in control of things unless they are taking direct and decisive action over a problem. Doing nothing for CWM is not doing something! That leaves them vulnerable in those situations where the best strategy, especially when no clear course of action presents itself, is simply to wait for further developments ("Don't just do something! Sit there!").

A secondary control orientation within a culture becomes a weakness when individual initiative and creativity are lost as a result of individuals becoming reluctant to follow their own lead when doing so might cost them standing within the group. A better idea is lost (to the individual, group, and society) as a result. A perfect example of the price that group conformity exacts on individuals is the workaholic lifestyle of Japanese executives that is the basis for the sudden death syndrome known as *karoshi*. Quoting from the *karoshi* Web site,

> Yoshinori Hasegawa, Vice Director of the Chiba Kensei Hospital and a recognized authority on karoshi, says that most of the victims of death from overwork had been putting in more than one hundred hours of overtime each. He said the victims did not receive any overtime pay for their extra work, but were members of the élite managerial class who worked themselves to death "out of a samurai-like pride." Because of peer pressure to keep up with co-workers, out-do competing groups and increase market-share at the expense of competitors, hundreds of thousands of Japanese managers are caught up in a vortex of psychological pressure that forces them to work at a frenzied pace. After years of such intense over-work, most managers find that they cannot rest even when they do take time off. They are so wound up that not working leaves them disoriented and suffering from serious stress. Masaaki Noda, professor of foreign studies at Kobe City University, says it is not difficult to understand why so

many of Japan's salarymen work so hard because they have shut themselves off from their families and have no place to go but to work.[8]

Japanese physicians counsel managers to relax more at home, but as former Prime Minister Nakasone said, "Following others is a social obligation in the Japanese scheme of proper behavior."[9]

A better choice for any culture and society is to foster and promote both primary and secondary control and not one at the expense of the other. A saying that captures this idea is "God grant me the serenity to accept what I cannot change, the courage to change what I can, and the wisdom to know the difference." Those committed to a primary control orientation, such as U.S. CWM, will have difficulty gaining "the serenity to accept what they cannot change." Those overly committed to a secondary control orientation, like Japanese, are likely going to have problems with "the courage to change what they can," when, for them to do so, risks their standing within the group. Culture A plus B offers a better set of options for an individual, group, or society, than having only the option of culture A or B.[10]

CWM define their identities through separation and individuation, becoming individuals with clear and distinct boundaries, informed and regulated by a morality of rights (noninterference). "Responsible" behavior for CWM is not doing for themselves when doing so might hurt someone else. Within a morality of rights, rules, and regulations become paramount—so does "playing the game by the rules." This pattern of socialization is a source of strength insofar as CWM see contests as part of the game in which individuals sometimes win and sometimes lose. One positive outcome of this pattern is that CWM can compete with one another without risking or destroying relationships. The game is not necessarily placed in jeopardy because of individual disagreements or disputes. Another positive outcome is that CWM are one of the few groups that can work well together without necessarily having to like each other. This pattern of socialization can also become a weakness for CWM. Insofar as identity (masculinity, individuality) is realized outside of the context of relationship getting close becomes problematic. For men, intimacy in relationships is risky when they see it as threatening individuality and self-identity. Carol Gilligan calls getting close for men "explosive connection."[11]

CWW define their identities within and through relationships, informed and regulated by a morality of responsibility within an ethic of care. Responsible behavior for CWW, and the extent to which it applies to women, generally, is doing for others even if that means not meeting their own needs in the process. This pattern of socialization is a source of strength insofar as CWW do not like to win at the expense of someone else losing. This opens up new possibilities in problem solving, leading to a creative search by these women for win-win solutions. This pattern of socialization can also become a weakness at work. By placing relationships first, CWW are reluctant to make independent career moves to achieve a separate identity, especially if it might put a supportive relationship at risk. Success is feared insofar as it produces social isolation. Carol Gilligan calls this "dangerous separation."[12] Overcommitment to any one cultural orientation is personally or organizationally limiting.

Cultures develop individuals along one path but leave undeveloped or underdeveloped other individual paths. If a goal beyond becoming an effective manager, strategist, marketer, and communicator is also to achieve greater maturity as an individual, then the development of multicultural flexibility also becomes a tool to access into new and different parts of one's self. To the extent that we can develop and integrate these differences into ourselves, we are better able to deal effectively with different kinds of people in different kinds of situations.

Applying Multicultural Flexibility to Situations at Work

This protocol is based on the therapeutic premise that feelings in themselves are not right or wrong—they either exist or they don't exist—and that no one really causes how you or another person feels.

One of the steps that we suggest when confronted with interpersonal conflict is to translate frustration into curiosity. This step has two parts. The first is to try to figure out what is going on for the other person that makes them behave the way they do. The second is to try to figure out for yourself what is going on that makes the other person's behavior problematic for you. The next step, which builds on step 1, is to own the problem that you're having with someone else's behavior as your problem. This entails not making the other person (or their behavior) the problem. Step 3 is to work toward an outcome with respect to what is culturally or individually at stake for both parties and then choose the best way to get there. The following is a training example of this process in action

In one training session, a CWM put on his "pet peeve" list that African Americans are "cliquish." The pattern of behavior that he was referring to was black men hanging out among themselves at the drinking fountain outside his office. I asked him what about their behavior was problematic to him. Since he could not answer offhand —people generally can readily tell you what bothers them but have to dig deeper to figure out why—I proposed the following: "Do you think they are talking about you?" He said no. I then asked him, "Is their behavior problematic because you see them as having a group and you don't?" He thought a bit and then said yes. I then asked him to consider how he might use that information. I offered the following hypothetical: "If you take the assimilationist approach then you would push for the African American men to start to become a collection of individuals" (like CWM). I then asked, "Would that solve your problem?" I then said, "What you have just identified about yourself is a wish for a group experience like the one you perceive African Americans having. You have shown a hunger for community—something that your own culture, perhaps, does not give you enough of. A more effective solution for your problem may be then, that, you, and perhaps other CWM, too, need to work toward satisfying a wish for a greater 'member of group' social experience."[13]

Once the CWM was able to identify the issue underlying his view of African American group behavior—his hunger for community—he was able to come up with a more personally satisfying strategy for dealing with the situation. One result was that the African American group behavior that he had an earlier problem with went away. In turn, the African American men who worked for the CWM were also able to congregate among themselves more freely—the negative vibes emanating from his office went away—as a result of his new understanding of what their behavior meant.

PART II
CWW at Work

This part of the book looks at the cultural conflicts that CWW have at work. It starts with value conflicts—how CWW values differ from the cultural standards of the larger CWM-dominated U.S. corporate culture—and then moves on to other issues of comfort/fit with CWM, with women of other groups, with other CWW, and, perhaps most of all, with themselves.

The literature is replete with discussions of differences between women's modalities and those of the larger male dominant culture. One example is Judith Jordan's description of movement toward relational resilience that reads like a proposal for corporate reorganization based on relational (female) rather than individualistic (male) values: from individual "control over" dynamics to supported vulnerability; from a one-directional need for support from others to mutual empathic involvement in the well-being of each person and of the relationship itself; from separate self-esteem to relational confidence; from the exercise of power over dynamics to empowerment, by encouraging mutual growth and constructive conflict; and from finding meaning in self-centered self-consciousness to creating meaning in a more expansive relational awareness.

For Jordan, self in relationship (or relational resilience) is achievable for both men and women, but the cultural challenges to get there are different. For relationally oriented women, the challenge is the development of the self. For autonomous, individually driven men, the challenge is the development of the relationship. As Bergman and Surrey put it, "There are strikingly different paradoxes in normal male and female development: young boys becoming agents of disconnection to preserve themselves; adolescent girls disconnect from their authenticity to try to maintain relationship."

Given their different starting points, one can understand the difficulties facing men and women as they try to become something other than what their own culture promotes and develops. But there is another matter to consider. Given their different cultural values and predispositions (individualistic vs. relational), it would seem reasonable to expect that white men and women would at least act in ways that are in sync with their cultural development. But that is not the case. Taking the workplace as a shared venue for both men and women, one sees Jordan's individualistic modalities—characteristic of the culture of white men—alive and well in the U.S. workplace, but not the relational modalities that characterize the culture of white women. The question is why not?

The feminist literature suggests that these relational female traits fail to surface because women operate in cultural environments that are controlled by the values of men, which are opposed—even hostile—to women's ways of being or behaving. Presumably if the cultural influence of men were out of the picture, then women's modalities would have greater currency than they presently do. There is no doubt that many CWW experience discomfort with aspects of mainstream U.S. corporate culture—among these discomforts are individual competition, self-determination, and self-promotion. Following Jean Baker Miller, "Using self-determined power for herself, to achieve her goals, has been described by women alternately as selfish or destructive." Anna Fels's study of women and ambition identified ways in which women avoid sounding ambitious. When asked to describe themselves, CWW differ dramatically from CWM in not attributing their success to either competitive drive or ambition. They say getting ahead is not about winning or beating out the competition; it's about the work or about others. Surrey argues that when basic relational needs are not valued or given outlets for development, there is a sense of being out of touch with oneself, disconnected, and unsupported. One successful CWW said, "The question is not how women get ahead; there's a clear path to do that, and most of them have done it to one degree or another. The question is whether, over the long haul, they can live with themselves acting out the 'success model' . . . that they have had to become to get where they got. Will they recognize themselves in the mirror anymore?"

CWW we have spoken to say, with a wish that it were different, "Who I am at work is not who I am really. At home I am more involved with relationships, concerned about taking care of others, how they're doing."

CWW often attribute the absence of more feminine values at work to not being the ones in charge ("Where has the bottom line really gotten us?"). They also complain about the pace of meetings in which CWM predominate. One woman in engineering said that in meetings with mostly male engineers it is hard to get a word in edgewise because of the competitive overlapping discourse and the difficulty she has jumping in. When she goes to meetings with the twenty women in human resources in her work group, she is more likely to participate because it's easier to come in. "There are more spaces, and no competitive discourse. People know me, trust me, and know my work." One CWW reported that when she worked in manufacturing, she was coached by her CWM manager to be more assertive. He said, "You'll never make it to the senior level because you get along too well with people." She showed him her budget, how everything was perfect, and explained how much her people liked her and worked hard for her. He said, "You need a thicker skin." She responded, "I have internal strength." Then, as an afterthought, she said, "I guess he was right, because I never made it to the senior level." Cultural factors arising from differences in gender styles play a role, to be sure, but they do not entirely account for issues around comfort/fit for white women at work. CWW report problems even when they follow standard CWM cultural protocols.

CWW understand that if they want to succeed in corporate America, they have to become a part of the "good old boy network" because there is no "good old girl network." Not only is there not a critical mass of women at the top with whom to network, but when it comes to connecting after work, they are less likely to develop networks around ball games, golf, or hunting. At best they might go to lunch together, but that's usually the extent of their out of office business networking. One CWW group organized a spa outing, which was a first for the company. However, because it was a first, unlike the golf outing, it was not one of the outside activities their company supported. Another reason it was a first for the company is that CWW, generally, often have less time to network with each other, because, like women cross-culturally, they also have to bear the brunt of maintaining family relationships at home. This double sense of duty adds a measure of stress to women's lives at home in addition to the shared level of stress they feel with men at work. According to one study, "Central to the development of conflict was commitment to both [work and home] domains."

Entrée into the good old boy network is often provided through powerful CWM, so it is in the interest of women to keep relationships with them intact. Membership in the boys' club also requires a style that is not threatening to men in the network. Those women who understand that try to fit in by being ultracompetent without appearing to be aggressive. This requires taking on a nonthreatening demeanor and even a willingness to be the brunt of jokes—thereby disarming men in the network. Joking and teasing is a vehicle for CWM bonding and trust building. Unfortunately, when CWM try to tease across gender lines they invariably offend. CWW learn to choose their battles. Given a choice between challenging every sexist provocation or joke and challenging someone who is stealing your ideas, CWW will opt for getting credit for their ideas. More importantly, CWM are testing them for the risk factor—how careful they will have to be—and ascertaining the extent to which the woman might pose a threat to their career by threatening charges of harassment. CWW report that when they begin to build a caring relationship with CWM at work, the men sometimes confuse friendship or discussion of family as an invitation to intimacy. One CWW said, "If a man is testing me with a sexual comment, I just ignore it and stay focused on the issue we're discussing at the time." CWW also complain that CWM leave them out of meetings and ask them to implement a plan they weren't involved in developing. This becomes especially grating when they have issues with the plan that could have been addressed had they not been left out of the meeting in which the plan was developed.

Other issues that CWW bring up relate to visibility and voice, especially over the difficulty they have being seen and heard at meetings. A frequent complaint is that CWM either ignore them entirely—sometimes diverting attention away from a female speaker by engaging another man in the room with a question—or, if they do listen, minimize their ideas on hearing them. Different communication styles also factor in here. Women's speaking style is narrative and contextual. Consequently, they often make their point within a story or use a story to provide background information on how they got to the point. When women listen to other women they nod to indicate that they are tracking the background of the story to the point being made. They also know that these seemingly unconnected points are essential to the understanding of the story and will come together at the end (fig. 2). Men's speaking style is linear and to the point

FIGURE 2. Narrative contextual conversation/presentation style

(fig. 3). Since men are not accustomed to tracking a story, when they listen to women they think each of the points that women are making is moving in linear fashion, like a vector heading outward (fig. 4).

This pattern of difference leads to a serious problem at meetings. CWM who expect the point to be made explicitly and quickly will either try to rush matters by saying to the CWW, "And your point is?" or they may lose

FIGURE 3. Linear conversation/presentation style

FIGURE 4. Narrative style as tracked by linear style

interest altogether. Should they listen with only half an ear and later register the point that was made implicitly by the CWW within the context of
the story, they often think, by making it explicit, that they were the ones
that made the point. When this happens, women think, "Didn't I just say
that?" The result and impact on CWW is that they are slighted and miss
getting recognition for their ideas. One group of women in engineering,
in anticipation of the dismissive manner of their CWM counterparts, strategically ask them before making a presentation, "Do you want the long
version or the short version?" When I asked them why they don't just give
the short version, they say, "If we did that, the CWM would challenge us
and say, 'Where did you get that?' If they know we have a longer version
upfront, we don't get the challenge."

Another gender difference that is problematic for CWW is the different way men and women manage, which is an outgrowth of the different
male and female discourse styles. We've all heard jokes about how men
refuse to ask for directions. I would change those jokes a little. I think
men do ask for directions, but they only listen to the first part and expect
to figure out the rest once they start down the road. This same pattern
causes gender problems at work. CWW not only want all the instructions
up front, they also want to know context: how their assignment fits into
the bigger picture. CWM give what information they think those who report directly to them need to know to start working on the task or project,
expecting them to figure the rest out by themselves or come to them only
when they are stuck (because they need more information or authorization to move forward). Another issue that CWW have with CWM is that
more often than not, CWW talk of being expected to accommodate and
follow the CWM's way of framing or thinking about a topic rather than
being treated as equal contributors in the sharing of ideas or the shaping of a plan. Given this litany of complaints, the rage that surfaces when
CWW discuss the difficulties and disrespect that they feel working with
CWM, and the cultural differences mentioned earlier, it is astonishing that
most of the CWW in our training programs (over a twenty-year period)
say they would, nonetheless, rather work with CWM than CWW.

So what is happening on the other side that leads CWW to prefer working with CWM? Some CWW say that they nurture relationships at home
with family and friends and don't want to do it at work. Work is a place
where other parts of themselves can flourish: those parts that want to ac-
complish things by tapping into a different skill set than their relational
expertise. They find this easier to do with CWM since they do not make

the same relational demands on them as CWW do. One CWW said that she wouldn't want to go into management unless "all those who reported to her were more independent and self-directed." She added that women, unlike men, "expect her to be more nurturing." Another woman executive said, "[Even though] I've felt excluded ... yet I say I prefer men. ... They don't mix work and personal. With women, if you give them constructive criticism, they worry that maybe you don't like them, not just that you didn't like their work on a project." But that is only part of the story. At issue for CWW are not only the relational demands that other women put on them but the difficulty they have resisting those demands. So what makes this and consideration of others, generally, such a problem for CWW?

CHAPTER SEVEN

Cultural Underpinnings

White female development has been described as a process of "relationship differentiation," the ostensible goal of which is to become an agentic and boundaried self in relationship, rather than a self that is only preoccupied with what others want or think. Miller notes with respect to the development of agency in girls: "In her internal representation of herself, I suggest, the girl is developing not a sense of separation, but a more developed sense of her own capacities, and her greater ability to put her 'views' into effect." Kaplan says, "The *process* of facilitating and enhancing connectedness with others . . . fosters the gradual evolution of a differentiated self, a self with its own clear properties, wishes, impulses . . . but a self that achieves articulation through participation in and attention to the relational process."[1] Somewhere along the way, however, the realization of agency and boundary gets subverted.

People pleaser CWW (hereafter PPCWW) and, before that, their white girl counterparts, learn early and often that the social goal for them is principally to serve and take care of others. The standard protocol for PPCWW is "I put your needs and wishes ahead of mine." One Ketchum Global Research Network survey noted, "Seventy-four percent of women 25–54 spend more time thinking about others' needs than their own."[2] This rule of etiquette applies across the board in various personal relationships that CWW have outside of work with husbands, children, parents, and friends. It also applies to interactions that PPCWW have with

other CWW, even those that they are meeting for the first time or don't
know that well. At work, these PPCWW approach each other cautiously.
They want to appear nice and friendly, so other CWW won't say bad
things about them behind their back, but they also don't want to get too
close, in order to avoid or minimize being sucked into a caretaking or accommodating role.

It is significant that PPCWW see themselves as givers rather than as
receivers in the encounters they have with other CWW—before, during,
and after the exchange—almost without regard to how much giving and
receiving actually occurs. Driving this view of others and themselves is
the image that PPCWW have of themselves as caregivers (more so than
care-getters), their consciousness of (and sensitivity to) the demands that
others make of them in their lives, and the actual amount of giving and
caretaking that they do, and have done, satisfying those demands. Putting
the needs of others first does not always lead PPCWW down a one-way
street. Reciprocal accommodation is also possible when they experience
other CWW also considering their feelings, needs, and wishes. Then a balance of give and take can occur. When that is realized and the quality level
is high—something realized with a few close personal friends—it becomes
a gratifying and delightful experience, both sought after and missed. Most
often, however, neither the quality nor balance of give and take occurs.
Then PPCWW find relationships with each other more exhausting than
satisfying—something to be avoided rather than engaged. Within the
workplace, as several PPCWW put it, they feel drained by the amount
of time they have to spend dealing with women's feelings, especially so,
when that entails being dragged into a web of intrigue, which includes cattiness, backbiting, and gossip in an effort to align relationships and avoid
or eliminate the competition. They say working with CWM allows them
just to do their job.

One CWW reported, "I'd much rather work with men. Women over-
read meaning into everything, and project their own insecurities onto you.
I was talking to our male boss about the challenges of parenting, and a female colleague came to me and said, 'I'm friends with him and his wife' . . .
as if to suggest there was something sexual [in our relationship]; she could
have just asked, and I would have told her there wasn't. She seemed jeal-
ous that he was talking with me."

CWW report that they go to men to share their problems and are often
likely to get a better ear. In some contexts, it is easier for CWM to listen because, unlike PPCWW, they don't take the other person's problem
home with them and are less concerned about who likes them or not.

One PPCWW said, "White men don't take it to heart if the boss is being critical or downright rude. They just repeat back to him what he said and just go about their business, whereas I was so upset about his tone that I spent three weeks drafting a letter about that problem to him."

The social demands placed on PPCWW are not limited to caretaking. They are also expected to assume a "be nice" demeanor along with their caretaking role even when that doesn't reflect who they are or want to be. They say they can be more authentic with their partners, but much less so with other CWW. So, again, what makes the social demands that other CWW place on them so irresistible?

Early on in their social development, white girls hear messages that promote giving others what they want, even when that is at the expense of them getting what they want for themselves. The literature often misses this aspect of white girl socialization. Harris, for example, sees "can-do" and "at-risk" girls principally along ethnic/class lines: one group "rarely able to fail" versus another group looking for "opportunities to succeed." This does not mean that "can-do" girls are without risk or "problem-free," however—just that their problems must be "dealt with quickly to ensure their success." However, the problems she cites for "can-do" girls are framed more as "individual" and "intrapsychic": relating to lack of self-esteem, eating disorders, depression, and anxiety.[3] The negative impact on identity and self-esteem coming from people pleaser white girl culture—specifically, not giving others what they want or expect—is an area that also needs to be considered.

My own example—one that rankles me to this day—occurred when I was thirteen years old. I was waiting excitedly with the group of single females who had gathered for the bouquet toss at my sister's wedding. Most of the young women were bigger and older than I was, but I caught it! I was thrilled. Another girl about my age had a grasp on the corner of it, but I had most of the bouquet, so with great excitement I took the prize back to my table. Unbeknownst to me, the girl who had her fingers on a couple of the petals began to cry at her table, at which point my father told me to go over and give her the bouquet. My dad said, "She needs it more than you do." I was furious and hurt inside and tried to argue that I had won the coveted bouquet fair and square. I can still remember my burning sense of injustice. I felt that my own father made me give up my sister's wedding bouquet to a total stranger. The message I wanted that I did not get was, "Good grab! Way to go! You caught it!"

What I took away from that on a deeply personal level was that I had to put other people's feelings first to get my father's respect. My dad implied that since I was the one who was stronger internally, I should be the one to give up what I wanted to take care of someone else. My own needs or wishes did not count. This proved to be a theme throughout my life. I was like him, strong internally. I would be the self-sacrificing caretaker. That was my father's message; my mother's message was even stronger.

The first mantra of people pleaser white girl socialization is "Be caring (of everyone)!" The second mantra is "Be nice! Don't hurt anybody's feelings!" Being "caring" is coupled with being "nice." The first socializing agents for these white girls to be "caring" and "nice" were mothers who strategically withdrew love if daughters did not align with their views or show that they were emotionally attuned to their feelings. One consequence of this pattern of socialization is for these white girls to feel guilty for not being attentive or empathic to the emotional state of others. If there is dissonance in the environment, they feel it is their fault or at least their job to fix it. As the nuns used to tell Catholic white girls in their classes, "When you grow up, and you get married, and you have kids, whatever kind of mood your husband and kids are in when they go out in the morning is your responsibility!"

Later, these white girls learn that the opinion that others have of them counts for more than the opinion they have of themselves. Shoehorned into behaving as other people think they should, they often lose the ability to see themselves independently of how others see them: becoming, in effect, the object of other people's lives more than the subject of their own. According to Mary Pipher in *Reviving Ophelia,* this shift in psychological development occurs between the ages of ten and eleven: white girls go from wondering "what do I like?" to "am I likable?" I have examples that suggest that shift occurs even earlier. However, there is no doubt that by the time people pleaser white girls reach high school, their predisposition to see themselves through the eyes of others is firmly established.[4]

As an example, I gave an assignment to groups of African American, Latina, and white girls at a Catholic girls' high school in Chicago, where the population was one-third white, one-third Latina, and one-third African American. Each group was asked to make a list of what it was like to be them or a member of their group at their school. The Latina and African American girls began their lists with the word "we." In contrast, the white girls began their lists with the words "they think we're ..." The African American girls went on to list several issues that had to do with pressure from other black girls to go out and to look perfect. Latina girls wrote about pressure to fulfill the role of traditional women and about strict fathers. At another meeting with adult Latina women, one of the items that they had on their list of things that were very important to them was dancing. I did not explore that further at the time. My initial thought was that they would say family. However, I subsequently learned that when taken outside of their role orientation, the subjective sense that Latina women have of themselves involves more than their responsibility to please other people. The white girls were preoccupied with what the girls of color thought of them: characterizing themselves in terms of how they were viewed by members of the other groups rather than by what they thought it was like to be a member of their own group.

Another aspect of white girl culture that became manifest from the way the white girls responded was that their collective sense of themselves—an artifact of the assignment—was not around being white females but, reactively, around a shared sense of how others were viewing them. White girls do not proactively identify themselves as members of a race/gender group but as a collection of individuals. Cliques of white girls are groups that white girls identify with. But cliques only develop after emotional or political alignment has been established. Those who don't emotionally or politically align with the group are socially shunned. For example, one woman reported she was in a male-dominated MBA program at a prominent university. There were so few women in the program at the time, they decided to form a women's support group. At one meeting, several women were complaining that one professor kept addressing the class as "gentlemen." The woman suggested to the group that they shouldn't focus on the negative but rather should figure out how to network with each other. Later, she was told by one woman that it seemed she had nothing to offer the group. After that, she felt invisible at the meetings and eventually stopped coming.

Within people pleaser white girl culture, being nice, caring, and considerate with respect to the feelings of others are conflated. To be nice means putting other people first. The opposite of being nice is being inconsiderate or mean. Being inconsiderate is putting one's own wishes and needs ahead of someone else's ("being selfish"). Being mean is more socially destructive of the other person, as when I eliminate the competition not because the other girl was mean first and so deserved what they got but simply because she stood in the way of me getting what I want. For example, in the movie *Mean Girls,* the clique was mean to other people, but within the clique, there was pressure at least to pretend to care about each other's feelings. The mean behavior that was ultimately exposed occurred through clique members backstabbing each other while pretending to be nice. Meanness seems to be on the increase among white girls, perhaps owing to the wish to self-actualize, which can only be done in an "anti" posture, or in learning to compete—even physically—with rival girls. In the TV show *Sex and the City,* one of the women used the term "frenemies" to refer to another woman who took away her boyfriend, all the while—through "fake nice"—pretending to be a "friend."

These white girls are also at risk socially by standing out and rising above the group. Pat Heim characterizes white girl culture as "power dead even,"[5] as opposed to the individualistic and competitive ("standing out," "create your space," "king of the hill") culture of white boys and, later, white men. In elementary school, if a girl becomes too popular, other girls will render her "invisible" by creating an "I hate so and so" club. Although staying attuned to the group is required of girls generally, it is especially true of people pleaser white girls. One way to stay connected for them is not to stand out.[6] White girls start feeling the peer pressure to conform early. For example, an eight-year-old girl asked her father if she could switch to another school. He asked her why. She replied, "So I can do what I want to do." When he asked her why she couldn't do that at the school she was at, she answered, "Because the other girls wouldn't like that." The risk of not being nice or standing out is to be socially ostracized. The form that this takes with regard to the targeted girl is to talk about her to like-minded peers—not to the girl herself—the effect of which is to align relationships along an axis of "you and me" against "her," or, with respect to white girl cliques, "us" against "them." According to Goodman and O'Brien, "cliques offer security to those who conform, and cause insecurity in those that don't."[7] This pattern shows itself clearly in the following example. On TV one morning there was a sitcom in which a junior high age white girl—girl number 1—is trying to bribe classmates to vote for her by giving away cupcakes. Another white girl—girl number 2—approaches "nicely" (appearing innocent, but framing what she sees going on): "If I take this, does it mean I have to vote for you?" "Oh, no, this is not a bribe!" replies the first girl, "I just get up early on school days and go pick up these cupcakes to give out to the needy and these are extras."

With an aside to the audience, girl number 2 addresses the TV viewer, who, in this case, is the surrogate friend with whom she is aligning herself. These viewers become her confidante in her effort to bring down the "not really nice" girl who has revealed herself as phony, stooping to bribery in her effort to compete and win the election at any cost. This is not a straightforward competition between the two girls; the second girl isn't running for office. She is, however, trying to outsmart girl number 1—the prize being the relationship and respect of her new friend, the TV viewer, by eliminating the "not nice" girl from the competition. Our new found friend, girl number 2, the heroine, is justified in getting girl number 1 and doing what she can to bring her down because somebody has to do it. After all, girl number 1 is "not nice." Girl number 2 would say she was teaching her a lesson or that she was saving the school from a conniving powerhungry candidate. At a deeper cultural level girl number 2 may also be punishing girl number 1 for being ambitious, another negative in white girl culture. "You are going to be pushing up daisies," whispers girl number 2 to the audience. Girl number 1 overhears the "pushing up daisies" comment, and asks, sweetly, "What did you say about daisies?" "Oh, I mean, there are rainbows and daisies in your future." "Oh, I hope so, I love daisies," continues girl number 2. Even though girl number 2 is justified undermining girl number 1 by white girl standards, both white girls play the cultural game of fake nice to your face but conniving behind your back.

The magazine *Seventeen* ran a piece called "Are You Too Competitive?"[8] What makes this article culturally relevant is its recognition of the difficulty that people pleaser white girls have with competition, especially in calibrating its outer limits. White male–identified women often become even more competitive than white men. But in mainstream people pleaser white girl culture, where any form of individual competition is discouraged, even competing a little can be seen as being "over the top." These white girls/women often use the term "competitive" not to describe a direct confrontation or contest but the steps taken to avoid or eliminate the competition. For example, PPCWW complain that other PPCWW compete with each other rather than help each other. When I ask how they compete, they say, "Well, they don't give you all the information you need, or they talk about you behind your back."

The advice that the psychologist Roni Cohen-Sandler gives in the *Seventeen* article is consistent with the protocols of people pleaser white girl culture.[9] She counsels those white girls who feel competitive with each other to acknowledge those feelings and find ways to defuse (not relish or celebrate) competitive situations. Part of the rationale is that these white girls, unused to engaging competitively, become easily bruised when they do. As an example, Cohen-Sandler cited a girl that she counseled who scored 1520 out of 1600 on her SAT but burst into tears when her friend got a 1580. This sensitivity is consistent with play studies of white girls compared to white boys. Carol Gilligan, following the work of Janet Lever, reports that in elementary school, girls play in smaller groups than boys, often playing games that require carefulness, like hop scotch or jump rope, and tend to stop playing together if there is conflict.[10] They won't play with their "friend" until they make up because someone's feelings have been hurt. In the following example a young mother reported that her seven-year-old daughter—girl A—came home from the block party and cried because her best friend—girl B—said she wasn't going to be her friend any more. Girl A was crushed, so her mom took her back to the block party, where the mothers created an opportunity for the girls to make up by teasing and pushing them together. Finally, girl B admitted that she threatened to end the friendship because by leaving the block party, girl A was "selfishly" doing what she wanted to do, instead of spending time together with girl B.

White Girl Culture in the Workplace

Avoiding or Eliminating the Competition

Within people pleaser white girl culture being caring and being competitive are incompatible. Consequently, to avoid being seen as uncaring, these white girls avoid competing with each other directly. PPCWW must also strive for competency and recognition without appearing to be selfish. Another reason PPCWW dislike competition (which they either withdraw from or try to eliminate) is that they cannot show themselves winning at the direct expense of someone else losing—an attitude that owes itself both to value conflicts and the people pleaser white girl cultural prohibition against individuals standing out. Some PPCWW are reluctant to acknowledge their ambition even to themselves, because to do so would violate their own value of putting others first, which in turn threatens connection and leaves them vulnerable to CWM who expect them to defer and other PPCWW who will undermine anyone who tries to leave the group (following the metaphor of crabs in a pot pulling each other down). If you do what CWM do—such as be competitive in pursuit of your own goals or assertive on behalf of your own views—you will be chastised as a bitch, or, more euphemistically, as "sharp tongued," "difficult to work with," or "having no sense of humor." These characterizations come from PPCWW as well as CWM. As Linda Carli says, "Women need to be tempered in their entitlement and self promotion, a challenge men don't even need to think about."[11]

For example, one PPCWW said that when she and her friend found themselves in competition for the same position her friend called and said she was withdrawing her name because it wasn't worth it to her to lose the friendship. When I asked if she thought that would have negatively affected the friendship, she said yes. If PPCWW are in different places in the organization, they may be supportive of each other, but when they are forced to compete straight up, the cattiness and backstabbing begin.

Compare this to white boys, who freely engage in competition and conflict without preoccupation or concern with how that might undermine the group or how others are feeling. For example, during a game of baseball, if boys argue over whether or not the runner is out or safe, one boy doesn't seek the other out later, as people pleaser white girls do, to say, "Listen, I hope you didn't take it personally when I said you were out at first; it's just that I really thought you were out." Besides being easily bruised, there is also the danger that direct competition between people pleaser white girls can become cutthroat. It is perhaps to prevent that from happening that beauty pageants have a category called "Miss Congeniality." If these white girls and women are going to be competitive, it should be as much directed toward "being nice" as toward winning. Whether increased involvement in team sports will change that remains to be seen.

A white woman in Seattle reported that her eight-year-old son and seven-year-old daughter were riding along in the backseat of the car. Her son asked her daughter, "Who's the smartest in your class? I'm the smartest in my class. It's already May and I'm the furthest in reading and no one can catch up with me." The daughter replied, "Jamie and me are the nicest in our class." "Yeah, but who's the smartest?" repeated the brother. "And you know why we're the nicest . . ." she continued. The mother was surprised, because, as she said, growing up in the Pacific Northwest, where there is generally a "Northwest nice" culture, she raised both her son and her daughter to be "nice." She didn't realize how differently the message of being "nice" was reinforced by people pleaser white girl culture, as compared to white boy culture.

My own example occurred when I read Carol Gilligan's *In a Different Voice*.[12] I, too, thought that there was no real difference between my daughter and two sons around being nice and considerate of others. Didn't I raise both my sons and my daughter to care about other people and their feelings? So I created my own test to see if my daughter and younger son would come out as caretakers. I asked Cristina, who was six at the time, "If you went out in front to play, and there were two kids standing together, and one standing alone, where would you go?" She said, "I would go to the one, because she wouldn't have anyone to play with." I thought, OK, Cristina thinks it's important to take care of others, including other people's feelings. I later asked Bill, who was eight at the time, the same question. "Two kids standing together, one child standing alone, where would you go?" "I would go to the one," Bill replied. "Why would you go to the one?" (I was thinking, "See, I've done a great job of raising this child; he is caring about the feelings of the person standing alone.") Bill explained, "What do you think, mom—so we'd have even teams!"

One pen pal study revealed that boys described themselves to their pen pals in terms of skills and abilities—"I'm smart, I'm a good soccer player"—while girls more often described themselves with regard to their character—"I'm caring and helpful."[13]

Backstabbing at Work

One of the items that CWW and women of color put on their list of pet peeves about CWW is backstabbing—which, at its most basic level, is for one CWW to talk about another person in their absence. For African American women, this pattern of behavior (seen as "going behind someone's back") is generally characterized as backstabbing regardless of motive—the appropriate cultural protocol for black women being to deal with personal matters between two people face to face ("And I'll say this to her face . . .").[14] For CWW, however, talking about a person when they are not present is only sometimes characterized as backstabbing. For PPCWW, confronting another CWW directly with a complaint is considered mean, and the PPCWW who is confronted will probably leave and go tell others how mean the confrontational behavior was, saying, "I don't know why she attacked me like that"—thus aligning others against the "mean girl" before the other woman aligns people against her. The option is to talk out hurt feelings with other sympathetic women.

It is considered backstabbing when I have been the target and socially hurt by what another CWW has done (regardless of the justification, who was really being mean to whom, or who was mean first).

It is not considered backstabbing when I am the one soliciting emotional support from another PPCWW for something that just happened to me or when I am aligning relationships to protect myself against the social ostracism that might be perpetrated by the other PPCWW (or the rumor mill). For example, when I ask CWW how they handle situations where another CWW has done something to upset them, they often report that they will vent with a friend. They report that this behavior is not backstabbing but is rather sharing frustration, hurt feelings, or anger with a friend or ally, often strategizing around how to proceed with the offending party, looking for any insights their listener may have to offer.

Third-party ("listener") PPCWW do not see themselves as participating in backstabbing when they are being empathic to someone that has just been hurt or when it is clear that the PPCWW being talked about is a recognized problem for everyone. For example, if the offending CWW who is the topic of conversation is a friend of the listener or someone with whom the listener has had more positive experiences, she may help the complaining woman understand and forgive this person by offering another interpretation of the behavior or by offering insights as to the character of the person who upset them, going to great lengths to explain what they know about the other person's personal life that might shed new light on their behavior. In the PPCWW world, this is a legitimate way to help a friend build their reputation as a nice, caring person, thereby improving their chances of support rather than attack from others who could eliminate them. Often this involves sharing information about how the offending party has been hurt or suffered in her life, because hurt/wounded women are cut slack, while competitive/ambitious women are brought down.

Another example of this: the listener may agree and offer further proof of the character flaw of the offending party and share her own similar experience, thereby confirming and validating the aggrieved woman's feelings, while at the same time, creating an ally against the other offending (mean, uncaring) CWW. In the future, the aggrieved woman and the listener may collude to eliminate that CWW; however, neither of them will let her know how they feel directly, because that would be mean and would create risk within the social mill by supplying direct proof that they are really the mean ones for confronting the other woman directly. This last response toward those who act mean—not just other women—was instrumental in turning things around for Hillary Clinton in the New Hampshire primary in 2008: "Women rallied to Mrs. Clinton . . . after what many perceived as an unfair piling on by Mr. Obama and Mr. Edwards in a debate."[15]

Also, since many PPCWW have been to psychotherapy, all of the above strategies can be augmented, or further complicated or exacerbated, by attempts to psychoanalyze any or all parties ("passive-aggressive," "solipsistic"), thereby adding a modicum of respectability and authority to the discussion about the targeted party whom neither PPCWW is approaching directly. Framing matters in psychoanalytic terms also suggests that a deeper chord has been struck. As Chesler says, "Mother-daughter dynamics continue to 'shadow' relationships between adult women at work" and "We never quite 'get over' our need for a Perfect Mother—some might say, for a loving God."[16]

Third-party ("listener") PPCWW do characterize that pattern of behavior as backstabbing when it is being done constantly by the same CWW about a variety of so-called offending other PPCWW. This is the time that third-party PPCWW stop being empathic and put their "fake nice" listening hat on. For example, the listener may pretend to agree with the speaker, choosing her words carefully: "I can't believe she did that to you." Since the listener's role is to listen empathically so as to be caring, she is reluctant to say, "I have a totally different experience with her" or "I like her," because acting contrary would violate the listener's prescribed role of offering empathy and connection. Afterward, the listener may share with a different friend or ally that the speaker was upset, but that she doesn't think she should be upset. However, you don't disagree directly to the person sharing with you, for this would be tantamount to refusing a direct request for emotional support. Not only would it be unempathic to disagree, it would leave you vulnerable to becoming next on her list of people talked about as mean, rude, inconsiderate, and not to be trusted for not allowing yourself to be an empathic "confidante."

So why are PPCWW reluctant to confront the other woman directly? When the culture mandates "be nice, don't hurt other people's feelings," even the most well-intentioned and constructive criticism can be misconstrued and leveraged as proof of malicious lack of compassion. Since PPCWW feel vulnerable to other people's opinions, they don't want to give anyone leverage to criticize on the basis that they hurt the other person's feelings. Up to this point, who hurt whom is open to the opinion of the rumor mill, but should you confront the other woman directly, you lose ground, since the rumor mill will be heavily influenced by the cultural view that sees any form of direct confrontation as an unjustifiable "assault" on the other person. As Mooney says, "When conflict or competition arises in the workplace, some women avoid engaging directly with their female colleagues.... Afraid of what might happen if they openly acknowledge tensions with their coworker, they shirk potential problems ... by way of passive-aggressive behaviors, attacking underground while continuing to appear warm and friendly on the surface."[17]

Moreover, for PPCWW, keeping what happened to oneself is also not a viable option. This is because keeping silent or simply addressing the situation directly and moving on is tantamount to social suicide—in effect, leaving the other PPCWW free to characterize what happened as she saw it to her group of friends/colleagues, with the result that she would be the one ostracized, not the other woman. Being ostracized at work means being "eliminated": left out of meetings, e-mails, discussions, and so on. Because of the fear and potentiality of becoming ostracized, PPCWW are wary when dealing with other CWW. Friendliness and overtures to alignment ("fake nice") become pragmatic efforts to minimize the risk of being undermined. What gets sacrificed at work is the positive side of PPCWW's relational orientation: women seeing each other as resources rather than as problems. So, with respect to the question posed earlier, what compels CWW to assume a demeanor and role that is out of sync with who they are or want to be?

One answer is the social isolation that they fear would follow if they choose not to assume the socially prescribed demeanor and role that others expect of them. As Carol Gilligan said, what creates risk for men is getting close ("explosive connection"). What women are afraid of is loss of connection and relationship ("dangerous separation").[18] Another factor is the extent to which other PPCWW are able to undermine their self-image as a caring, nurturing person. The more PPCWW see themselves as others see them—those with permeable boundaries and an external locus of control—the more accommodating they will be to do what others want and expect of them. Many CWW fall into the people pleaser category, but there are also those who don't.

Key Characteristics of CWW in the Workplace

Table 1 shows a cultural taxonomy of CWW at work. The table reflects the extent to which CWW have adopted or resisted the patterns and values of white girl/women socialization. While the categories are not exclusive of each other, one of them will emerge as dominant for any particular woman within or outside the U.S. mainstream work context. One exception is white male–assimilated women who display masculine values primarily at work. For example, one white male–assimilated woman who worked at an

TABLE I. **Key characteristics of CWW in the workplace**

	Please others at expense to oneself	Go along to get along	Power dead even vs. competition/recognition	Let others define them as nice/caring; permeable boundaries	Follow the letter of the law	Able to let go of gossip/making others people's problems their own	Get ahead by eliminating the competition (gossiping, backstabbing) consciously or unconsciously	Interests of the group/organization are more important than own interests	Competitive joking; individually ambitious	Collectively ambitious—interests of the group are equally important to own interest; true empathy to superiors, peers, and to subordinates, while maintaining own boundaries
People pleasers	X	X	X	X						
Male identified/ assimilated						X	X	X	X	
Obedient/ rule governed					X			X		
Narcissistic/ egocentric						X	X			
Evolved						X				X

investment house said that one of the women she worked with "acted just like a man: arguing vociferously without any concern about their feelings. Yet, when I had the aneurism, she called and offered to bring food. She also stayed longer with me in the hospital than the other women that I regularly had lunch with."

People Pleasers

CWW people pleasers are preoccupied first and foremost with caring about other people's feelings. Their concern with what other people need or want is motivated by their own need to be liked, loved, and accepted and to protect themselves against backstabbing, which leads to loss of relationship and social isolation. People pleasers grew up with direct or indirect messages that pleasing mother was more important than pleasing oneself. This pattern was reinforced in school by peers along with a "go along to get along" mindset. Part of being a people pleaser is to stay attuned to power dead even. What is important is not to have more than others. Direct competition, which requires mastery and leads to recognition, is not valued.

White Male Identified/Assimilated

These CWW either identified with father/brother and rejected the role of people pleaser early in life or have assimilated—learning how to play the CWM game in the workplace because that was the ticket to getting ahead. The difference between these two groups of women—identified versus assimilated—shows up outside of the workplace rather than within. White male–identified women—polar opposites to people pleasers—repudiate the caring side of themselves when taking on the white male persona. White male–assimilated women assume both the male and female personas but compartmentalize them, taking on the white male persona at work and the white female persona outside of work. Because they assume the same persona at work as white male–identified women, we group them together here. More of the white male–identified/assimilated women can be found among members of younger cohorts (the generation X and generation Y group rather than boomers), although the majority of young women in our sessions still identify themselves as people pleasers.

A subcategory of the above is the white male–identified strategic people pleaser. This category is for women who are white male identified but have found for practical reasons that they need at times to assume the persona of a people pleaser ("fake nice") with white men in order for them to do their job. For example, a female technician from the North who was white male identified, when working in the South said that if she did not assume the people pleaser persona with some white men, "Bubba Gump would say, 'I want to talk to a man'—wouldn't talk to me. After three years of this, I learned to say, 'Hey, hon [honey]. How you doin'? How's your wife feelin'? Then they would start to trust me, probably saying to themselves, 'Well she's a nice girl. Let's see if she knows anything!'" She added, "I tried to get into Sales: kept notes on those clients that I had to get personal with: know their wife and kids names, what they were ailing from, or how far along the kids were in school. It worked but it was hard. I hated the pretense of it."

Obedient/Rule Governed

Obedient/rule governed women were never allowed to think for themselves. They were taught that power comes from positional rather than personal power, and when they attain a position of power, they play by that rule, not allowing themselves any discretionary authority. These are women who, when giving performance reviews, give them exactly at the designated time (little mentoring along the way) and go by the letter of the law as they understand it and their role even if that violates the spirit of the law. For example, an obedient/rule governed waitress in an airport restaurant carded a couple of senior citizens who ordered a beer because of a rule that all customers had to show their ID. She said that "if they didn't, I couldn't serve them." In another instance, I asked an obedient/rule governed woman in charge of the velvet rope that kept the line in check as people were waiting to get in to see the next show if, "I could quickly use the restroom." She responded, "Do you want me to lose my job?"

Narcissistic/Egocentric

Hotchkiss describes the narcissist as follows:

> Developmentally arrested before having achieved the ability to see Self as separate from The One Who Meets My Needs. Internally, these individuals remain in a state of psychological fusion with that all-powerful, all-nurturant caregiver, and this becomes the working model for their interactions with others. They

treat people as if they exist only to meet their needs, and they have little regard for anyone who can't be used in some way. In a psychological sense, they don't really "see" anyone else, except when a person can do something for them. They may have developed well in other regards, may be smart, funny, accomplished, even lovable, but you still sense that quality of childlike narcissism by the way they relate to the people around them. There will be inevitable violations of boundaries. More than vanity, arrogance, self-absorption, or any of the other traits we commonly think of as narcissistic, this is your biggest clue to another person's narcissism.[19]

In the workplace, narcissistic/egocentric women don't want competition from other CWW. For this reason, they often prefer to be the only woman and don't hesitate to compete by whatever means necessary to get to the top. They rarely form coalitions with other CWW. Rather, when they have the inside track with a man who holds power, they will use him to eliminate other women whom they see as threats to their position.

Evolved (Self in Relationship)

These CWW have developed a self-image that is independent of how other CWW see them, having a well-developed agentic self. Agentic selves know what they want as the subject of their life and have no qualms about pursuing their goals.[20] Their goals include big picture thinking where they can do well and do good at the same time. Their relational self always has the well-being of the group in mind, but they are also able to include their own self as part of the greater humanity. In contrast to the white male–identified/assimilated women who either repudiate caring for others or compartmentalize caring for oneself and others, the evolved woman does both at work as well as home. These women either grew up—through the luck of the draw—with incredible parenting, where they were encouraged to develop a self in relationship, or somehow in the course of their life, they had a significant relationship, perhaps a grandparent, teacher, spouse, friend, or therapist who helped them to evolve. The younger women who are white male acculturated often report that their fathers encouraged them and/or that they attended all-girl schools where competition for intellectual mastery rather than competition for boys was highly valued.[21] One thing is sure, if you have not been socialized well into this way of being, it requires an enormous effort to keep from slipping back into earlier people-pleasing patterns.

Evolved CWW at Work

Many CWW who have moved up in corporate America report that to do
so they have had to let go of several ("people pleaser") behavioral traps.
These are (1) letting go of the kind of gossip that is used to align relationships against other "not nice" women; (2) letting go of the need for other
people's validation of themselves as a caring and nurturing person; and (3)
letting go of the habit of making other people's problems their own. These
evolved women still see themselves as "selves in relationship," espous-
ing women's core values—such as, being nurturing and connecting their
own personal success to the success of the group. But, in contrast to their
people pleaser counterparts, they are able to set personal boundaries that
enable them to successfully withstand being drawn into what they regard
as the dark side of CWW relationships. One CWW executive remembers
the exact moment when she realized that to continue on her career path,
she would have to let go of the need for personal validation from others as a caring and nurturing person. In fact, she would have to develop
a thick skin because she was already being negatively characterized by
female colleagues as "aggressive and competitive"—adjectives that might
be positive if used to describe a man. She overheard others saying these
things about her and had to pull over in her car on the way home from
work to weep. She did not let it deter her, however, and learned that she
had to develop an internalized sense of her character regardless of what
other PPCWW might say.

Another time, an evolved CWW reported that a PPCWW colleague
was consistently sharing information with her that she didn't think the
subject of that information would want shared. She tried to dissuade this
colleague tactfully by saying that she wasn't comfortable hearing this kind
of personal information, but the woman persisted. She finally decided to
distance herself from the relationship when it became clear that this colleague wouldn't respect her boundary around being told other people's
personal information.

Evolved CWW approach a person directly, framing their views in a
way the receiver can hear them without them becoming defensive. If the
receiver does become defensive anyway—responding to the candor with
a cold shoulder, disbelief, or tears and anger at the perceived confrontation—then the evolved woman may seek the support of a friend with
whom she can vent or strategize. Even here, the goal is not to manipulate or eliminate but rather to understand and strategize, trying to bring

about the well-being and success of the group. In the following example, Ms. E sensed that Ms. P was upset with her, but didn't know why.[22] When Ms. E approached Ms. P directly, asking if she were upset with her, Ms. P responded, "I'm not upset," but clearly she was. Ms. E resorted to indirect communication and discovered through a third party that Ms. P was upset because Ms. E had requested (and received) the vacation weeks Ms. P also wanted. Ms. E did not believe that she had done anything wrong in acting on behalf of herself, but, understanding where Ms. P was coming from and to maintain good will, she apologized to Ms. P for not having thought of her when making her own request. She also suggested that, from then on, they create a protocol for requesting vacation time that would allow everyone's wishes to be considered. You can tell from this example the extent to which CWW spend time working out the nuances of building good relationships in the workplace. Had Ms. E not demonstrated the ability to deal with things directly, the work group may well have become mired in aligning relationships—one group of CWW pitted against another group of CWW—to the detriment of the work group as a whole. Because evolved women can set personal boundaries, they are often among those CWW who say, when asked if they prefer to work with men or women, that they prefer to work with other CWW or that it doesn't make a difference, while PPCWW are more likely to say that they prefer to work with CWM.

Women from other cultural groups face similar challenges resisting the social demands of others to establish an authentic sense of self. For example, a Latina woman from a traditional background talked about "how painful" it was for her to have to move away from her family in order to get what she wanted for herself. Likewise, a white woman from a conservative religious family had to constantly remind herself that she was not "sinning" when she made decisions for herself even if others in her family saw her as being selfish.

Challenges to Becoming an Evolved Woman

The challenges for the different types of CWW listed above are different. Obedient/rule governed women need to develop an agentic, boundaried self and to create intersubjective types of relationships. Intersubjective relationships are ones in which women see themselves and others as fully entitled subjects of their life and not simply as objects to either be served or to serve them.[23] People pleasers need to develop a boundaried, agentic self. White male–identified women need to develop a relational self. White male–assimilated women need to integrate their (compartmentalized) agentic and relational selves at home and at work. Narcissistic women need to put the skids on their unboundaried, self-absorbed, or intrusive self and learn to develop intersubjectivity by becoming more aware of their impact on others.

People pleasers have a special challenge with narcissistic women, because their propensity to please others feeds into the narcissist's wish that others fulfill their wishes. Evolved women can be sensitive to the fragility of the narcissist, while maintaining a sense of personal boundaries. It is possible to be compassionate, while maintaining internal and external boundaries. External boundaries are managed by limiting interaction with the narcissist—internal boundaries are maintained by depersonalizing interactions and remaining psychologically distinct as a separate self.

Healthy Relationships

Reciprocity is critical to the development of a boundaried "self in relationship." Hotchkiss describes reciprocal relationships as follows:

1. In a reciprocal relationship, each person contributes something and each person benefits in some way. The contributions and benefits need not be spelled out or exactly equal, but it is important that each person feels he or she is receiving good value in exchange for what is offered.
2. There is flexibility in the role of giver and taker. Whether it is an unspoken intuitive understanding, a formal contract, or something in between, there is a mechanism by which each person knows when to give and when to receive. Over the course of the lifetime of the relationship, both parties have a sense of fairness about this aspect of their interactions.
3. Both parties are able to feel valued for their contributions and to express appreciation for what is received. [As one white male identified woman put it, she "loves working for evolved women because they develop her, give training opportunities and talk work/life balance."]
4. Separateness and boundaries are valued on both sides. In the event of conflict, both parties attempt to work out their differences with respect for one another's feelings and points of view.
5. There is no need to "keep score." Scorekeeping—keeping track of who's done what and who "owes" whom—is an indicator that someone feels the relation-

ship is not reciprocal or has difficulty with the sometimes irregular flow of give and take.[24]

Women take great pleasure in relationships and can learn to be tactfully candid. We can share, vent, and strategize with like-minded others without allowing those conversations to become backstabbing, catty, and gossipy. Strategizing can cripple you and block productivity, or it can open the flow to creativity and growth.

Don'ts and Dos

The following list of don'ts and dos can be useful for anyone, but they are designed with CWW in mind. Any individual may be catty, backstabbing, and emotional, but CWW's socialization to be "fake nice" to avoid attack on the basis of not being caring fosters indirect communication ("telling others"), being inauthentic, and allowing oneself to be vulnerable to manipulation by others. Latina and Asian women use indirection too, but they are less likely to lose authenticity when doing so, being "coolly polite" rather than "fake nice." African American and Eastern European women are more likely to be direct. CWM may eliminate the competition maliciously, but, unlike CWW, they can to do so publicly as well as privately or through use of the rumor mill. For example, a bold statement in a meeting—"He/he isn't management material"—can be career damaging for that individual, as can comments from anyone in power (sometimes over a beer); but CWM who are peers of women don't spend the same amount of time as CWW aligning relationships or manipulating feelings through narrative sharing.

Don't: Denigrate or demonize others as a "type" behind someone's back as a power play.
Do: See people in more nuanced ways. Strategize with allies on how common issues/concerns can be raised tactfully. Remember "timing and tact."

For example, once you stereotype someone, you will react to that characterization of them even when it doesn't apply. Evolving women often go through growing pains where they think they are acting from principles—perhaps reacting to a boss who is rigidly authoritarian—but then find that they have painted themselves into a political corner.

Don't: Try to manipulate outcomes in an effort to eliminate the competition.
Do: Feel comfortable acknowledging your expertise and stating your goals.

Don't: Barter other people's personal information for self-enhancement, trying to demonstrate that you are "in the know."
Do: Respect personal boundaries.

Don't: Put all the issues in the offending "other's" court.
Do: Look at how you and others may be reinforcing problematic communication.

Don't: Take it personally.
Do: Stay focused on the work issues.

Don't: Assume that you are stuck.
Do: Strategize on how to move the company forward.

Don't: Focus on eliminating the problematic other.
Do: Strategize to leverage the "offending other's" strengths.

Don't: Let others steal your ideas.
Do: Let it be known publicly when you have done the work.

For example, if the boss takes credit for your idea, don't complain to everyone behind his or her back; rather, tactfully, let the boss know how much you appreciate the kind of leadership that validates your contributions and ask if there will be a problem with that. Continue the dialogue.

Don't: Offer only emotional support.
Do: Speak up at meetings to support others with whom you agree.

Don't: Be afraid of the "bitch" characterization as long as you are not acting so.
Do: Remember: If you stick up for yourself in an unemotional authoritative manner, sticking to the facts, without attacking the character of others, you will demonstrate integrity, competence, and leadership.

Don't: Make yourself the victim in the "story."
Do: What African American women do culturally: Make yourself the hero—the one who didn't take it, or the one who spoke up, or the one who dealt with the situation masterfully.

Don't: Put the blame elsewhere, acting helpless, when you have to make tough decisions.

Do: Make tough decisions with honest information.

Don't: Try to do it all yourself.

Do: Look for role models, if not at work, then in your personal life or in counseling.

CHAPTER EIGHT

CWW and Women of Color

U.S. mainstream culture and traditional ethnic cultures shape mother-daughter relationships differently. Diana Baumrind has identified three styles of parenting: authoritarian, permissive, and authoritative.[1] These parenting styles correlate to different types of white women. Obedient/rule governed women grew up with authoritarian parenting, people pleasers with permissive parenting, and evolved women with authoritative parenting. Authoritarian parenting demands obedience and respect and prepares children to know their role, which in turn prescribes behavior. It is the parenting model for most of the world. Our South Asian Indian colleague is the fifth daughter in the family; she knows that at family functions she must behave like the fifth daughter: deferring to those of higher rank in the family. Authoritarian parents demand obedience and respect. Children should be seen and not heard and should speak when spoken to. Behavior is controlled based on an external threat of justice meted out by parents, rather than through the internalization of guilt. This does not necessarily impede the development of agency. For example, African American parenting, while authoritarian, encourages agency and relationship for both boys and girls.[2]

In permissive parenting, the mother does not have a clear boundaried self and creates a symbiotic relationship in which the daughter is to care about everyone else's feelings (especially her mother's) at the expense of her own. There is little or no external control, which can lead to impulsivity and lack of clear boundaries in children. It is the opposite end of authoritarian parenting in that children do not know what is expected of them. As a result, they often have trouble with self-discipline. Guilt is used to manipulate children in this system; permissive parents withdraw love when children don't comply and promote feelings in the child that they have selfishly hurt or disappointed others. This consideration of others at the expense of one's agentic self is reinforced by white girl culture. One consequence of that is girls withdrawing from connection in order to avoid facing disagreement. In authoritative parenting, parents have a clear sense of boundary themselves. Their goal as parents is to create agentic, self-directed children with an internalized locus of control. Authoritative parenting is gendered insofar as female children grow up in relationship and connection to mother but not at the expense of agency. The result for girls is a boundaried relational self. These girls are not invulnerable to cooptation by white girl ("be nice") culture, but with authoritative parenting, the odds of developing agency are greatly improved.

Authoritative parenting is viewed by mainstream U.S. culture as the optimal way to prepare a child to grow up to be autonomous, self-reliant, and self-directing. The parenting style reflects the U.S. system of rule by law. There are consequences to choices made by children. Shame and guilt are minimized in favor of a rational system of laws/rules and consequences for breaking them. In support of rationality and an internal locus of control are mainstream U.S. cultural values of self-reliance and self-determination. Both the authoritarian and authoritative models foster obedience. The difference is that the authoritarian model promotes obedience to the person, while the authoritative model promotes obedience to the rule. The terms "positional" versus "rational" are also sometimes used to differentiate the two styles. "Don't talk back to your father" is positional and rooted in an authoritarian style of upbringing. "Don't talk with your mouth full of food" is rational and rooted in an authoritative style of upbringing. The mainstream U.S. workplace tries to move people from a more authoritarian model of communication to one that is more authoritative (from who's right to what's right). The transition in moving from an authoritarian to authoritative modality is filled with transference issues.[3] This mainstream middle-class authoritative parenting style, which shifted from the more traditional authoritarian standard, became popular in the post-WWII Dr. Spock years, where the interior life of children became important and childrearing was no longer focused only or even primarily on obedience and preparation for ascribed roles.[4]

One effect of these different parenting styles described above is on individual autonomy. For example, CWW—from either the permissive or authoritative parenting style—are not as role driven as women from traditional patriarchal families. Traditional Latina and Asian women will say they must consult with their families before making any personal decisions. Self-development, autonomy, and identity are mediated by prescribed roles and obedience to elders. For example, our South Asian colleague said that when she got her masters degree in anthropology her advisor asked her what her plans were after getting the degree. She mentioned that was the first time in her life that anyone had asked her what she, herself, wanted to do. In true South Asian fashion, she responded that she would get back to him after consulting with her family. Her advisor, being Afghani, perfectly understood her response. She also provided another example. When her son said he wanted to change his undergraduate major from engineering to philosophy the decision to do so had to go through the family. His father was against it, but his grandfather supported the decision. Without the grandfather's support, our colleague said, "It would have been very difficult for her son to have changed his major."

Another effect is the power distance between mother and daughter or the extent to which achieved (professional) status outside the family can override ascribed status within the family. Within the U.S. mainstream family structure, the power/status difference between mothers and daughters is small compared to other cultures and is equalized or reversed as daughters reach adulthood. In place of having an ascribed role, white women achieve status within the family by acting as, and being identified as, the one who is caring and nice. What they achieve professionally outside the family within the wider society is of secondary, and sometimes only marginal, importance. Families governed by the authoritarian model prepare children to be respectful and obedient and to know their place. Individual status/power distance—based on family position, gender, birth order, and age—is transparent and fixed, qualified, but not overridden, by the professional attainments of family members within the larger society. For example, an older black woman working as a domestic would nonetheless have higher status within African American culture than a young professional black woman. By way of contrast, for white women within U.S. mainstream culture, professional achievements confer higher status than age.

Early Messages That Impact Self-Image and Cultural Style

CWW and women from other cultural groups were asked to share the messages they heard the most from their mothers when they were growing up. The most frequent responses from CWW are "Be caring [of everyone]" and "Be nice and don't hurt anybody's feelings, especially Mom's." The number 1 message African American women report having heard growing up is "Be strong; be self reliant." Obedient/rule governed women who grew up with authoritarian parents also report receiving similar messages of self-reliance (e.g., German Baptists) but, unlike African Americans, within an ascribed role that emphasized duty and obedience over subjectivity and agency.

For example, one African American woman reported that when she got married and left Mississippi after high school, her mother warned her, "You're grown now; you can't come running home." A woman from St. Louis was advised, "Make sure that it is your name that is on the lease, because you have to rely on yourself." The second message that African American women heard most frequently was "Don't let anyone disrespect you."

Traditional role-oriented Latina women report hearing, "A woman is good if she is submissive. She is supposed to serve others. Nobody wants a woman who is for herself; you have to learn to cook and sew and clean house." One traditional Mexican woman said, "The thing that I hear my mother saying in my head is: 'Always make fresh tortillas.'" In another instance, a former Latina migrant worker reported having asked her mother if she could work inside spraying vegetables instead of outside in the hot sun. Her mother said, "Other people know better what is best for you."

The American Association of University Women tracked a group of African American, Latina, and white (non-Hispanic) girls from grade school through high school and asked them at each level, "Do you like yourself just the way you are?" In grade school the self-esteem of Latina girls was the highest (68 percent) of the three groups, followed by African American girls (65 percent) and then white girls (58 percent). Although the self-esteem of all girls dropped in high school, the African American girls had the highest self-confidence/self-esteem of the three groups (58 percent), followed by white (non-Hispanic) girls (45 percent); Latina responses reflected the greatest drop in self-esteem/self-confidence (32 percent).[5]

Although the data was not accompanied by an analysis, I would suggest that the high school responses reflect the degree to which agency is encouraged or allowed within each group of young women. African American socialization (messages to be strong and self-reliant) encourage agency. White girl people pleasing undermines agency. For Latina women, it is people pleasing that undermines agency accompanied by pressures to satisfy traditional role requirements and being subjected to increased levels of parental control stemming from the father's responsibility to protect the virginity of daughters.

Workplace Application

The corporate version of the traditional Latina orientation to serve others is "I will do whatever my boss needs me to do. I will give him/her my very best." An extension of this pattern is the predisposition of Latina women not to refuse their boss when he/she asks them to do something. One consequence of this is that they take on jobs and responsibilities above and beyond what they were hired to do, to the point that, when they leave a job, the company often has to hire two or three people to replace them. Since traditional Latina women also neither complain nor self-promote— they expect the work to speak for itself—they not only end up being overworked but overlooked for salary raises and promotions. Referring to this pattern of behavior, a panel of Hispanics at an HACE (Hispanic Alliance for Career Enhancement) conference several years ago addressed the career drawbacks of becoming indispensable. East Asian women talk about the profound sacrifices made by their parents and what they owe them. They also talk about never receiving praise and being accountable to strict mothers and grandmothers who expect perfection in everything. For example, our Vietnamese colleague Lan Nguyen Roberts remembers her Vietnamese professor saying, "When a young man is telling his mother that he wants to marry his girlfriend, the mother will then advise him not to forget the 4 female virtues from the Confucian culture. They are: CONG: Hard work: contribute to the family; stay at home and take care of all things; be submissive; forget oneself and think of others; DUNG: Beauty; NGON: Language, she must know all the right things to say. She is not allowed to laugh loud; HANH: Personality: be nice, polite, and do not talk back." The first-generation Vietnamese women who have come though our training programs recognize and relate to these words. Lan, commenting on the above list said, "What they are looking for is a woman who will be submissive and obedient to the husband's family."

The cultural style of Latinas is closer to the U.S. mainstream model in promoting attunement to the feelings of others but is different in that honoring and obeying mothers takes precedence over anything else. As identified by Rogelio Diaz-Guerrero, Latina women almost uniformly agree with the statement, "It is more important to obey one's parents than to love them."[6] U.S. mainstream women say just the opposite. Latina, Asian, and African American women also resonate with the parental expression, "You may not love me, but you will respect me!" This is not an expression white mainstream mothers typically say to their daughters.

Nature of Caretaking

Women in every culture care about their mothers, but the nature of caretaking is different. White mainstream women are rewarded and punished on the basis of how nice they are and how caring and attuned they are to mother's feelings, rather than—as with ethnic white women and women of color are—how respectful and obedient they are regarding their mother's behavioral expectations or how respectable they make their mothers/family look in the wider community. African American women, for example, also receive messages that they should be caretakers, but the nature of the caretaking is situational and concrete rather than emotional. On a day-to-day basis, African American women deal more directly with matters that affect the physical well-being of others, saving emotional caretaking for more dire situations.[7] The different focus of caretaking—feelings versus physical needs—also leads to different levels of preoccupation. White women's emphasis on feelings leads to a constant monitoring of other people's feeling states to ensure their emotional well-being. So it is not surprising that a common topic of white woman gossip is who is or is not being caring and nice. In contrast, parental responsibility for African Americans is being attentive to other people's physical needs when the need presents itself. It is preoccupying within a set time frame but is not a constant (cultural) mindset. So, it is also not surprising that for African American women what is important and upfront is not caring for other people's feelings and being nice but being strong and "on your game."

Among authoritarian women generally, behavior is more the focus than feelings. So it should come as no surprise that first-generation Russian American women, parented by authoritarian mothers, should only discover the focus placed on feelings, or interior states of being, on arrival to the United States. For example, when our Russian colleague Tatyana Fertelmeyster began to study clinical counseling, it shocked her that there actually was such a subject as an interior self that could be doing things in the present that were caused by behaviors in the past. Up until that point, she did things because she had to for her survival and that of the family. This was a new concept of feelings and interiority. I asked her if, in Russia, little girls would say, "You hurt my feelings." She replied, "Are you kidding? Maybe they would say to someone else that so and so hurt them, but it wouldn't be feelings." The monitoring and repairing of feeling states is distinctively a category of mainstream U.S. white women. African American girls also do not acknowledge hurt feelings. For Asian women, hurt feelings are connected to shame, and for Latina women, to shame, suppressed anger, and resignation.

These patterns express themselves in the different ways parents discipline their children. At one women's shelter, a woman from Sweden and an African American woman were discussing what they do when their children refuse to put on their seatbelts. The woman from Sweden said, "I tell my daughter, if she doesn't put on her seatbelt, we can't go to the store, and then we won't have any dinner when Daddy gets home from work." The African American woman said, "Oh, no, I tell my kids, 'Then get out of the car!'" The Swedish mother used guilt based on consideration of other people's feelings, while the African American woman used fear and shame by threatening abandonment as a result of disobedience. The manipulative technique that CWW use in the workplace, when they see other CWW as an implicit threat, is the withdrawal of love/relationship (a form of personal shunning or social elimination). Latina and Asian women can also be schemers and manipulators, but when someone is a friend, it is clearly marked. At work, developing friendship and loyalty is possible for Latina and Asian women, but much less so for CWW who are more pragmatic and focused on business and relationally oriented only when they cannot otherwise avoid it. African American women also do not see the workplace as the place to make friends.

Affecting (or Being Affected by) Other People's Feeling States

The different attitudes toward caretaking described above affect the degree of influence that women have (or believe they have) on how others are feeling, as well as the degree of influence that others have on them based on how others are feeling. The protective focus and priority that white women give to the emotional well-being of others—and indirectly themselves when they are the "other" person whose feelings deserve principal consideration[8]—develops a susceptibility that sets them apart from women of other cultural group, most notably, African American women. For example, when CWW say, "I'm sorry if I upset you" to black women, the black woman's (almost knee-jerk) response is "You didn't upset me" (or "If you did, you would have heard about it loud and clear.").

The issue for black women is handing over to someone you do not trust or do not have a relationship with the power to hurt you. This is shown by the dictum, "Never let them see you cry." In effect, black women are saying, "I am in charge of what and how I feel, not you or, for that matter, anyone else." This protective layering—one African American woman characterized it as a "Teflon" coating, others as a "coat of armor"—is what enables black women to navigate and survive corporate America. This different susceptibility to other people's feeling states became apparent during a class session in the 1980s, in which a group of women were discussing the research that was done on the responsibility they felt to take care of the emotional state of others. A black woman in the class challenged the research. She said, "This is a book about white women." The group leader then proposed the following: "Let's say you wanted to divorce your husband, but he said he would kill himself if you left him, what would you do?" A white woman in the group said that that might cause her to change her mind. The black woman replied, "He's dead." Unlike the white women in the class the black woman was not going to allow herself to be "manipulated" by the husband's emotional neediness, which she characterized as "emotional blackmail."

Being Forthright/Assertive/Acting Contrary

People pleaser white girls/women are careful not to act contrary, even with their close friends. "If you can't say something nice, don't say anything at all" is the proverbial mantra. But for white girls/women being nice is more narrowly defined, because something "not nice" is anything that disagrees with the speaker. So white women wait until later and then test the waters with like-minded peers, rather than disagree to another woman's face. For example, a young white woman grew up with brothers and went to an integrated school where she was one of the few white girls who was as comfortable with the African American girls as she was with the white girls. She considers herself white male identified—her father is Italian/Greek—and assertive and capable of telling people directly what she thinks. This approach backfired on her at a school meeting. An older white female colleague offered a solution to a problem that was posed to the group. The young woman said, "Oh no! I totally disagree with that because ..." and received the support of the group. The woman who was "totally disagreed with" leaned back from the table, did not speak for the rest of the meeting, and avoided speaking to the young woman for several days afterward.

Not only are disagreement and being critical avoided because they signify lack of alignment or attunement, white women go out of their way to convince women they don't like that they like them. One of the ways they do that—part of fake nice—is to agree with everything they say. This "agreement," of course, is not a real alignment of views. Rather, it is done to avoid the appearance of being contrary, which, in white girl culture, makes you not nice. If you must express a dissenting view, such as at the above school meeting, it has to be couched in language that is protective of the other person's feelings, such as, "That's an interesting idea *and* I would like to offer an alternative"(using "but" instead of "and" is often seen as dismissive and offensive to a people pleaser).

By way of comparison, African American women don't have a problem disagreeing or being critical of what is going on. They will say what's on their mind: sometimes directly ("Girl, what are you wearing!"); sometimes critically, through signifying ("Girl! I know you didn't *buy* those shoes?" The implication here is "You didn't really pay good money for those [worthless at any price] shoes"). Showing anger is also permissible among friends. African American women say, "If we have a relationship, we ought to be able to handle each other's anger!" African American women will also let you know directly if they don't like you. Latina and Asian women will let you know by avoiding you. If Latina and Asian women can't avoid you, they will be polite, but keep conversation to a minimum. Eastern European (Serbian, Polish, or Russian) beauty technicians in the salon I go to do not hesitate to be direct with each other and their clients. Recently, I heard one of them say to one of their customers, "You look awful! What happened to you?" Compare that to mainstream white women, who, if a friend comes out of the dressing room wearing something awful, will smile and say, "That's nice, but I like the other one better." The Eastern European women at the salon also do not try to have the same opinion as their clients or coworkers. It is absolutely acceptable to say, "No! I totally disagree!" at a volume several notches up from mainstream Anglo discourse style. This statement occurs much more frequently than "I know just what you mean" or other white women people-pleaser language.

For example, our Russian colleague Tatyana Fertelmeyster and an Iranian woman training participant and I were chatting after a seminar. The Iranian woman shared a theory. Tatyana said, "I totally disagree." The Iranian woman's face was taken aback at the forthrightness of the statement. Since I was present, I was able to clarify what was going on culturally. One of the things I said was, comparing the Iranian woman's reaction to that of CWW, "When mainstream white women disagree in an informal discussion, they generally say something like, 'I see your point, but I also think maybe . . .'" Tatyana characterized that way of framing disagreement as using "social lubricants"—something she said she had to learn to do as part of her U.S. acculturation to make for smoother exchanges in the workplace. For her part, the Iranian woman said the level of forthrightness that Tatyana showed would be possible with someone with whom she had a close relationship—this sets her apart from mainstream white women—but not with someone she was meeting for the first time. That was not the case for Tatyana and other Russian women, however, who can lead with "I totally disagree" without such a relationship first having had to be established. As for myself, I don't think I've ever said, in the acquaintance stage of chatting with another woman, "I disagree, because . . ." That is already too much of a "confrontation" for mainstream white women and hard to do even with close friends.

Irish Women

Irish women are like U.S. mainstream white women in at least one respect but also different from them in two others. They are like CWW people pleasers by being "fake nice" with people they meet, until they are publicly disrespected. Then they will confront that person directly and belligerently. As my Irish mother told me, "Never take any shit from anybody!" Consequently, she will confront anyone outside the circle of close family relationships who is disrespectful, especially if the person represents authority. At age eighty-eight, she'll get out of her car and argue with a truck driver if she thinks she has the right of way. However, if a person within that circle is upset with anyone else, no one ever says so directly. These relationships are protected by avoiding confrontation, which, following the Catholic model, can end with excommunication from each other's inner circle for years, even for their entire lives. Consequently, if one of my sisters is upset with my other sister, there is no way she will go directly to that sister and tell her what she is upset about. Instead, she will call me and say, "I'm so upset with [sister 1]"; I will then call my mother and tell her what sister 1 said; then my mother will call sister 2 and say that sister 1 is upset. Each of these conversations begins with the words, "Now don't say anything, but . . ." Guilt is used to decide who should do what, and the cause of the guilt is insufficient caring about the other person's feelings. As a result, a great deal of time is spent gossiping about who didn't show enough care and concern for the feelings/personal suffering of others in the network.

My mother's Irish cultural influence came forth when I confronted the school librarian as a child, something I would never do with another girl. My offense was that I had disagreed with the white woman librarian and wouldn't back down. The librarian's view of a book called *Ghosts, Ghosts, Ghosts* was that it was a scary book.[9] I insisted it was a humorous book. That disagreement earned me a detention after school. I served it with another boy who had hit somebody. In an example from the workplace, an evolved CWW reported that she spoke up at a meeting offering political support to a CWM colleague. When his statement was dismissed by their CWW boss, she countered with, "I think we should go back and listen to his point carefully." Later, offline, her CWW boss commented, "Catherine, your passion concerns me."

People pleaser white women have a harder time standing up for themselves than evolved women. Note the following example of a people pleaser "confrontation." Each white woman stood her ground but framed it as being considerate of others, which is what "nice" and "caring" people pleaser white women do.

As about three hundred teachers were leaving the conference for lunch a line started to form at the buffet table. There was not a lot of room so there were almost two lines forming. One line went straight back from the table, and the other sort of wrapped around. At some point the two lines joined, and there was a little confusion over who was going to go next. One woman said something to her friend like, "This was the line first, so we're fine where we are." Then another woman in the other line said, "Well, think of all the people behind us that are waiting, and they thought they were in line too."

The Power of Women

At a conference for victims of domestic violence, a Kikuyu woman from Kenya said, after having been in an abusive relationship, "I have to get my power back." A Swedish woman, on hearing that, responded, "You talk about having to *recover* your power. I need to *discover* mine."

Black and white men both say to their kids, "Don't upset your mother!" but they mean something different by it. African American fathers don't mean, as mainstream white men do, "Stop it, your mother will be emotional, sad, and destroyed." They rather mean, "If you upset your mother, there will be hell to pay. You don't want her to have to get in it." For Latina women, the issues are, first and foremost, respect for mother and then obedience; for Asians, obedience first and then respect, rather than emotional turmoil or fear of reprisal.

The day Chicago mayor Harold Washington passed on while in office, I struck up a conversation with an African American woman about his death. She surprised me by saying, "I guess he couldn't take it." This was a double-edged commentary on the pressure of racism and on the cultural value that he be strong enough to withstand it. In that regard, one aspect of their socialization that produces self-reliance for African American women is the value and importance of being able to display strength in the face of adversity.

On Backstabbing

Backstabbing rarely shows up in our training session as a peeve about women of color, although for Latina and Asian women that may be due to the relatively small number of them in management, since the pattern of behavior does occur in the culture. Black women do talk about each other; however, unlike white women, there is a protocol for engaging each other directly when they decide to do so. It can take the form of teasing or constitute a real disagreement. As a way of promoting face-to-face communication, African American culture, as noted earlier, considers it a cardinal breach of etiquette for someone to go behind someone's back to talk about them.[10] Should that later be discovered, the black woman who has been talked about will often confront the alleged perpetrator and say things like, "If you have anything to say about me you better [or please have the decency to] say it to my face."

On Competition

The number 1 peeve about African American women, by outsiders of the group, is that they are "loud" and "bossy." The number 1 peeve by black women of black women is that "we don't support each other." One reason for that is that African American women see each other as competitors. For example, one black woman said that the question that goes through her mind when she meets another black woman at work is "Will she be out to get what she wants without regard to me or others"? Another African American woman reported, "There aren't enough of us at work to know what we would do. But in my church, for example, when I meet another black woman, I know she'll be polite, but I also know we're sizing each other up for competition. We will compete directly, and we certainly can disagree and be forthright."

One black woman said, "I always assume black women will compete but the only stories I have are competing over men [smile]. At work, I have so few situations where black women were bosses, my peers, or competitors. Most times, they were my subordinates and saw me as a mentor/advisor or as a boss they were pleased to be reporting to and they did whatever they could to support me. As for myself, I came from an era where competition was expected and encouraged. If I saw someone as my competition, I was willing to work harder, longer, smarter, to achieve what I wanted . . . but with fair play. I believed in a greater good: that the best 'man' would win . . . or that other doors would open for me if I didn't. Maybe that's naive . . . or idealistic."

Expressive Behavior: Cross-Cultural Perceptions

Black Women of White Women

ANGER AND CRYING   African American women and CWW have different views on anger and crying. African American messages (and that of other women of color) included "Don't let them see you cry." "Them" was anybody white. For CWW, crying mainly occurs when they feel their words or ideas are ignored or dismissed without having been properly heard or considered. When that happens, crying is a substitute for confrontation and anger. However, since African American women can get angry, crying in place of direct confrontation or showing anger is seen either as a sign of weakness or being manipulative. For example, an African American woman was trying to get information from a CWW, who said, "I don't like being backed into a corner" and cried. On reporting the story the African American woman said, "I hate it when white women cry, because I can't cry, and it seems weak." Another time a CWW began to cry in a seminar and left the room and went to the hall to regroup. A black woman joined her outside the room and gave her a pep talk, "You're stronger than that! Don't let them see you cry." When I saw that, I thought that a CWW would have said, "Are you OK? I totally can relate. I get emotional, too. That other person was insensitive to hurt your feelings." She would demonstrate alignment and attunement rather than send the message "Be strong, be self reliant/sufficient." Not surprisingly, given these different attitudes, African Americans regard white women as emotional "lightweights"—weak and spoiled—in part, weak because they are spoiled.

An African American woman at work who also happens to be a minister said that she hates when white women cry to a white man about a problem they are having with her, rather than come to her directly, because the man then intervenes on the CWW's behalf, telling her, the black woman, that she has upset someone and needs to tone down and be more approachable. She not only is asked to change her communication style, but she now has become identified as the problem instead of the performance issue that she identified to the CWW—what she saw as the real problem—that brought on the tears.

This example also illustrates the vulnerability that African American women experience in the workplace as a result of CWW going around them to get the ear of a CWM boss. It also plays on CWM susceptibility to CWW. CWM are accustomed to getting character assessments about other people from their wives, mothers, and sisters. Their typical response is either to ignore the complaining woman or to act on an opportunity to make their colleague's life easier by eliminating or minimizing the power of the woman who is the target of the complaint. CWM are especially likely to use their position/power if the CWW makes her case based on work-related criteria, such as "The person is not a team player," "She's too self assured," or "She doesn't take constructive criticism" or is "confrontational" or "aggressive."

These characterizations are especially damaging for African American women because CWM typically view their more self-confident, forthright style through the same cultural filter as CWW. Furthermore, CWM are more likely to accept the word of a CWW without getting another opinion, since African American women and other women of color don't have the same credibility with CWM as CWW do. This "getting the ear of a white male boss" not only negatively impacts African American women when the issue is their communication style but decisions relating to who gets a particular job. For example, a black woman was given an assignment to go to Atlanta to help train a CWW for a new position. Six months later she was called back because the CWW called her manager and reported that she could now handle it herself. It was a position the African American woman also wanted that she was training the other woman for, but she never had a chance to compete for it. The CWM who sent her to Atlanta called her back without explaining why; she didn't find out until months later that the CWW had influenced that decision by having gone to her manager behind her back.

Another time, I came into an office building elevator in which a black woman had her hand on the back of a Latina woman who was crying into the phone. The Latina woman said, "A car came through the window. I was so scared. I was on my way to a meeting." The black woman said, trying to comfort her, "Are you OK? I heard you say you have business to take care of, so you need to be OK." I would have said, "Are you OK? What happened? Do you need to talk? I can stay with you till you calm down enough to get home." Where I would have tried to restore her emotional state through talking and listening, the black woman encouraged and supported what she needed to do for herself.

In yet another instance, I was conducting a workshop for victims of domestic violence and a white woman, who was in a relationship with an African American man, said he told her, "A black woman wouldn't have to go to a therapist; a black woman could handle it herself."

I overheard a similar message while I was sitting on the "el" train heading down to the Chicago Loop. In front of me was an African American mother and her young daughter. The daughter, around five years old, was squirming and whining, and her mother said, "Now you can quit acting white." The message was clear: white girls are spoiled brats, and black girls are not. Perhaps this suggests the opposite message, too: black girls are supposed to be tough, strong, persevering, noncomplaining, and in charge and control of themselves.

I have been out to dinner with African American friends who roll their eyes when a young white waitress comes to the table with a "Suzy Snowflake" manner: superficial, flighty, and smiley. As an insider to the culture, I read it as "I'm harmless" or "Please don't take me seriously." My black friends, however, see it as phony and childish. Perhaps that explains the appeal of the Hillary character on the show *Fresh Prince:* black viewers taking delight that a black woman can allow herself to be spoiled and clueless—something they are not allowed to be themselves.

ON SMILING A friend of mine grew up in Iowa in a German fundamentalist Baptist family. Her father would leave three-by-two note cards around the house, which said, "Smile." She also remembers visiting a very stern grandfather's house, where there were no toys, and they had to just sit in the living room. She also remembers her mother leaning over and hissing in her ear, "Smile." She recounts this with great pain, remembering the rage she felt at the commanded inauthenticity. My friend suggested this smiling rule must have come from many generations of Puritans. Perhaps, she said, her father was concerned that a gloomy appearance reflected a certain amount of spiritual bankruptcy that would be displeasing to the Lord. Women in Renaissance Christian art were portrayed with beatific smiles. She said maybe being nice was a way to display to others that all is well with you—a state of righteousness or grace—which reflects well on the family. "After all," she said, "everyone wants to go to heaven." This pattern of behavior was especially reinforced among women, who often are the keepers of traditional values. Note the lyrics to the Brownie group song: "I've something in my pocket that belongs across my face. I keep it very close at hand in the most convenient place. I'm sure you'll never guess it if you guess a long, long time, so I'll take it out and put it on; it's a great big Brownie smile!" White women who don't do the smile are often criticized because of that, most often, by other white women.

One CWW reported working on a bulb farm. She said, "I wanted to work in the clean building, but was told I couldn't because I didn't have a positive attitude. But my face is just like this; I'm not smiley, so people think I'm unapproachable. The woman who told me that then told me to look at another white woman who was coming toward us saying, 'See how her eyes and her mouth are smiling?'"

MEANING OF THE SMILE TO BLACK WOMEN African American women, who got different messages, have queried about the white woman smile, "Why is it that when you walk past white women in the grocery store they smile this funny little smile at you?" They imitate the smile, lips closed: a smile that I often find myself doing in the grocery store. Polite greetings are very important to African Americans. Children are taught to "speak," which means to be sure to say hello to people. However, African Americans don't know how to interpret the smile without the greeting. Another difference between black and CWW greeting patterns is that one daily greeting is enough for African Americans. Black women have wondered why CWW smile at them every time they pass by their desk, not just on the first greeting of the day. CWW have asked why black women are so "mean" when they don't smile and give off what seems like unfriendly vibrations every time they pass. Both African American men and women have asked me why white people approach them and say, "Smile." Their interpretation of this command to smile is "If you're not a happy black person, then maybe you're dangerous"—a legacy of forced inauthenticity reminiscent of slavery days and of Paul Lawrence Dunbar's poem "We Wear the Mask."[11] Nonetheless, one black woman said, she tells her daughter to smile to offset the workplace view of her and other black women that they are unapproachable. She does it because she thinks that view of her and other black women has hindered the progress of African American women within the workplace.

CWW of African American Women

HAIR   White women notice each other's hair as a way to show interest and a sign that one is acting in a caring way about someone. One white woman was shocked, therefore, when she complimented her black coworker on her new hairstyle and was told (only somewhat facetiously), "You better be careful or you'll get your white butt beat." Since they were indeed friends, she took it as advice to be heeded with other African American women but was curious as to why it caused offense.

Black women are generally wary of comments on their hair made by a white woman, unless you happen to be a close friend. Otherwise, casual observations are taboo, carrying with it judgmental undertones, such as implying that their hair didn't look OK before. In other cases, black women see it as a form of objectification: being seen as exotic. For example, one black woman noticed that each time she wore her hair differently at work she got a different response from the CWW. They were used to her wearing her hair straight. One day she came in with her hair in corn rows. The response she got from them then on was—even while the CWW complimented her on the new look—that they seemed more intimidated by her and less likely to approach her. She got curious as to why the CWW responded so differently to her on the basis of her hair. So she decided to change her hair style again as an experiment to see what effect that would then have. She found that when she began to wear her hair natural, she was increasingly avoided. One CWW commented, "You have a new hair style every week." Black women hear this kind of comment (likewise comments such as "Is that real?") as voyeuristic and judgmental—a form of signifying or implying criticism—especially when coming from some-one who doesn't usually speak with them.

Most CWW feel rebuffed by hostile reactions to observations or com-pliments they make on black women's hair. Curiosity, in white woman culture, is met with openness, even when it is unwelcome, because it isn't nice to show suspicion or to be unreceptive, even if you, in turn, may gos-sip about that person later as having been phony or intrusive. CWW view the reproach they get to their inquisitiveness as mean, and, once a person is identified as mean, there is no longer a requirement to be nice to that person, because they have "struck the first blow." The more a culture de-mands "niceness," the more it punishes or isolates those who don't meet that requirement. And while a CWW won't likely say directly, "I'm sur-prised and hurt"—thereby allowing a verbal exchange that could lead to a confrontation—she will afterward report to her group of friends how "unreceptive and "mean" the black woman was while she was simply try-ing to be "friendly." For black women, what isn't nice is to be intrusive. But since they also know CWW will shut down if rebuffed, they may instead of saying directly, "Why are you disrespecting me?" respond to the invasive question as if they are speaking with a child. For example, a white woman who was intrigued at the particularly interesting way that a black woman had done her hair asked her how she had done that. The black woman saw her curiosity as genuine and explained the process to her. However, when talking to another black woman about the other black woman's hair and her curiosity around how it had been done, the white woman was met with a condescending, "And what did you learn from that?"

In the workplace, African American women who don't share personal information or who don't smile are viewed by PPCWW as mean and an-gry. Also, because the discourse style of black women is more direct and forthright than theirs, PPCWW think of black women as especially strong and powerful (often suggestive of their first experiences with black girls in high school). For example, one white high school senior said, "The black girls intimidate us; they sometimes walk by in the hall and suddenly stamp their foot and say, 'boo.'" At this point, a black girl in the group said, "Well, you know, when you first come to a white school, you're surprised by how much power you have compared to white girls."

One of the difficulties that CWW have with black women who work for them is around how to handle the direct, forthright manner that black women use themselves and expect from others. One white male–identified CWW characterizes black women bosses to be "less flexible and out to prove themselves—as if saying, 'I worked hard to be here and demand your respect.'" In the following example, a young African American woman was hired by a PPCWW who thought she was great. In fact, she was great, and the CWW began to feel threatened. When an important meeting came up, she didn't tell her about it. Not telling her follows the pattern of white girl/woman culture, which is to deal with direct competition by trying to avoid or eliminate it. When the African American woman found out about the meeting having happened without her, she confronted her CWW boss by saying, "Why wasn't I included in that meeting?" Her boss said, "Because I didn't think you were ready, that's why." Down the line, white girl/woman culture will kick in again in the way the CWW boss will frame (or rationalize to herself) what went on: telling others that the black woman is too self-assured and cocky and doesn't respect authority—even, that she was totally out of line to "confront" her in that manner—suggesting she is an "angry black woman" who "could be trouble" down the line.

STANDARD OPERATING PROCEDURE   The following example reflects a cultural clash ending in a confrontation between an obedient/rule governed CWW and an African American woman. The African American woman was placed in charge of a program that was failing and managed to turn things around. She thought she had discretionary authority in changing the plan that was in place. African Americans frequently say, "Tell me what to do, but not how to do it!"—believing that the person who directly executes the plan is in the best position to know what changes need to be made to ensure the outcome. Also, African Americans, coming from a "performance-oriented" cultural mindset, believe that performers are "granted great license to improvise with regard to the text" in the interests of getting the text/plan accomplished.[12] The O/RG CWW, coming from a "plan the work and work the plan" "compositionally oriented" mainstream organizational mindset, said that the black woman needed to get prior approval for the changes that she made to the plan. The confrontation that developed from that—the black woman expecting praise for having turned a failing plan around and the O/RG CWW feeling disrespected at the black woman's disregard for her role/position—led to a breach in their working relationship.

At the same time, even while PPCWW attack and punish black women for their more forthright manner, they also admire black women for being authentic, direct, and forthright—something they wish they could be themselves. These CWW lay awake at night worrying about what they said that might have offended someone. Black woman say that they're more likely to lay awake thinking about what they should have said but didn't. As one African American woman said, "I play back what I don't say, not what I say. At least I know I was true to myself."

CHAPTER NINE

Gossip and Community

Women's networks both in and out of the workplace are generated and sustained through gossip. According to Meijer and de Bruin, gossip is concerned with questions of identity and cultural citizenship. It is part of knowing that people belong to a community and share a common language.[1] The sense of community within and among different women's groups at work is mirrored by a common language: specifically, what women talk about, the way women represent themselves and others within the gossip context, and how they position themselves (hero or victim) within the stories they tell. The presence or absence of a common language (subject matter, tone, and style of gossip) among women of diverse cultural backgrounds directly affects their ability to network and connect with each other at work.

African American Women/CWW

Narrator as Hero

African American gossip in the workplace positions the narrator as the hero of the story. This differentiates their informal talk from that of white mainstream women who tend to focus on what someone else did rather than on how they, themselves, responded or acted. For example, when I taught at a Chicago middle school on the predominantly black West Side,

African American teachers would tell stories about how a particular administrator or teacher might be ineffectual, then go on to say how they handled a situation with that individual, because they wouldn't take that from anybody. Gossip often included, "He/she wouldn't try that with me." In James Brown's immortal words, "Papa don't take no mess." Even when African Americans talk about racism at work, they don't promote themselves as the victim. Black women may start gossip with, "Am I crazy?" followed by an account of what may be racist treatment. This frames the situation as a question, reflecting the constant guessing game African Americans play, especially in the North, where racism is often covert or unconscious. The listener or teller of the story may signal the obvious racism by saying, "Hello!" ("Hello!" = racism greets us once again). But the gossip is about the lameness of the racist or clueless person, rather than the helplessness of the storyteller. The power of the black person to endure in such a way that they don't let racism get to them has to follow up with what they are going to do about it. Listeners will say, "And what did you say/do?" thereby encouraging the storyteller to display their strength or sharp thinking in the face of difficulty. By way of contrast, when I sat with white middle-class teachers, stories would more often characterize how frustrated and victimized they were by ineffective administrators or bemoan the behavior of mean, rude colleagues—positioning the storyteller as heroic for their endurance, rather than for their ability to aggressively confront the situation, since direct confrontation is not valued in the culture of white women, because it isn't nice.

Gossip Styles in Conflict

These different approaches collide when black and white girls get together. For example, when I spoke with diverse students at an integrated girls' high school, the African American girls said that they were surprised when they went to an integrated slumber party that the white girls spent so much time and energy talking about who did what mean thing to whom. On another level, it was also frustrating that they didn't do anything about it. So when white women share how upset they are with someone by reporting what someone else said, black women respond by saying, "And what did you say?" For black women, the story is (or should be) about how powerfully you handled yourself in one or another situation. For white women, it is to get emotional support for an assault on hurt feelings and appreciation that they managed to handle the situation appropriately (in consideration of the other person's feelings) despite that assault. The reasons that white women give for not challenging someone directly—concern over loss of relationship for having hurt someone's feelings—is seen by African American as weak; likewise, black women see white women's desire for "peace before truth" as a cop-out.

Within my Irish family, as mentioned earlier, one woman (sister A) calls her sister (B) to complain that a third sister (C) isn't helping enough in the care of their aging mother. B calls C to tell her what A said. C explains that she is doing what she can and also says why she can't do more. B explains to A what C said, and that conversation involves considerable evaluation of whether C has a valid argument. All the time each sister is communicating their side of the story to the mother, which creates further avenues of gossip as each sister debriefs the conversation that they had with mother with another of the sisters. When I share this pattern with black women they often say, "Why wouldn't sister A just confront sister C directly and tell her to step up?

The reason black women respond that way is that African American woman's cultural style is oriented around "doing something about a problem." For women from other groups, this is occasionally seen as forcing matters to a plan of action before they have been fully processed. For example, when our culture club met—it consists of a white woman, a black woman, a Japanese woman, and a Mexican woman—it was the black woman that was out of sync because she kept pressing to move the problem forward to "What are we going to do about it," instead of—where the rest of the women were—focusing on how everyone felt about the problem.

Irish Women as "Heroes"

Irish women can be either heroes who fight the system or victims of personal meanness. Irish culture has a place for bragging about what you do when it is behavior that co-opts authority. Celts, like African Americans, have a social legacy of oppression and a cultural style that values personal power and display (e.g., "the Fighting Irish"). It is not surprising, therefore, that Irish women are often the most likely to create relationships with African American women since the level of assertion in their styles can be similar. Irish women, like West African women, share a history of a cottage industry in Ireland and West Africa and share an acculturation that "raises daughters and loves/spoils sons." In the following example, an

African American woman was intrigued by an Irish American woman. Their white colleagues were whining at a meeting, so the Irish woman banged her fist on the table and said, "This is what it is—deal with it." The African American woman was impressed by the display of personal power and thought there were possibilities for friendship. When both of them attended our training seminar, the Irish woman realized that although she and the black woman had different styles, they did have a common language to understand each other. The African American woman reported that she needed two things before she could gossip with the Irish woman: respect and trust. She got both. Consequently, when they started talking with each other, they could be direct, truthful, and honest and didn't have to beat around the bush. The black woman noted that "because we could be forthright and direct we didn't have to share the same point of view or have a common style." The Irish woman would call me and say, "My people pleaser mode is dead." She found her connection to the African American woman to be empowering because she discovered that she could also begin to be more forthright in relationships she cared about without concern that the relationship might be at risk.

CWW Storytelling and Gossip at Work

The following story from a young CWW executive exemplifies what I have heard over the years from many white women in corporate America:

> Mostly, I find that white women gossip about other women. Occasionally, you hear about the philandering man. The married ones usually gossip about the poor professional etiquette of the single ones. The single ones gossip about the unfortunate or torrid personal lives of the other single ones. If it's strictly business gossip, it often revolves around who is visibly ladder climbing, too bossy, or too self-assured. There is lots of gossip about poor performers, rumors about them having to go, and wondering about who will put them in their place. I can not think of many examples where women characterize themselves as heroes. However, I do often find myself saying, "Not to pat myself of the back, but ..." Both men and women seem to get a kick out of that—I suppose since it's unexpected. Of course, when giving myself credit, I'm sure to be a bit tongue-in-cheek about it so as not to offend the other white women. I can't say that only women are put off by a bossy woman. Men are equally put off by a "bitch." However, you have a 50/50 shot with men. If they agree with you they welcome the assertiveness, if not ... here comes the big B. Know what I mean?

It took me years to build up enough of a positive reputation before I felt free to take complete charge, e.g. act bossy: give direct orders, have strong opinions without using apologies or disclaimers, and be confident. Now people just seem to think I'm "eccentric." Of course, eccentric is just another way of saying "high ranking jackass."

Previously, my standard mode was to approach co-workers and subordinates softly, working up to a more directive tone. Now, I don't often waste time warming people up. Frankly, this is extremely liberating and, without a doubt, the best way to get shit done. However, at this point in my career—being established, but not showing visible grey hair—I am still conscious of offending others with a direct approach. More often, this is the case with peers rather than those that I manage. In those relationships where I am clearly the boss, I like to establish hierarchy quickly. This helps eschew the occasional confrontation with the [white male] departmental know-it-all that inevitably occurs when a young woman in charge takes the let's-be-friends approach.

This all becomes much less complicated if you are a man or significantly older than those you manage or work with. For those types, far less finesse is required to maintain control/authority without losing the likeability factor. Honestly, it's an incredibly delicate ecosystem to maintain. Although I wouldn't trade my estrogen for anything, it must be nice to be an old dude when it comes to the world of business. I love operating in the get-shit-done mode, fearlessly. That's my version of "being in the zone."

African American Women's Gossip and Storytelling at Work

African American women say, "We gossip about how committed individuals are to reducing racism. One issue is, how does so-and-so's behavior make us look, and the other is, what is so-and-so doing for the group? Or is so-and-so too self-centered, promoting him or herself more than the movement. If somebody is too bourgeois, they are gossiped about. The question is, are they committed or not, or are they doing more harm than good in terms of racism. We also talk about politics."

Another young African American woman who works in human resources said that the common elements within African American female gossip structure are damage control, bonding, exclusion, addressing perceptions, and correction. She said,

A lot of the time our gossip is centered around how we are perceived and about cultural/racial injustices. We are not above talking about one of our own. Within our gossip there is also opportunity to bond when you find common ground with one another or find connection when sharing a similar experience. When we gossip it is usually about a particular topic, person or the event that is of substance or meaning to our culture. Gossip serves a purpose for us; it's rare to gossip about something that won't go anywhere or won't result in something. It's rare to share personal stories when gossiping unless the person you're gossiping with is a close and personal friend. Gossip is also a form of "taking action" against an injustice or wrong doing especially in the workplace. Often when African-American women are gossiping, they will form a plan of action to address or resolve the issue. An example of this would be if another African-American woman were not representing us correctly, a plan would be formed to let her know or address it in some way so that she understood her behavior or actions weren't appreciated by the rest of the community or population. Often during this gossip session, we also talk about what approach would work best and decide who among the group should be the one to carry the message to the offending party. If the person who is exhibiting the offending behavior has already been warned or addressed, then often the gossiping portion or gathering is done to send the message that that person is excluded.

Appearance

Appearance is gossiped about, in part because of the cultural value of personal style, but because African Americans see themselves both as individuals and as members of a group, individual group members have a stake in wanting other members of the group to appear sharp, as it reflects on the group. One black woman said her boss, a successful African American executive, admonished her for not having her hair and makeup sharp enough. African Americans sometimes say they feel pressure to dress nicely when they go anywhere, because dress impacts how they are treated. While that is true for people generally, it is especially true for groups that suffer social oppression. It is easier for a white person to count on good service even if they are dressed in work-around-the-house clothes. The cultural point about being well dressed, however—Harrison's term "vitality of imagery" comes to mind—should not be overlooked just because being well dressed also has race/class/status implications.[2 3] Talking about anyone or anything that is publicly visible is fair game and can even become a source of play when African Americans engage in signifying.[4] For example, as I was riding with an African American colleague in downtown San Antonio, we both noticed a woman wearing a skirt that was way too short. My colleague said, "Doesn't she have any friends?" (Implication: To tell her how to dress.) Likewise, when I taught at the Chicago middle school, back in the days of "stacks" and "floods" (towering shoes—good; short pants—not good), Meta said to Charlotte, who came into the room wearing stacks and floods: "Charlotte, if your shoes caught on fire, honey, your pants wouldn't know nothin' about it."

Gossip and Other Women's Groups

Latina Women—Recognition and Trust

Latina gossip follows a pattern similar to that of white women, except that Latina women seem to gossip even more than white women do. Perhaps the more conflict avoidant a culture is, the more it relies on gossip as a way to deal with issues and align relationships. A common gossip theme of Latina women in the workplace (Hispanics, generally) is over recognition and parity (or lack thereof). For example, at a week-long training program in Southern California, Latino participants were unhappy with the representation of the Latino segment that began the second day of the program. This unhappiness was registered quickly with the resident Hispanic diversity focal who, acting as the authorized and designated broker, brought the matter up to those of us in charge of the program. At issue was the amount of information that was covered and the amount of time given to the program relative to the amount of time that had been given to the African American segment the day before. The matter of representation and proportionality—respect or *dignidad* is the ultimate issue—was especially strong because the program was being done in Southern California, which, demographically, is heavily Hispanic, and the considerable number of Hispanic participants in the program. Culturally relevant was the collective way the matter was handled among Hispanics themselves and then, through a broker or mediator, communicated to those in charge. Also relevant was the difficulty in trying to repair the damage after the fact. At issue were not only matters of proportional representation (we were ultimately able later to create a better program balance there) but residual matters of hurt pride and anger that the group felt over having been initially disrespected—feelings, which, no matter what we tried to do afterward, we were not entirely able to dispel.

Another gossip theme revolves around trust. Deep levels of trust develop among insiders, often by creating personal relationships outside of the workplace. Insiders of a clique spend time creating solidarity and getting to know each other's families. Latina women have their *chismes* or gossip. Sometimes whispering even happens in the presence of others. Covering one's mouth with fingertips is sometimes considered "private." For Latina women, it is not considered rude to do this in the presence of others. One Latina woman talked about connecting with another within the company. She said, "We kept each other sane. In order to survive within the company, and try to get ahead, we would process collectively, going over data points and information, trying to figure out white people. She had an amazing work ethic. She was also very nurturing, taking care of both people and things. Once you have loyalty with her, she is fiercely loyal!"

One Latina woman observed, "While I believe the term 'alliance' is appropriate, I see Latinas being a bit more *tribal.*" Those tribes of women are typically small, and it has been my experience to see how some Latina women can form a close bond to one another, built around a shared belief, experience, or cause. The alliance builds off of that and a commitment to each other grows. Latina women have different levels of trust with individual women, and gossip varies depending on the level of friendship. Because cultural changes for traditional Latina women (as well as traditional women from other groups) happen at work before they happen at home, a common gossip theme among close friends is the challenge of trying to reconcile the different self/role expectations at work with those at home.[5] Some information they will willingly share with others, and other information they will keep secret to their grave from even their closest family members or friends. One Latina woman said that "trust within the tribe is an expectation. If the trust is broken, rebuilding that relationship will be a long process and may never be the same. This [breach of trust] is taken hard by Latinas. I believe this may be due to the Latino family experience. A breakdown in loyalty and trust by a family member is very hurtful."

For example, sister A didn't speak to sister B for five years because there was no longer *confianza* (trust) between the two of them. What caused the breach was that sister A had wanted sister B to just listen to her gripe about sister C but didn't want her to bring in sister C to tell her directly what she was upset about. When sister B told C to talk to A because of what A was upset about, A felt that B forced the conflict into the open. The preferred mode for Latina women, like white women, is to pretend that everything is OK with another woman face to face even though they and everyone else who knows them knows that a problem exists between them. What differentiates Latina women from white women, however, is that it is almost impossible to repair a relationship once trust has been broken. With respect to the above situation, after five years, sister B went to sister A and said, "Look I want to have a relationship with you. Do you want to discuss what happened or not." Sister A chose not to discuss what happened. And while A has begun talking to B again, as B says, "It's not the same as it was before."

Latina women who are from different countries see each other as very different. Culturally speaking, Caribbean Latinos will be more assertive than Mexicans, for example, as a result of the African influence in the Caribbean versus the Indian influence in Mexico. Adler and Garaitonandía discuss some of the communication breakdowns between the more assertive Cubans and the more harmony-oriented Mexicans in Mexico.[6] One Mexican woman said that her godmother referred to a Cuban woman as a *guzano,* which translates as "worm." This woman said to her godmother, "We have to stop doing that." Her godmother didn't speak to her for six months after that. Ethnic solidarity and communication style can also get in the way of creating trust. One Latino group that reported to the mayor's office couldn't get along, because they divided along lines of nationality and levels of assertion. Establishing a social connection with white women at work is difficult for Latina women because they see white women as not really interested in getting to know them personally. They are generally put off by the perfunctory "Hi, how are you?" that white women give in passing them in the hallway ("who never stop to find out how you really are doing"). One Latina woman said, "I eventually left my job because my co-workers were so cold. I once won an award, and people congratulated me, but they never even asked what I did to get the award."

East Asian Women

A critical issue and common theme for Asians generally, and East Asian women specifically, is over how to get ahead at work. One of the key reasons is that the majority of East Asian women find the political and networking aspects of getting ahead not only difficult to figure out but also extremely difficult to do. As one East Asian woman executive who did manage to navigate the corporate terrain to get to a top senior-level position put it,

> I have had many conversations with Asian women who struggle to understand
> the strategic aspects to getting ahead. Usually this conversation happens when

they come to me to complain about "so-and-so" having gotten a promotion even though they are not that good, smart, qualified, etc. And even after I point to the need to be political and strategic about getting ahead, they balk at the idea, not only because they haven't yet developed the skill set to do it, but also because getting ahead by being "political" is not seen as a respectable thing to do. It conflicts with their value system which is based upon the belief that hard work, honesty and integrity and loyalty to the boss are the proper means to get ahead. As a result of that, and because it is not natural to them, they default to their work ethic and false belief that their bosses will recognize and reward them.

Our colleague Adrian Chan, when in graduate school, was startled to learn that a fellow Anglo male graduate student "who had come to him and his Asian friend for help in statistics" got a higher starting salary on graduating than they did. As he and his friend put it, "He came to us for help. He wasn't as smart as we were." But what his Anglo counterpart did that the Asian graduate students did not, or not as much or as well, was network and promote himself with prospective employers.

Part of the reason that Asians (Hispanics and Middle Easterners, too) resist the U.S. style of networking is that it is strictly business related and impersonal. As the Asian woman executive put it with respect to what loyalty means in the United States compared to what it means elsewhere:

Loyalty in the U.S. corporate arena is a business arrangement around position and power. There is a tacit agreement that you scratch my back and I scratch yours. If you don't, then, there is no relationship to have. For East and South Asians, it's a long-term human relationship based on trust, admiration, etc. It has little to do with rank or position and all to do with what we owe each other. I have experienced this quality with both East and South Asians from business associates, corporate leaders, clients, and suppliers. We call this *on* in Japanese. We are taught to return *on* to those who have taken care of us, our families, etc.[7]

Because Asians are on the lookout to get help with their careers from those who are senior to them within the organization they will also gossip among themselves about which managers whom they can get and expect help from and which they cannot. For example, a Southeast Asian woman reported, "If a non-Asian woman is going out of her normal duty to help other people with their job, the Asian women would go around the building and spread the good news about that particular person. However, they will also tell on people whom they view as selfish. So Asian women often come to me and tell me, 'Don't bother to ask so and so about something that you don't know because she is not going to help you out.' Rather we fear that she will tell other people that we are so incompetent." Often Asians—East Asian women especially—communicate their needs or wishes indirectly. Implicit in wondering out loud or making a complaint is a request that the person they are addressing do something to remedy the situation. There is also the expectation that the person will be sensitive to the request implied in the message. East Asians call this mode of communication "stomach talk." What often happens with white women is that they assume that what the Asian women are doing is simply sharing and asking for commiseration and emotional support. Asian women, however, assume white women are picking up on the indirect request and just don't want to help. On the reverse side, when I am talking informally with Asian women, I occasionally observe them trying to figure out whether or not there is an implicit request hidden within what I am saying. Because I know their cultural style, I often stop and say, "I don't mean more than what I'm saying; I haven't thought this through, and I don't expect you to do anything." Even so, they often still go deep to search for a hidden meaning. While the confusion is equal on both sides of the fence, the impact is not. The failure of white women to pick up on the implicit request for political support undermines trust building, especially since Asian women (and women of color generally) assume that white women's voices carry more clout with CWM than their own voices.

Asian Indirectness and the Absence of a Gossip Network

East Asians often prefer an indirect method of communication when making a request specifically to avoid the shame that might result from someone having to say no and generally to preserve harmony. This approach flies in the face of advice that Asians get from their white coworkers who occasionally counsel their Asian coworkers to be more direct in asking for a raise and promotion. But this is extremely difficult for Asians, especially East Asians, to do. For example, when we started our training at one company we noticed a first-generation Korean woman at the beginning of the first day going to each table and asking her work cohorts for a million dollars. When we asked her why she was doing that she explained facetiously (trying hard to gloss over what in fact was a serious problem for her) that since she was told by her Anglo peers in her work group to "simply go to the boss and ask him directly" for the raise that she had confided to them that she wanted, she was practicing hearing no to prepare herself for rejection, in case her boss said no.

Since U.S. mainstream Anglos tend to register requests only when they are direct and (verbally) explicit, East Asians—women in particular—are seriously handicapped when they don't have other Asians in their work group to gossip with who will understand the request that is implicit within their indirect communication and act as a mediator on their behalf with the boss or colleague who is the target of the request and from whom they expect remedial action to come. First-generation East Asian women also don't realize that third-person communication or the use of mediators, which is common among Asian and Latina women, will be looked on negatively by CWM, who will ask, "Why doesn't she come to me and speak for herself?" Moreover, "If she can't speak up for herself, how can she be leadership material?" CWW who are white male identified will also react the way CWM do. White women who are people pleasers might also wonder whether they did something to upset the other person and assume that is the reason why they are using third-party mediation instead of coming to them directly. But they would still expect the woman to come talk to them face to face either to deal with why she couldn't come to them directly the first time or about the raise, promotion, or other issues generally. In that regard, the white woman sees third-party communication not as someone playing a broker role—petitioning on someone else's behalf—but simply as chitchat, and, thus, not something that necessarily requires any action on her part. This, in turn, as noted above, leads to Asian gossip about her not being willing to help.

The failure to properly read indirect communication also occurred when a well-known Asian American female columnist took a position at a new paper. The paper was short on office space, however, and, since she did not speak up for herself, she ended up with a desk out in the hall. No one else spoke on her behalf, because (a) when they asked her if things were OK, she said, "It's fine, I can work here"; (b) they did not read between the lines to know that she really was not happy with the situation but just didn't want to force the issue; and (c) she ultimately felt it was someone else's responsibility to initiate action to remedy the situation, especially since, given her status at the paper and in the community, she should not have been put in that situation to begin with. Moreover, since there were not others to gossip with at the paper, especially someone who would be able to read her situation correctly and act on her behalf, she unhappily stayed where she was put while keeping her feelings to herself.

International Example of Indirect Communication

A Hong Kong Chinese woman working in Korea reported to a Japanese American woman (born and raised in Japan who worked and resided in the United States). One evening the Hong Kong woman called at a time when the Japanese American woman was busy with family. The timing of the call was unusual. The Japanese woman knew to try to figure out what was going on. She began asking open-ended questions, knowing that one difference in the Korean office was a new Korean male manager who the woman reported to. She asked, "How is everything in the office there? How are you doing? Is everything OK?" The woman replied yes a couple of times, even after she asked her the same question in different ways. Oddly, the Hong Kong woman wanted to discuss various other topics and prolonged the call as if she did not want to end the conversation. This was unusual as the Hong Kong woman knew how impolite it was to keep her boss busy late at night. The Japanese American woman asked, "Is the new manager saying or doing anything to make you feel uncomfortable?" The answer was not sure. She then asked, "How about the other women? Are they uncomfortable?" The answer was yes. The Japanese American woman flew to the office, discovered what was going on, and removed the new manager before his three-month trial period ended.

A white woman (or mainstream U.S. Anglos generally) would not only have missed picking up on the request that was implicit within the call but also the other cultural piece: that, contrary to U.S. mainstream telephone protocols and discourse style that require the caller to be direct and explicit and, given the late hour, quick in giving the reason why they are calling, the East Asian protocol requires that the person called—in this case the Japanese woman—try to figure out what was behind the call. The Japanese woman, knowing the East Asian protocol, did just that, also knowing that something important was going on for the call even to have been made.

South Asian Women

In the workplace, peers are viewed as competitors—thus not someone with whom to form social alliances. Our colleague Gudy Grewal gave the following example of this perspective from a discussion that she was having with another Indian couple at home. She reported,

> My husband and I had a young couple over for dinner on Saturday. They are South Indians and both work in India. He is here on an assignment with his company and she has taken a leave of absence from her consulting group to accompany her husband to the U.S. When I started talking to her about KMA and our work she was surprised that people would have to go through "diversity training" in order to work with people from diverse backgrounds. According to her, "People should just adapt, according to whatever their boss/customer wants." So, when I asked her about cooperation/relationship among the peers, she immediately said, "Why do you have to have a peer relationship? That is not important! What is important is that you do what your boss has asked you to do or what the customer wants you to do." When I asked her, "What if something is not clear and you want your peer to help you?" She said, "I don't think that the peers will help you."

Gossip often revolves around who is not fulfilling their role properly, because of the value placed on role fulfillment, but also—self-servingly— as a way to position oneself ahead of the competition. Gossip over the competition is generally critical and can be done within a work group of peers or with the boss regarding the work performance of a peer. In personal life, gossip is about other people's families. How successfully or unsuccessfully they have raised their children is commonplace, as is gossip about other women's jewelry, since it is also a sign of family status within the rigid hierarchy of South Asia. They also gossip about whose daughter or son is the most successful or who shamed the family. As a result, Asian and Latina women are often reluctant to share information that might be embarrassing with family members—sometimes not letting other family members know when they are laid off, for example.

Gossiping within Mixed Groups

Three women were seated at a table: a Latina, an Anglo, and an African American. The Anglo woman laughed when I talked about how white women meet new people, because she had done exactly that with her tablemates: "Where do you live? Are you married? Do you have any kids?" I asked the Latina if she asks personal questions. She replied, "Oh,

I'm gonna find out. I would preface it by saying first, 'You have such an open friendly manner. Do you have brothers and sisters?'" It was interesting that her questions didn't ask where the black woman lived or if she was married, but rather her questions were about family and didn't require answers that could be seen as qualifying a person one way or the other, which is often how African Americans read those questions that white women ask. She also began with a question that was designed to show why she asked, not leaving it open to speculation. Note also that by giving the reason why she was asking a question first the Latina woman also addressed the other issue that African Americans have with respect to being asked personal questions, which is "Why do you want to know?"[8] My sense also is that the Latina woman's question would likely be better received in any case, because African Americans in the United States do not have the same history of discrimination with—therefore, less reason to be suspicious of—other women of color as they do white women.

CWW Gossip about Black Women

Black women are criticized for being angry, mean, or unfriendly or for having a chip on their shoulder. The level of assertiveness that garners respect among African American women causes stress among CWW. African American women also come under attack from CWM and CWW who apply their standard of appropriate assertive behavior and leave African Americans (not just black women) wondering if something racist is going on. Consequently, they are often surprised when their performance reviews reflect a perception on the part of white supervisors that they are "too assertive," "think too highly of themselves," or are "overconfident."

CWW Gossip about Latina Women

CWW (also CWM) often make disparaging comments about Latina women (also Latino men) as being "too social," implying that Latino people are thereby not taking their work "seriously" enough. This comment reflects the Anglo cultural view that compartmentalizes work and personal life—believing that work and personal life should not be mixed—and, by implication, that individuals cannot do two or more things at the same time without one (work) being sacrificed in the process. What Anglos miss here is not only the level of expertise developed within Hispanic culture at multitasking, but that for Latino women—coming from a culture that integrates work and personal life—the social element often is also what drives the work process. What is distracting to Anglos is motivating to Hispanics. For example, our colleague Ilya Adler, in doing survey research for a Mexican newspaper, found that when he sent interviewers out by themselves the average number of interviews done at the end of the day were between one and two. When he sent two interviewers out doing interviews, he found that the average number of interviews done at the end of the day were between four and five. The interviewers were more productive and efficient when working together than when working separately.

CWW (and CWM) also make comments about Latino women being "too political." This attitude grows out of the different ways that Hispanics and Anglos network. For Hispanics, opportunities grow out of personal/ friendship networks. Because they also do not separate work from personal life—they see helping someone in their personal life also helps their work life (and vice versa)—Hispanics often informally take on the broker role of putting people together who can use each other's help. Notwithstanding the informality Hispanics have a personal stake in how things turn out between the two parties as well as an expectation of credit/acknowledgement of favors having been done. Anglos, who compartmentalize work, personal life, and politics, see networking as a pragmatic business activity with its own distinctive time and place—disconnected not only from work proper but also from long-term personal/friendship obligations.

CWW Gossip about Asian Women

CWW do not typically gossip about Asian women. As one white woman commented, "The quiet-busy types rarely get talked about. Hence, I don't hear much about Asian women—sorry to stereotype—that is, until they get into real positions of power. At that point women like me wonder why they don't assert themselves more often." Sometimes, the way Asian women micromanage gets talked about. One CWW said that she would not want to work for an Asian woman because she would be afraid of "detail demands" and not "being able to live up to her expectations."

Gossip and Native American Women

While white women gossip in order to build or align relationships with others, a Pan-American Indian conceptualization of gossip views it as an indication that the person engaging in gossip has encountered a problem and is struggling to deal with it. Dealing with it requires rebalancing the self. Our American Indian colleague says that "folks who have mastered remaining in balance fairly well describe it as being empty, not tied to anything and not personalizing anything" and sees it as the "primary way to address 'problems.'" If necessary, a person who is unhappy with another person might feel the need to engage a medicine person or an elder whose role it is to help them get into a proper relationship within themselves. However, she added, "This pattern of going to another person is very rare. When people do that they are usually sent back to handle things in a ceremonial way themselves." She gave an example of a Native woman sharing a concern with another Native person whom she trusted about working with a third woman whose character she didn't trust. The Native woman hearing the concern responded with, "Are you going to tell the teacher what to teach you?" She explained that thinking about what other people think or who they are is a way that we trick ourselves into staying simplistic—believing that there is safety in that illusion of "dangerous illusions" of the limited world we mortals exist in, which is only a small part of reality. She suggested that the person she was "gossiping about" probably had something to teach her about herself, and she shouldn't allow herself to be sidetracked from her role by thinking about this other person. In sharing this story the Native woman said that as a result of this conversation, she learned that 99.99 percent of what she worries about during a day is not worth caring about with that degree of focus and consternation.

Since CWW align relationships by talking to third parties about other people at work, they may be suspicious of Native women who withdraw from such conversations, seeing them as closing the door on networking opportunities. Traditionally minded Native women, however, would see not wanting to engage in gossip about third parties not as a lost opportunity but as a necessary means of staying away from imbalance and as being respectful of others. However, should CWW see that withdrawal as a general sign that Native women do not wanting to network with them, rather than as a signal relating specifically to third-party gossip, CWW may be the ones who end up closing the door on networking opportunities with Native women by not considering that other forms of networking may still be open. In sum, the Native rule when you are upset with someone is (in the following order) (1) get in balance; (2) enlist a medicine person or elder whose role it is to help you do that; and (3)—in rare and extreme cases—find a third person who will mediate with others. Contrast that with the pattern and sequence that white women people pleasers follow when they are upset with someone: (1) talk to other people to get their view, enlist support, and align others on your side against the offending other person; (2) discuss with a therapist/religious advisor how to deal with the person/situation; and only lastly, (3) engage in prayer, meditation, and self-examination. What Native women do first, people pleaser white women do last.

CHAPTER TEN

Other Cultural Contrasts and Lessons Learned

When I first arrived at Douglas Middle School on the West Side of Chicago in the 1970s—I was there for seven years—I tried to get to know the African American women I was working with. Part of my initial presentation of self was trying to show myself as an empathic, caring person. I called on my "white girl antennae" to pick up dissonance in the environment and go on "search and rescue." One morning a black woman colleague seemed upset about something. I read this by the way she sat down, her expression, and the manner in which she tossed her attendance book on her desk. In white girl/woman culture, you are at risk if you don't respond to these signals, which are interpreted as distress signals. If you ignored such obvious cries for help from a white woman, she might talk about you later behind your back. So, following my white women cultural protocols, I asked the black woman how she was doing. She looked at me in a way that told me it was none of my business. I was shocked at the rebuff of my attempt to show myself as someone who was caring and considerate of other people's feelings. So I went and sat down, all the while thinking, "I can't believe she did that"—a common white woman expression that became the title of Mooney's book.[1] However, as the new kid on the block and dissatisfied with the way it went, I approached her again and asked, "Have I done anything to upset you?" She said, "Jean, you're really not that important." Later that day I went home and said to my white women friends, "I can't work with *them. They* are so mean!" The black woman's view of what happened, no doubt, was equally uncharitable toward me. As I came to understand the culture, she probably thought—since validated by other black women—"First, you think that you can come and ask me how I'm doing (as if we had the kind of relationship that would allow you to do that), and, second, you think you cause everything that happens."

My other approach to show myself as caring and friendly also failed. White women build relationships and make friends by soliciting and sharing personal information. On meeting someone for the first time—part of the getting acquainted stage—white women typically ask questions such as, Where do you live? Are you married? Do you have any children? African Americans view such questions on first meeting someone as violations of personal boundaries. Consequently, when I asked African American women these kinds of questions, I got a cold, disbelieving look and the comment, "You got any chips for all that dippin' in my business?"

What I subsequently learned through many trial-and-error attempts was that soliciting personal information and showing that one is considerate of other people's feelings is a way to start a friendship or relationship—things that worked in my white woman cultural group—only happened with African American women after a trusting relationship has been built. So how does one then start to develop a trusting relationship with black women? The answer is by being personally helpful and supportive at work, not by being inquisitive.

The other mistake I made with African American women—this part also applies to Latina women—was sharing information that I had learned about that person with others. This was not "telling tales out of school" or gossiping about someone in the traditional sense, but rather a well-intentioned move on my part to correct a wrong impression that another woman had of the black or Latina woman whom I had come to know—a move perfectly acceptable in white girl/women culture. For example, if an African American woman (Ms. A) shares something with me about a struggle in her personal life, and a third colleague (Ms. B) comes to me to say, "Ms. A is being so mean," I will share what I learned about Ms. A so that Ms. B won't continue to spread mean things about her. Bringing Ms. B into the reasons why Ms. A is acting as she is, requires Ms. B now to be protectively considerate of Ms. A's reputation and emotional well-being in relationships that she may also have with others, not just herself. If the shared information is not to be shared with others white women mark it by saying, "Promise not to share this with anybody." Women of color, on the other hand, assume that you will not share their personal information.

Consequently, regardless of my motive to "save someone's reputation," this behavior was taken by African American and Latina women as malicious gossiping—not only a breach of confidentiality, or tattling, but more seriously—disloyal backstabbing. I later discovered that women of color will often test white women for trust by sharing personal information and wait to see if it comes back around.

This breach of trust becomes especially egregious if the information that is shared was meant for your ears only. For example, Latina mothers have been known to counsel their daughters to keep their divorce a secret even if that would mean, after the divorce, the couple would have to continue to attend family and community functions as an ostensibly still-married couple. For white women, this information would fall in the category of common knowledge—who hides that they got a divorce in mainstream white woman culture?—and thus, though personal, still shareable, unless the person has marked it as confidential. Other breakdowns around information sharing revolve around trust and cultural style. For example, while Latina women, like white women, share personal information on first getting to know someone—such as, "Do you have any kids?"—unlike white women, they won't share personal or family problems until trust has first been established. For example, one Latina woman reported, "A man is good if he puts a roof over your head. I learned to be *submissiva* [submissive] and to accept that men have their little affairs, and fathers must protect the virginity of their daughters. The family is central, and problems are hidden, since they reflect badly on the whole family, and future marriage opportunities."

Black women are taken aback at the premature sharing of information by white women. Because they are also socialized to be strong, they are also shocked by what they see as a weakness by white women sharing personal problems over things that others did to them. White women in turn are taken aback when black women try to distance themselves from the conversation, expecting the same kind of empathic response they get from other white women—"I know just what you mean"—when they do that kind of sharing. Black women, in characterizing white women's solicitation and sharing of information as simply being nosey, misrepresent those white women who use such overtures as a way to network and connect.

Another kind of cultural breakdown occurred at meetings; it was started by a black woman expressing an opinion about something that opposed what was going on at the time. After the meeting was over, I often would go to the woman who spoke and say, "I'm so glad that you said something in there!" Her response was, "Why are you telling me here out in the hallway? Why didn't you say something at the meeting?" This happened so many times that I finally asked myself, "Why *am* I saying it out in the hallway, and why *didn't* I say something at the meeting?"

The answers I came to were several. The first one was that, as a white woman, I was culturally programmed to give (private) emotional support, but not (public) political support. Additionally, I thought that, since white women are a collection of individuals, like white men, they are not required to take political risks, simply in support of another person. In fact, to do so, in my cultural group might imply that the person was either not sufficiently articulate or (in needing my support) was not able to stand on their own two feet. That last implication might even invite the rebuke: "If I needed your help I would have asked for it." Another thought I had was whom else I might be offending by speaking up. All of these were reasons enough for not volunteering political support on behalf of someone else at a meeting. Finally, since speaking up at a meeting—whether or not you agree or disagree—is not a requirement in my culture, there is also no penalty attached if you don't speak up.

I quickly learned from my African American colleagues, however, that there were penalties attached to not speaking up: their cultural rule being that silence means consent and that if you disagree with what is being said, as Kochman noted, speaking up becomes an obligation, not simply an option.[2] That's why black women regularly said to me, "Why didn't you say something at the meeting?"

Given that prevailing view—I was getting the reputation there of being mealymouthed—I decided that I was going to offer public/political support at the next meeting for those points that I agreed with. This was already countercultural for me, but, since I was agreeing with the person, I thought that there would not be that much of a personal risk in doing so. However, I also thought, what if I disagreed with the point being made? Or what if, after agreeing with that person, another black woman disagreed with me as well as the person who said it first. That scenario felt really risky. The reason for that sense of risk, as already said, is that white women are not socialized to disagree openly with what is being said or directly to the person saying it. Their cultural pattern is to gather their group of like-minded friends after the meeting is over and say, "Did you hear what she said in there? I don't agree with that at all!" Like Madame Defarge, who recorded names of enemies of the French Revolution in her knitting, white women people pleasers are also chronicling who is nice and who is mean, hurtful, or insufficiently considerate of other people's feelings—that person being aligned against (and socially shunned) after the meeting was over. So if it was already somewhat risky to take a publicly assertive political position on behalf of someone else's point, it felt especially risky (and countercultural) to do so in disagreement.

However, in that cultural environment, I was not being praised for being nice, but rather I was criticized for being insufficiently forthright—African American women not only are not bothered by disagreement, they expect it. I came to the conclusion that if I was going to get personal respect in that environment, I had also better be able to disagree with what was being said openly and to the person saying it. So, at the next opportunity, I mustered some courage and said (somewhat qualified), "Well, I don't necessarily agree with that." But after having said that, I was then faced with another problem. The black woman I was disagreeing with said (much louder than I was comfortable with), "Well, why *don't* you!?" My initial (cultural) response was, "Now don't get angry!" The black woman said, "I'm *not* angry!" Initially, that response "did not compute" since it seemed angry to me. However, I heard, "I'm *not* angry!" from different black women in like situations so often that I finally started to think, "Maybe they're really not angry! Maybe that's just the way I'm hearing it."

Then another light bulb turned on. I watched two black women disagreeing with each other at a meeting. I initially saw it as arguing and expected them to behave as arguing people do in my white ethnic (Irish, Jewish, Italian, and Greek) culture. That is, to dig in your heels and hold your own ground even if you think your opponent's points are better than yours—the goal being to establish "who's right," not "what's right." However, in the midst of the exchange, one of the black women said to the other black woman, "That's true! I agree with that!" I was flabbergasted! My first thought was that she surrendered! Then, I realized that what was going on culturally for them—and also those times with me—was that they were still doing sincere truth seeking but at a high level of energy and passion.

What I ultimately learned how to do—by accessing some of my white ethnic arguing techniques and changing the way I framed what was going on—was to keep an open mind to the other person's point of view. However, there were other problems beyond that that I also had to work out. I became aware that I still wanted the exchange—however contrary and passionate—to end "nicely"—"agreeing to disagree," as it were. At the same time, I observed that African American women, generally, did not feel that they had to do that. So I started to wonder why I did. I came to realize that when the bell rang, and we left that meeting without some kind of resolution, I felt vulnerable. The source of that vulnerability came from my experience with white women, where the next move—if you are in the midst of a disagreement—is to react personally and begin to align relationships within the work group with like-minded others after the meeting is over. A key strategy of alignment is for each white woman to get to her friends before the other woman biased them with her point of view. It is also common to bring in the manner in which the other person disagreed if they weren't sufficiently sensitive to your feelings. Thus starts the rumor mill and the so-called cattiness or pettiness around what others said or did.

However, African American women didn't do that, because—as I came to learn—they didn't take the disagreement personally. African Americans make a clear distinction between a confrontation that is issue oriented and one that is a personal attack.[3] They might talk about your idea, but it didn't mean they had to worry about being friends with you in the future or backstabbing you because of a disagreement or insensitivity to feelings. For example, a dispute over an issue between two white women at work became a dispute between two groups of white women—each woman got all of her friends together to take her side—ultimately leading to a shut down of the production line. By way of contrast, when two black women got into a dispute over an issue—they went toe to toe over it—the matter ended once each woman had her say.

Once I was able to see the more direct, "Why *don't* you agree with that?" as a real question and not the start of an argument or fight—which are the meanings that such contrary, passionate, confronting behavior would have in my U.S. mainstream/white ethnic culture—I became more comfortable asserting myself at those meetings. Moreover, once I realized that I wasn't vulnerable to attack if I left while we were still in disagreement and that it wasn't personal—the nonverbal disdain was for my idea, not for me—I was able to be more candid.

Note, however, that it is important to differentiate publicly disagreeing with someone in a meeting where the truth of the matter is all that counts and where the relationship between two disagreeing parties is not at stake and public disagreements that occur within the workplace that have or might be seen as having ulterior motives and that produce public embarrassment. Because of the political ramifications that might develop from that situation—African Americans would consider public disagreement in that context as "fronting someone off" (not sincere truth seeking)—it would be taken personally and put the relationship between both parties at risk.

Lessons Learned from Training Sessions

At one of our training sessions a CWW said, with considerable feeling, on viewing the list I had of some social and cultural perspectives of black women, "That's not cultural, because it's true of me too." She looked over at me, expecting that I would support her. When I didn't—I was even a bit critical, explaining that her comment could be heard by the African American women as minimizing the impact of racism that they were describing—a veil came over her eyes. She expected me, another white woman, to emotionally align with her. When I didn't, she "eliminated me," giving me the silent treatment from then on. At the same time, had I done it the way the CWW wanted at the time—choosing emotional alignment over truthfulness—I would have been in trouble with the African American women. The way it got dealt with was to deal with the truth of the matter in the training session and then go to the CWW offline and talk to her one on one, in the hope of bringing her back on board. In this case, that worked. It does not always. For example, I was running a training program at a company when one of the CWW took offense at something someone said and left the room. Two of her friends followed her into the bathroom and reported that she was in tears and that I, as the one running the meeting, should do something to show support for their friend's hurt feelings. I did not stop the course of the training to do that, however. Because I did not I was effectively shunned ("eliminated") by the CWW in the group from then on, notwithstanding my attempts to deal with the situation afterward.

The next time something similar happened, I sent someone into the bathroom to speak with the woman and make sure she was OK. Because of that, the CWW returned at ease and participated freely now that I (as the responsible leader) had proved myself to be a caring presenter.

When CWW go into their homogeneous gender and culture groups to discuss their issues relating to men—and the "us" was CWW and the "them" was CWM—white women stayed longer than any other break-out group. They also presented a more united front when reporting what their lists were. However, when I presented the information on CWW as a group divided along lines of people pleasers, white male assimilated, and so on, there were problems. In one session, the people pleasers, overly concerned about how the rest of the group was going to hear their complaints, excised the angry tone off the lists—under the rubric of wanting to sound professional—thereby offending the other CWW in the group who had no problem having others see and hear exactly how they felt. The result was a watered down presentation. Real and important problems were rendered less so. Consequently, when the group reported to the larger group there was a general level of misrepresentation of the seriousness of the issues CWW were having at work.

After the session was over, the subgroups of CWW divided offline and began talking and e-mailing along lines of "us and them." One people pleaser wrote to me explaining her position. My own e-mail back to her was authentic, but written very carefully and indirectly in line with white woman people pleaser protocols. The woman knew, nonetheless, that I had identified her as a people pleaser and that she had in fact undermined the goal of the process, which was to be as candid and authentic as possible. In another session, the CWW said they were anxious to get to their families, summed up quickly, and left. They didn't know how to create solidarity, warmth, caring, or an opportunity to vent shared issues vis-à-vis men. Without a common "enemy" they could not build community. Nor could they create a sense of community by strategizing around issues they might have with each other—it wouldn't be nice!

It became clear that for CWW to create solidarity, they needed to be able both to feel good about themselves and have someone to unite against. So the next time when the breakout groups were focusing on the issue of backstabbing I asked facetiously, "How many of you see yourselves as backstabbing white women?" As expected, no one raised their hand. Backstabbing is only something other women do, not something they do. I then explained what white women think they're doing when they listen empathically or ask for someone to listen empathically and how that seems different from backstabbing. I also say what has been true for me, and that white women have sustained me throughout my life. They are often isolated in the workplace because women of color see them as spoiled, other CWW may potentially eliminate them if they are ever in competition, and CWM often view them as too emotional or circuitous in their communication style. This framed the assignment from "What do we want white men to know about us?" to "What do we want all three groups—CWW, people of color, and CWM—to know about us?"

The next task was to create a "them" or "other" group whom the present group of CWW could unite against. This group became "other white women" who weren't in the room because they hadn't been through the training yet and couldn't talk candidly about these things. The "us" were the CWW in the breakout group. Even though they were secretly assessing each other for how they fit the different categories, it didn't become the dominant (and divisive) theme within their group as it had with other groups. They could and did unite around imagining themselves as evolved women or as women who wanted to be evolved. Another contributing element was that I had given them the direction (and authorization) to act like evolved women—to be candid and direct and to have them place the locus of control within themselves to decide whether or not they thought they were caring enough, irrespective of how other women (or for that matter, men) might see it.

CHAPTER ELEVEN

Styles of Conflict Resolution

Black/White

In the "reality" TV series *Black.White.* two families are transformed by makeup to look like members of the other race. Their interactions are taped as each of the family members prepares to experience what life is like as their counterpart in the other's race. Some of the most dramatic footage occurs in the preparation stage between members of the two families, who are living together for the filming of this documentary. In one scenario, there is a powerful culture clash between the mothers of each family. The white mother, Carmen Wurgel, offends the African American mother, Renee Sparks, when—perhaps in imitation of what she has seen other black women do with each other—she tries to "get down" by greeting Renee with "Yo! Bitch!" Renee is furious, and Carmen responds by crying and feeling hurt, saying that she "didn't know" that what she did was inappropriate.

Carmen's Position

Carmen feels (not just thinks) that Renee should understand that she was well meaning. White women people pleasers, like white men, begin conflict resolution by explaining their intent, but unlike white men, they don't expect to be cut slack for inadvertence unless they accompany their explanation of intent with a sincere apology for having "upset" or "hurt the feelings" of the other person. For white women, situational impact—the specific offense that negatively impacted another individual—is quickly turned into a weighing of emotional impact, and that emotional impact involves a two-sided analysis. The offender and the offended each have a role to play in "being nice." For white women, admission of fault, whether sincere or not, is both a protection against others viewing them as uncaring and a willingness to put the demands of the relationship before their need to get all their personal cards on the table. However, when the apology requires that white women swallow their pride and their real feelings—this is more a sign of reparation than sincere regret—and is then rejected, all the issues that were submerged will reveal themselves in the context of angry self-defense and reciprocal attack. As one southern white woman said with visible anger, "I always extend courtesy and kindness, but once someone backstabs you, then you don't owe them nothin'; the first time shame on them, but the second, shame on you." This is not to say that white women don't make heartfelt apologies, but sometimes the apology grows out of a strategic programming to put other people's feeling above their own, and to avoid backstabbing.

The scene typically plays out like this: once someone acknowledges that they're sorry they upset the other, the other "nicely" says they're sorry too, just to create "power dead even," and the two parties either truly reconcile or pretend to reconcile until their inner emotions catch up to their words—which is dependent on each individual's subsequent behavior—so as to be able to continue working together. If the words of the apology are "I'm sorry I upset you," it is an admission of disrupting the harmony of the relationship. If the words are "I'm sorry *if* I upset you," on the other hand, it means that I'm not sure I did anything, but you are saying I did, so I must have at least inadvertently done something, and I just wish you wouldn't be so quick to think ill of me. If the words are "I'm sorry you took it that way," it translates as an attack and puts the shoe squarely on the other person to assume responsibility for what happened. It says, "Why are you purposely distorting my words and making negative assumptions about my character? You are the one who misunderstood, and then maliciously misrepresented me." Reciprocity of apology is a part of the balance of power that is critical to white female relationship. If woman B brings a criticism to woman A, then woman A may remind B that she did something just as offensive to her, but she was "nice" enough not to bring it up. However, now that it is all out in the open, both can equally apologize and the relational balance restored.

When white women are not met with a similar "I'm sorry, too" response, they feel angry at the repudiation of their overture to apologize. Applying this general cultural pattern to the above conflict situation, Carmen's expectation is for Renee to "nicely" explain that what she said was an offensive, stereotypical view of how black women speak to each other. If Carmen had similarly offended a white woman, Carmen would apologize for her ignorance and say she was sorry she offended her and maybe cry to demonstrate the intensity of her remorse. The other white woman would say, "That's OK," which doesn't mean it's really OK but does mean that she has done what was expected even if she still feels offended by what Carmen said. Carmen, in turn, is expected to be equally "nice" by accepting the ostensibly forgiving "that's OK," regardless of who still feels offended or who did the worse thing in the exchange. White woman apologies generally have as an underlying focus how feelings were disrupted. In that regard, Carmen goes along with the expected protocol, even though she might still feel Renee was being hypersensitive and mean since she was well intentioned and "only" meant to be playful. It is an open question whether individuals across all cultures would like to be cut slack based on their good intentions and also like others to acknowledge when they have adversely impacted them—a cultural universal, as it were. The difference here is whether, because of cultural programming, people can expect to be cut some slack or not. The white mainstream cultural expectation in conflict resolution is to give as much or more focus and weight to clarifying intent as to assessing impact or damage done.

Renee's Position

Renee's African American cultural position holds people accountable for what they say and do and the impact of that. Her culture also holds people accountable for what they should have known. For African Americans generally, ignorance is no excuse for bad behavior. It is definitely no excuse for "stupid" behavior ("And you couldn't have figured that out!"). In the present example, not only would not knowing not have been an acceptable excuse for Carmen to do what she did, Renee also doesn't believe that Carmen didn't know better, because it seems to Carmen "common decency" not to call a woman "bitch." Therefore, from Renee's perspective, what Carmen did was seen, at best, mischievous and, at worst, malicious. Also at issue for Renee is that Carmen thought she could "take liberties" by assuming a familiar tone with her given that they were still at the first stage of relationship building. From that perspective, Carmen's

approach came across as presumptuous: as suggesting a stage in their relationship that had not as yet actually been reached. Renee was probably
also miffed that Carmen saw her as only a black woman and not someone
that she might also need to get to know on an individual basis to learn
what she could and could not say. For example, Renee might be the kind
of person that would object to the word "bitch" if said by a close friend
(regardless of race or ethnicity) and would expect that friend to know that
about her as an individual and not use that word with her.

The view of African Americans as a homogenous group was also an issue underlying the flak around the comments of Don Imus referring to the
black women on the Rutgers women's basketball team as "nappy-headed
hos" without regard to the different tastes and attitudes that exist among
African Americans along class, gender, or individual lines around the social
acceptability of the use of that phrase, especially the term "ho" (whore).
For example, at one conference I attended where hip-hop music was part
of the after-meeting entertainment, the black presenters were strongly re-
buked by African American professional women there for characterizing
women—especially African American women—that way. Another issue
for African Americans is that of social entitlement. The black position is
that just because you hear others using a term does not automatically en-
title you to use the term yourself, especially if you are an outsider to the
culture.[1] This issue also underlies the interpersonal conflict that comes up
when whites use black slang, especially when talking to blacks, when it is
not naturally how they talk. The following statement by Al Sharpton also
addresses the issue of Imus's right to use the term when he says, "One of
the things I think is the most bogus thing he said, when he [Don Imus]
and I debated on 'The Today Show' . . . is that it comes from black music.
I attacked black rappers and hip hoppers that used it. Most hip hop is not
using it. Most hip hop is positive. But he acts like he got it from black music
and I think that's a cop-out. . . . It seems he is very selective from what he
gets from black music."[2] Actually, what did Imus in was less his selective
use of the term than his global assumption that because some black people
used the term he could, too. This assumption also guides the "zero tolerance" policy in the workplace: the view that if some people were allowed
to use a particular phrase regardless of their ethnic group membership or
insider status, then anyone within earshot is also entitled to use the term,
which was also Carmen's position regarding her use of the term "bitch."

Renee's cultural expectation on how the conflict might be resolved
would be for Carmen to apologize for having said that and not to do it

again. African Americans apologize and expect an apology for what was said and done ("I'm sorry I said that" or "I'm sorry I did that") and in the case of a more egregious transgression will also apologize and expect an apology for any disrespect that has been shown. Respect/disrespect language is an important component of conflict resolution for African Americans—"respect" often occurring as a theme in African American music lyrics. Note also, however, that repairing the damage for African Americans—Renee, in the above example—will take some time. The time it takes to make up will also be an issue for white women—Carmen in the above example—who want resolution ("kiss and make up") to happen right away.

Moreover, compounding the problem for Renee is that Carmen breaks down and cries—what black women call "white women water power." For Renee, Carmen's tears are seen as manipulative—as if to suggest that she, Carmen, was the injured party, and not Renee. For Renee, it also puts Carmen's feelings on center stage and deflects attention away from what she did and the effect in had on Renee. In that regard, it is also seen as self-serving and devious. From Carmen's perspective, Renee's angry reaction (that was so unforgiving of her "not knowing" and her basically "good intentions") seemed far too strong for what she considers a learning blip: something relatively minor that she should have been corrected for doing, but not attacked for doing. At another level, Renee's angry reaction implies that she, Carmen, was not being considerate enough of Renee's feelings.

This implication is especially powerful for mainstream white women because being viewed as a well-intentioned caring person is such a strong identity piece that when that self-image is impugned, they dissolve into a protestation of their goodness with the result that nothing else can happen until that image is restored, preferably by the very person they have just offended. Also, because of the implication that they may not have been considerate of someone else's feelings—and because of what that says about their identity as a good and caring person—Carmen and mainstream white women generally often refuse to consider that what they said or did, had, or could have had an adverse impact. The key issue for Renee and for black women generally is "never let anyone disrespect you." Any time a people pleaser whose identity is built around "be nice, don't hurt anybody's feelings" is interacting with a "be strong; be self-reliant, don't let anyone disrespect you" person, this kind of conflict is bound to happen.

Given their different views of what happened, Carmen and Renee each felt that what the other person did far exceeded what they did, although Carmen was probably the only one to think that she had done anything. Renee probably saw her angry reaction as proper and justified—something that Carmen ought to be able to handle—and therefore not something that should cause Carmen to cry. This view is also affected by the different cultural positions of mainstream white women and African American women about the appropriateness of showing anger. For Carmen and mainstream white women generally, anger is seen as outside the framework of a good relationship. African American women (and African Americans generally) see anger as something that is part and parcel of a good relationship: anger is something that makes a relationship real and that individuals committed to the relationship should be able to handle. From Renee's perspective, therefore, she did not do anything that she needed to feel sorry for or try to repair. Carmen, of course, did see Renee as having done something. From her perspective, Renee's angry reaction maligned her character, which caused her to cry and which was far worse a thing to do to her than anything that she had done to Renee.

Parallel Play—the Bar Scene

An office group goes to a bar after work on a Friday to celebrate a coworker's birthday. The group places their drink order. The waitress, who is white, brings the drinks and on distributing them to the group discovers that the black woman's drink is not on the tray. When this becomes apparent, the waitress says, "Sorry!" and asks the black woman what she ordered. Also, since she is just about to collect the group's money for the drinks that she had just brought, the waitress asks the black woman if she wouldn't mind also paying for the drink "up front" (before she actually gets it) to "save her a trip." She adds that, it being happy hour, she is "really busy." The black woman complies, and the waitress then brings her the drink. The black woman says afterward to her work group that she thought what had just happened was "racist." None of the white workers in her group agrees. In the training context, we ask participants (working in groups) to pretend that the waitress overheard the black woman's comment and ask them, "What do you think the waitress would (culturally speaking) think and do upon hearing that comment?" We also ask them to represent the black woman's cultural position.

The White Waitress

The white waitress would not confront the black woman directly but would go to her cohort group in the kitchen and complain, "All I did was forget her drink and she accused me of being a racist." Her position is that what the black woman did—slandering her moral character—was far worse than what she did (forgetting her drink). It probably would not occur to the waitress that asking the black woman to pay first also factored into the black woman's comment. Another possible scenario is that if the waitress could not avoid dealing with the comment directly, insofar as the black woman was saying it to make sure that the waitress would hear it—blacks call this "fronting someone off"—she might say to the black woman, "I'm sorry that you took it that way." This way of framing it places responsibility for the meaning of what happened entirely on the shoulders of the black woman and exonerates the waitress of having done anything wrong, either by mainstream cultural standards that defines racist behavior in terms of what was meant (intent) or by white women cultural standards that implicates them in someone else's feelings having been hurt as a result of something that was said/done (whether intentional or not).

This last part separates white women from white men (or African Americans, for that matter), insofar as these groups are less concerned over hurt feelings than with the specifics of what was said and done and the principle of right and wrong behind it. Consequently, they also do not feel personally implicated in having caused someone else's feelings to have been hurt. Nor are they as susceptible as white women are to being accused of having been insensitive to demands of the relationship. For white women, admission of fault, whether sincere or not, is typically both a protection against others viewing them as uncaring and a willingness to put the demands of the relationship before their need to get all their personal cards on the table. However, in the above example, the waitress did not have the same stake in keeping the relationship on an even keel, given the context—it was not an interaction that was going to continue beyond that encounter—especially so, given her assessment of what happened.

The African American Woman

The African American woman's social and cultural position is to view what happened as an example of different (inconsistent) treatment and something that happens to her (and other African Americans) all the time.

African Americans in the training group also say that the waitress asking her to pay first—given the social history of harassment and discrimination of African Americans in the United States—probably affected the black woman's characterization of what happened as racist rather than just forgetting the drink. She also wants an acknowledgment that something different happened along with responsibility for making sure that such different treatment does not happen again. Also, since African Americans equate what you did with what you meant, they see the attempt to separate what was meant from what was done—as in, "I didn't mean it"—as a way of deflecting attention away from or refusing to take responsibility for inconsistent treatment, especially along racial lines. She may also hope for a general awareness of the impact that this different treatment has had on her, specifically, and on African Americans, historically,[3] not only from the waitress but also by her white cohorts, who, despite their working relationship, took the side of the white waitress, whom they don't even know.

When I first started working at an African American middle school in the 1970s, a black parent of one of the students in my class asked me if I was a racist. I reacted to that question defensively—as if my moral character had just been impugned. I said, instantly and without regard to what was behind the black parent's comment, "I'm on the Peace and Justice Committee of my church. My best friends are black." The comments and the emotional tone of my response said to the black parent that a chord had been struck, which for African Americans is a sign of guilt, not innocence (see chap. 3, pp. 42–43). I could see the black parent's disbelief of my protestations in her eyes and manner; she was probably saying to herself, "Yeah, she's like that." Later, I came to understand that the question, "Are you racist?" was code for, "Are you going to treat my son fairly?" The black parent, unaccustomed to having a white teacher for her child, only had her previous experience with whites—in Chicago's mostly black West Side and previously in Mississippi—as reference. Subsequently, I came to understand where she and other black parents were coming from and learned to stay with that and not make my moral character the issue. I started saying, "I've been white all my life. Tell me what you're concerned about and let's deal with that." That response turned things around for the black parent, and ultimately for me, in representing myself as a caring person.

In a recent training session, I was sharing the above experience with the group to advise them on how best to respond if a black person at work characterizes something that was said and done as racist. A CWW came up to me afterward to discuss a similar situation that had happened to her.

She said a black woman who reported to her told her that her decision to promote a particular CWM was racist. Her reply, like mine many years ago, was immediately defensive. She said, "I don't think it was racist." I asked the CWW how the black woman responded. She said, "She simply rolled her eyes, ended the conversation, and walked away." I pointed out to the CWW that her comment, in effect, closed the door on an issue that the black woman, and blacks generally, want to have seriously considered. The CWW said that the black woman's statement constituted an assault on her moral character, over which she was still smarting. Her focus on the power of the accusation kept her from dealing with the perception that led to it. The black woman, in turn, took the response that the CWW gave as an indication that she was unwilling to deal with the issue of race as a factor on decisions that are made at work. One group—whites—see the one who makes the accusation as implicating moral character; the other group—blacks—see the way a person reacts to the accusation as implicating moral character.

Iranian/African American Conflict

An Iranian woman engineer managed an African American woman engineer. The Iranian complained, "She took my criticism personally and reported me to human resources. I was just operating directly out of my role." We didn't hear the other side, but often when African Americans go to human resources, it is because they feel singled out and treated differently. In this case, the Iranian said she was critical of white men who reported to her, and they didn't mind, while the African American woman took it personally.

Both Iranians and African Americans can be forthright, but misunderstandings occur when a woman from an Asian, Middle Eastern, or Hispanic hierarchical culture (South Asian, Iranian, Latina, etc.) is in a role where an African American woman reports to them. The conflict arises because African American women are forthright in disagreement (based on "what's right"), regardless of their position. However, since authoritarianism within hierarchical cultures is driven by positional considerations ("know your place")—the boss in those cultures is the only one in that encounter who is authorized to be direct, forthright, and "right"—the African American woman's (more egalitarian) direct approach is seen as disrespectful. Beeman notes that the behavior that characterizes unequal status in Iran from high to low is dispensing favors and rewards and giving orders; from low to high it is (dutifully) rendering service, paying tribute, and making petitions.[4]

Latina Boss and a CWW Subordinate

A similar collision owing to differences in cultural styles occurred between a Latina boss and a white woman at a Latino agency. For example, the CWW was in charge of putting together the agency newsletter. The established protocol was to show it to the Latina boss and, on getting her approval, send it on to be printed and mailed. In this instance, the Latina boss was not around to approve the newsletter—her involvement in the approval process was more pro forma than substantive in any event—and the deadline for getting the newsletter to the printer was imminent. Because of that, the CWW decided to send the newsletter to the printer, figuring that her boss would not only understand the pressure and need to meet the deadline but applaud her for her initiative in taking the lead in this matter. When her Latina boss returned and learned that the newsletter had been sent to the printer without her approval she removed the CWW from her position.

Bosses in traditional hierarchical cultures do not cede functional (operational) decision-making authority to subordinates when delegating responsibilities, unless they expressly say otherwise. By way of contrast, U.S. mainstream Anglos do cede functional authority to subordinates when delegating responsibilities, unless they expressly state otherwise. One way of characterizing that is that in traditional hierarchical cultures the traffic light governing subordinate behavior is "red" until the boss says "green." In mainstream U.S. culture, the traffic light governing subordinate behavior is "green" until the boss says "red." These different attitudes and values underlie the above conflict. The Latina boss saw the CWW's acting on her own as disrespectful of her authority. The Latino respect for and concern with chain of command is especially revealed when it has been violated, regardless of the functional role the boss may or may not have, in the operation itself. They also view the more independent actions of Anglos in making decisions that are not, by virtue of their position, theirs to make as attempts to take over the job of authority. The CWW, in turn, saw her functional role and responsibility in getting the newsletter out as primary and her boss's supervisory role, insofar as it was simply ceremonial, as inconsequential.

In working the cultural conflict, both sides need to consider what is going on for the other party. What can be addressed immediately are the inferences that each party is drawing from the other's behavior. The Latina woman should consider that, for the CWW, acting independently does not mean that the CWW necessarily wants to take over her job. The CWW, in turn, should not think that, because the Latina woman's involvement in the approval process was simply ceremonial, it was, therefore, not important. What might take longer to work out are issues of trust and loyalty. However, if those are addressed and resolved, then greater acceptance of each other's cultural style at work can develop.

For example, a Latina boss, Angela, had problems with Liz, a CWW, coming up with proposals at meetings without checking with her beforehand. For Angela, this was seen to undermine her authority as the one in charge of the meeting. At the same time, she appreciated the energy and initiative that Liz was bringing to the project in moving things along. The way the matter got resolved—Angela said to Liz after the meeting, "Liz, No surprises!"—was to request that Liz simply tell her that she had some ideas that she wanted to present before the meeting. This way, Angela, with respect to her position and role, could authorize Liz's entrée by saying to the group, "And now Liz has some ideas about the project that she wants to propose." Note that Angela did not need to evaluate the ideas that Liz would propose beforehand—it was more about showing respect for Angela's position and role by having matters going through her, not around her. From Liz's perspective, going to Angela ahead of time to tell her she wanted to bring things up at the meeting was not a major control issue, especially since she was trusted to proceed independently in matters that were important to her: creativity and the ability to define her own role with respect to the development of the project.

CHAPTER TWELVE

Networking and Getting Ahead

According to Catalyst—a nationally recognized organization whose goal is to research and maximize opportunities for corporate women in management—the primary goal of women's networks is to strategize about getting ahead. In the formative stage, some members may even see each other as the competition (to be eliminated), as they seek to create venues where they can network with executive women, whom they hope will take them under their wing. Since women are accustomed to creating cliques of like-minded others, there are pitfalls to be overcome. Catalyst includes the following issues in their list of considerations as women's networks are developing.[1] (1) Is there a lack of interest on the part of members or groups of members in what the group is doing? (2) Do members display a negative attitude toward change, people, and team building in general? (3) Can opposing views or negative feelings be expressed without fear of punishment? (4) Are discussions in the hallway after the meeting freer and more candid than those that take place during the meeting?

As women of color are included in the developmental stages that Catalyst identifies for women's networks, the items above become more complex. It will be helpful to understand from the beginning that white women and women of color have different issues around social inclusion, building relationships, ways of integrating work/life issues, and strategies for getting ahead.

One mistake that white women make trying to connect successfully with African American women is either—from an African American perspective—not considering when race matters or putting race into the situation where it does not apply. In corporate America, this often occurs around the development of women's affinity groups. Although women of color may join a women's affinity group, there is often an assumption on the part of white women that women of color will deal with issues of race and ethnicity in a different affinity group and deal with their gender issues in the women's group. Women of color don't separate these out. African American, Asian, Latina, or Native American women are seen and see themselves broadly as "women of color" not just "women."

For example, at a women's executive retreat, two African American women brought up the issue of race, to which the white woman leader responded, "We're not talking about civil rights in this session." She framed the retreat exclusively as one that dealt with the problems that women were having with men. What she missed was that the African American women wanted to include issues they face as black women, which, first and foremost, means talking about racism vis-à-vis CWM within the larger society and, perhaps to a lesser extent, issues at work with black men (the latter being something that black women are often reluctant to share outside of their own black women's network in any event, especially with white women).

The categorization "women and minorities" also imposes an either/or dichotomy. In the previous example, race and gender are separated by CWW through the excision of race. In the women and minorities classification, putting women of color only in the "minorities" category excises their gender. As Sojourner Truth said, "Ain't I a woman, too?"[2] One result of this dichotomization led to a confrontation between a white and black woman at a federal agency. Both were executives, yet when the African American woman read a local newspaper article on the agency she was startled to read that her white woman cohort referred to herself as the only woman at the executive level at the agency. The compartmentalization of race, ethnicity, and gender is reinforced in U.S. mainstream English where the use of "woman" alone suggests white woman. If the woman is not white, then a race/ethnic qualifier—Asian, African American, Hispanic—is typically added. Yet it is a dichotomization that only exists for white women. The conflation of race, ethnicity, and gender, and the realities that stem from it, is such as to have made them inseparable for women of color. As Yamada says, "The two [ethnicity and gender] are not at war with one another; we shouldn't have to sign a 'loyalty oath' favoring one over the other. However, women of color are often made to feel that we must make a choice between the two."[3] Similarly, Bell and Nkomo write,

"Black women perceive that their white colleagues feel more comfortable with blacks whose racial identity is suppressed, yet African-American women managers often want to maintain a strong 'visible' racial identity at work."[4] Because of that pattern of usage (and either/or way of thinking around race and gender), women of color often find themselves rendered "invisible" when gender issues are considered. Yamada writes, "A movement that fights sexism in the social structure must deal with racism, and we had hoped the leaders in the women's movement would be able to see the parallels in the lives of the women of color and themselves."[5] Chin and Sanchez-Hucles also see the need to attend to "issues of diversity and intersecting identities as they pertain to leadership."[6]

Building Relationships

Asking "Member of Group" Questions

CWW as well as CWM offend African Americans by asking questions that compel them to either speak for their entire race or for another black person such as:

"What do black people eat for Thanksgiving?"
"What do you think is going through Rodney King's head about now?"
"What do black people think of Jesse Jackson?"

Some African American responses to the above are

Condescending: "Are you asking me what *I* am having for Thanksgiving?"
Dismissive: "I don't know! Why don't you ask Rodney King?"
Dismissive/mirroring: "I don't know! What do white people think of George W. Bush?"

As these answers imply, one of the big issues for African Americans in the workplace is being seen as individuals, not just, or primarily, as members of a group.

"It's a Black Thing—You Wouldn't Understand"

Given the reluctance of African Americans to speak for other black people, the question arises, under what circumstances would it be possible for a CWM or CWW to utilize the social or cultural expertise of a fellow black employee on problems that they may be having with another black employee at work? Some answers that African Americans give to that question are "It depends upon the kind of relationship that I have with the person asking me. If they're just asking me, because I'm black, then it's a definite no-no. In addition to the above it also depends upon how I am approached, and whether I think this is really a 'black' problem or a situation that any manager ought to be able to deal with." The absence/presence of an ongoing relationship was also key in the following example. A CWW insurance claims adjuster felt nervous about going alone into an all black area in the inner city to settle an auto claim. She explained her situation to a black woman who also worked in the office—they knew each other only in passing—and asked if she would accompany her. The black woman declined, saying, "Why do you think I would be any safer in that neighborhood than you?" During the break, I asked the black woman to talk more about what was behind her comment. She said, "We didn't have the kind of relationship that would allow her to ask me something like that."

Sometimes fear of a confrontation is the issue. A black woman said, "I am especially wary and reluctant when I am asked if I 'would talk to this other black person,' especially if I think the CWM is trying to avoid dealing with the black employee directly. I have no respect for that—I see it as a weakness and that person refusing to assume his or her proper managerial role. I usually tell them, 'Just go and talk to them!'"

Failed Empathy

White women often use the expression "I know just how you feel" as a way to show empathy and support for what another person is saying. African American women view this statement as hollow and presumptuous. For African Americans to say you know how someone else feels stakes a claim to have lived a life like that of the person you are saying it to. The view is, "How can you really know how I feel if you are not black?" I notice that white women do something similar with me when they try to identify with the grief I've experienced over the loss of my son. They will say, "I know what you're going through because my friend lost her child." I know the goal is to be supportive, but it also comes across to me as hollow, since I also believe that until a person has gone through such a loss, they can't really imagine what that feels like. In that regard, I also see that statement as presumptuous. I also find it interesting that African American women are more likely to say when showing sympathy, "I was so sorry to hear about your loss" than "I know just how you feel."

Another example of failed empathy happens when CWW cite personal or family examples of suffering or difficulty in response to those offered by African American and Latina women. The examples that follow are indicative:

MEXICAN AMERICAN: My parents were all migrant farm workers. I was the first person in my family to graduate from college.

CWW: So was I. My parents didn't finish high school.

AFRICAN AMERICAN: My sister was the first black person to integrate a white high school in Baltimore. When she went on stage to sing the National Anthem all of the white students in the audience started booing.

CWW: My dad had to drop out of school when he was sixteen to help support his family. He loved learning but never had a chance to get a formal education.

The basis for the mismatch stems from African American and Latina women not only talking about their individual and family trials and tribulations, they are also making a social statement about the struggles that they have experienced by being members of an ethnic minority group. As such, they are not just speaking for themselves but others of their group as well. In that regard, the personal or family examples that CWW give, while parallel, are not equal. What's different and missing is the social part: an awareness and acknowledgement that CWW's personal experiences, however dire, are never totally comparable because, as members of a relatively privileged group, they are still able to engage the system without having to deal with the stigma of color. Until that acknowledgment happens, African American and Latina women will consider the "matching" personal responses that CWW make "clueless" and, at times, even disrespectful.

Likewise when a white woman said to a Latina woman, "I was in Mexico and my heart went out to those people. Our nanny took some shoes out of the trash. I felt so sad that anyone had to live like that." Showing oneself as caring can also come across as clueless if it misses the larger social picture.

Failed empathy along the same lines also occurred in the previously discussed bar scene. Since race was not on their radar screen as an explanation for the different treatment that the black woman got, the white women saw forgetting the drink as an honest mistake. Consequently, the CWW people pleasers in the group reacted by saying—in their attempt to make their black colleague feel better—"I was here once and the waitress forgot my drink, too." This approach framed the different treatment that the black woman got as unintentional—as well as an individual, as opposed to a collective member of group, experience: therefore, without regard to the number of times this kind of thing has happened before to this woman and black people generally. Consequently, the approach taken by the CWW to be empathic fails—in effect, they are saying to their black colleague, "Your reality and experience as an African American woman are invisible to me."

White Women and Privilege

CWW, because of their own experiences under patriarchy and their view of themselves as just women, are often blind to the racial privilege they have vis-à-vis women of color. Like U.S. CWM, CWW do not have an upfront racial awareness of being white.

During one multicultural executive women's retreat, the session broke into seven groups: black women, Asian women, Latina women, Muslim women, and three groups of white women—Gen X white women, "baby-boomer" white women with children, and "boomer" white women without children. At the end, one black woman noted that the white groups spoke of their experience as X-ers or parents or nonparents (with a rich life), but none of the white groups spoke of their "whiteness." She asked if they would also address that part of their identity.

At that point, white women responded as if they heard the request to hear more about the experience of being white as a request to match the stories they heard of others' racial oppression, rather than as a request to hear about white privilege. The conversation turned to the honest sharing on the part of white women of what was on their radar screen: issues of personal hardship, poverty/class, or ethnicity—but no white women spoke to white privilege.

The occasions when CWW do become racially aware occur when they are the ones on the outside looking in, which runs counter to their accustomed ("privileged") position of being on the inside looking out. For example, in one racially mixed senior building, white women residents became upset when black women put up photos from a dinner they hosted, where mostly African Americans attended. The white seniors responded by putting up photos from another party, before the facility was integrated, under the caption, "Remember when . . ."

The following example occurred at a classified sales department of a newspaper that was racially mixed—consisting almost entirely of women—in which a CWW headed the department for many years. One of the white women in the department was best of friends with the supervisor, and they often went to lunch together. When the CWW department head left she was replaced by a young African American woman. Like her predecessor, she had friends within the department whom she invited to attend her wedding and to her home for a Christmas party. These friends were African American, however.

In addition, because of her open door policy, her African American colleagues felt free to stop in. Someone also left Avon literature out in the common area advertising African American hair and skin products. The CWW in the department saw the matter in entirely racial terms. Someone in the department wrote an anonymous letter to the publisher to complain that there was favoritism and exclusion of whites based on the fact that only blacks were invited to the supervisor's wedding, blacks were spending time in the supervisor's office, and only Avon books with African American products were left out in the common area.

Other issues also started to surface. Although the previous white supervisor had a close white friend reporting to her, the other CWW were not concerned that they would not also be considered when it came to situations like days off, vacation time, performance evaluations, referring new hires, and so on. It was not until a black woman became supervisor that these matters became a cause of concern. The CWW's fears were intensified by concerns as to whether or not whites at the paper were losing control generally. They mentioned that the publisher of the paper was black—another sign that "things were changing." The CWW were afraid of being excluded on the basis of their race.

Another instance of this pattern happened when the editors of the book *Female Subjects in Black And White* organized a conference around the themes psychoanalysis, feminism, and African American contexts.[7] They reported that on the last night of the conference at a party hosted by one of the organizers at her house the gathering had split along racial lines. The black women, most of whom were meeting each other for the first time, were having a critical discussion out on the deck. The white women had either gone home or were sitting inside in the living room.

As they put it: it was a case of the insiders (white women) experiencing themselves as the excluded outsiders. One of the white women, watching the discussion that the black women were having out on the deck, came out to ask if the white women who were inside could join in. The black women said "in a little while." Since a "critical discussion" was just under way, they wanted to protect it against interruption. "After waiting another half hour, the white women . . . burst out on the deck with their paranoia, their wounded feelings, their sense of . . . painful [racial] exclusion" even though the black women said that they had not been talking about or consciously excluding them; nor had they "registered their absence . . . in racialized terms."

What these examples show is how quickly the white women framed matters along racial lines—and cried "foul"—when the African American women had something that the white women wanted or were simply not getting. At the same time, the white women were totally unaware when they got things that African American women and other women of color were not getting. While it is generally true, as a matter of perception, that people tend to notice what other people get or have that they don't and not what they get or have that others don't, it needs to be said that there is a real material difference in the things that whites get that blacks don't. By way of contrast, the things blacks seem to have that whites covet fall more within the cultural realm—a sense of connection and community— things that whites have the means to create for themselves if they have a mind and will to do so. White women are aware that in corporate America white men play down race and gender, don't see it, and want to get on with the business at hand—it's difficult for white women to realize that our dominant experience with whiteness aligns us with white men, not with women of color. When white women endure poverty, grief, illness, immigrant experiences, minorities can speak of those too, but in these situations, the reality is always compounded by minority status. We must learn to let go of invidious comparisons. We see it when white men do it: when white men are up in front of a group of minority people, and asked to speak of their privilege, they often talk instead of "reverse discrimination" or their personal hardships, perhaps comparing a battle with cancer to a black person who has not faced this struggle. The point is not to compare one-on-one personal stories, but rather, to show an understanding of broad social realities around race as well as gender.

We also recognize, however, that white women are often asked to become aware of white privilege at the very moment they are most out of their comfort zone, having taken a risk to share painful, personal life experiences. This vulnerable moment offers a rare opportunity. It is a breakthrough moment in white identity development: accepting white privilege, even as our personal stories are organized around "overcoming." This does not diminish the personal stories of overcoming that white women hold dear, but it does ask white women to expand awareness of how minority women's stories of hardship are exacerbated by virtue of not being a member of the dominant group.

The journey of diversity and inclusion requires us to make mistakes along the way. Dominant group women who feel passionate about diversity welcome the opportunity to learn what is out of our awareness. As new learning is brought to our attention on this path of awareness, there is always that horrible feeling that there was something we didn't "get," that moment of failed empathy, and then there is a moment of decision. We may use the opportunity as a moment of growth, or we may retreat. Sometimes we retreat for a bit, and then re-engage. Some people react to these learning moments defensively: "Screw this; it's always about 'them.'" Others, who are developmentally ready, and have sufficient self-esteem to be learners, can withstand not having known. This is a place where, culturally speaking, white women have an advantage over white men, insofar as we are acculturated to be listeners/learners, while white men are more likely to have been socialized to have their identity invested in "knowing."

Women's affinity groups, whose mission is to empower women, cannot avoid unconsciously privileging white women. While mainstream gender issues are on our radar screen, those of other women generally are not. This ignorance of minority women's realities is destructive to all women, because it inadvertently divides women, and conquers those who are left out. The moment of realization requires great personal introspection, and the ability to stand in the space between privilege and oppression.

Once CWW can recognize their racial privilege, women of color can also start to listen to them. Without that, there is not much chance of any meaningful network or sustained relationship happening between these two groups.[8]

Other Mismatches

At a newspaper a white male editor said, "I need someone who can be aggressive, and get the story in time for me to meet deadlines. A quiet Asian woman just doesn't fit the bill." I asked an Asian woman in the room at the time if she could get the story that was being discussed. She replied, "My aunt knows people in that neighborhood. I could find out what happened very quickly." The point was powerful: there is more than one way to meet business goals. Newsrooms generally reflect a U.S. mainstream cultural bias—favoring individuals that are verbal, visible, and assertive—and need to be reminded from time to time that Asian news reporters also meet deadlines and Asian newspapers also come out on time.

With respect to differences in communication style, the U.S. mainstream pattern emphasizes "Be explicit! Say what you mean!" The East Asian communication style emphasizes "Go deep! Try to figure out what is meant!" These styles conflict when East Asians read more into what is being said than what the speaker meant or, conversely, say less than what they mean, expecting the listener to figure it out. East Asians call this style of communication "stomach talk." For example, our colleague Adrian Chan told of an Asian woman who, approaching one of her work cohorts, said, "I have a letter that has to go to our downtown office"—she knew that the white woman drove by the office on her way home, but didn't want to ask a favor directly. The white woman commented on the literal meaning of what was said, by responding, "Why don't you just fax it?" She missed the indirect suggestion: the Asian woman was making a request to have it delivered personally. The Asian woman also did not want to remind the CWW that she had done her three favors the week before, so the CWW, in effect, "owed" her.

A similar "read" is necessary when an East Asian or Latina woman comes to the boss's office. What is implied by that action, but not made explicit, is that it has taken a lot of courage and trust and many sleepless nights for the East Asian woman to make this kind of move. If the boss is a CWW who doesn't know how difficult it was for the Latina or East Asian woman to come in, she may too quickly dismiss what may initially sound like a small issue but is really just the tip of an iceberg.

A South Asian woman started to share with a CWW, "My daughter is in school at Washington University, in St. Louis." The CWW said, "Oh, my daughter is in school at Purdue." The South Asian woman wondered why she didn't ask more questions about her family before changing the topic to talk about her own family.

For people pleasing CWW, the accommodating style of Latinas (being simpática—"personable," "charming," "likeable") suggests to them that they need help. This leads to the complaint about CWW from Latina (also from East Asian) women, "Why are white women trying to give me advice as if I am weak or helpless, when what I am being is pleasant and nice?"

Negotiating Work and Lifestyle Differences

As tables 2–4 show, CWW and women of color have different ways of managing their work/life environment. These differences affect the kind of networking and relationship building that occurs between CWW and women of color or between different groups of women of color. For example, CWW and Latina women both share personal information about themselves and their families on first meeting each other. CWW do this to be friendly; Latina women, to create trust and establish the basis of a real friendship. For Latina, as well as Asian, women establishing friendship often means connecting outside of work, not just at work. This will be an issue for CWW as well as for African American women who look to create alliances at work but not friendships. Establishing trust with African American women comes from being helpful at work, not from being inquisitive. Sharing personal information comes after a relationship has been established, not before. There are also different rules about sharing personal information with others that have already been discussed in the "Lessons Learned" chapter above. Latina, Asian, and African American women also look to establish a relationship along hierarchical lines. Latina and Asian women are especially loyal and supportive of the boss and expect the boss to reciprocate in kind. All three groups believe that it is the boss's responsibility to initiate action on behalf of the employee and that good work should speak for itself. This impacts the degree to which these groups will self-promote.

CWW, African American women, and South Asian women will be more direct in asking the boss what it will take to get to the next level and make their case to be sure the boss knows what they have been doing. Latina and East Asian women expect the boss to know what they have been doing and, in effect, make their case for them.

Key Characteristics of Women of Color at Work

African American Women

POLITICAL These women play by the rules after finding out what the rules/requirements are. They are strategic and meticulous, cover every base, and avoid pitfalls. This may also partially explain why they tend to be more highly credentialed than their white women counterparts. In a sample of three hundred black women managers and four hundred white

TABLE 2. **CWW/women of color taxonomies**

	Political	Isolated	People pleaser	Narcissistic	Evolved
CWW	WM identified/ assimilated	O/RG—obedient to rules/job expectations	All about other people's feelings	Others have no subjective reality—they are only more or less useful	Authentically committed to success and well being of both self and group
African American	Highly credentialed; navigate racism; avoid pitfalls	Keep to self; work hard; avoid politics	Go along to get along	Dominating queen bee and her court	Authentically committed to success and well being of both self and group
East Asian	Strategic—long-term planning; hard work; develop alliances	Fulfill role; nose to grindstone; expect boss to notice	Self-effacing; deferential to authority; harmony above all; caretaking	All about me and how well I perform my role; insist on personal respect/obedience	Authentically committed to success and well being of both self and group
South Asian	Strategic—long-term planning; hard work; ally with power person (boss)	Act out of prescribed role; expect boss to notice	Deferential to authority; fulfill role	All about me and how well I perform my role; insist on personal respect/obedience	Authentically committed to success and well being of both self and group
Hispanic	Hard work: show loyalty; develop alliance	Fulfill role; nose to grindstone; wait for boss to notice	Nurturing; loyal; caretaking	All about me and how well I perform my role; insist on personal respect/obedience	Authentically committed to success and well being of both self and group

TABLE 3. **Differences that impact networking and building relationships**

	Share personal info without trust being established	Share family problems without trust having been established	Look to extend work relationship outside of work	Look for relationship across hierarchical lines	Test for trust and support	Test for loyalty, willingness to build alliances	Test whether sharing of information will be considered confidential	Test for willingness to help with career	Readily talk about issues of race and ethnicity with friends
White women	X	X							
African American					X		X	X	X
Hispanic	X		X	X	X	X	X	X	X
Asian			X	X	X	X	X	X	X

TABLE 4. **Support and strategies for work, life, and getting ahead**

	Who/what sustains me outside of work	Work/life strategies	Strategies for getting ahead
White women	Husband, close friend	Institutional	Network with key players
Hispanic	Extended family	Extended family	Build alliances with boss/peers; work hard; demonstrate loyalty
East Asian	Extended family	Extended family	Build alliances with boss; promote themselves through hard work; maintain harmony; show respect
South Asian	Extended family	Extended family	Build alliances and develop personal relationship with boss and other powerful people
African American	Family and church	Family; institutional; church	Learn role/requirements; work twice as hard; don't make mistakes

women managers, the researchers Bell and Nkomo found that "black women in this sample group have a higher educational level in terms of MBAs and Ph.Ds."[9]

ISOLATED   These women keep to themselves, work hard, and avoid politics as much as possible.

PEOPLE PLEASERS   These are women who "go along to get along." They are generally friendly to everyone, smile and engage in pleasantries with associates, and only broach real feelings about racism at work with a few trusted friends.

NARCISSISTIC   These woman are authoritarian and dominating. They use rules to establish and enforce personal power. They also exhibit a queen bee/"I do for me, and you do for me!" attitude. For example, in one cross-cultural communication class at the university the instructor was framing CWM social etiquette as "I do for me, and you do for you," and members of other cultural groups as a more reciprocal "I do for you and you do for me." By way of contrast, an African American woman said that her social life is governed by the protocol of "I do for me, and you do for me." The instructor said, "That sounds like the 'Queen Bee,' pattern." The black woman said, "That's right!"

EVOLVED   These women can be authentically who they are in any situation; multicultural flexibility doesn't threaten their identity as an individual or as an African American. Cross discusses the connection between personal identity and reference group orientation.[10]

East and South Asian American Women

POLITICAL   The approach here for East and South Asian American women has been to engage in long-term strategic planning and to pursue goals that they have managed to achieve—for those who have successfully made it into management—through hard work, display of loyalty, and the forging of alliances with powerful people at work. As discussed earlier in the chapter on gossip, traditional East Asian women are often reluctant to engage in the political aspects of networking and self-promotion that go beyond displaying hard work and loyalty to the boss—the boss representing their chief (and sometimes only) means of getting ahead. Consequently, bosses are often seen and related to as mentors ("gurus"). Consequently, as one of our Asian American colleagues put it, finding Asian women who do think and act politically and have made it into executive leadership roles as a result is very rare. For South Asian women and South Asians generally, peers are seen as the competition, with whom one is friendly, but not someone with whom to connect or relate to as allies.

ISOLATED   These women are very role and task oriented and generally don't make waves. The goal is to fulfill one's role as best as possible and despite a wish for recognition—for South Asian women this may be more of an expectation—(Lebra calls this "quiet endurance") to persevere even if there is no immediate reward in sight.[11]

PEOPLE PLEASERS   Knowing their prescribed place and role is something Asian women learn early on in their socialization, to the point where, as adults, it seems quite natural to create the roles they play. These are, in conjunction with their collective, harmony orientation, those that will best serve the work process and fit within the work team. Consistent with their role/harmony orientation, they are always working to figure out what others want or need. Nose to the grindstone, these women are also hierarchical and obedient. As part of their collective group orientation, they often take care of others' work in addition to their own. Note also—while role/harmony are core cultural values for both East and South Asians—

relative to each other, East Asians emphasize harmony more, and South Asians, position and role more.

NARCISSISTIC   These women are all about themselves and couch this attitude in how well they fulfill their role and how others are never good enough and never quite meet their standards.

EVOLVED   This woman is authentically committed to the achievement of both self and group. One Asian woman commenting on this point said, "I agree!" She also added, "This achievement orientation is killing us."

Latina Women

POLITICAL   The positive attitude that Latinas have on the strategic/political aspects of networking is similar to South Asians—both cultures consider it necessary and appropriate to getting ahead—but differentiates them from East Asians who view such politicking as unnatural and also sets them apart from African Americans who view playing politics more defensively: as a necessary and protective measure against being overrun. Latina women hope to get ahead by working hard, by demonstrating loyalty to the boss, and by creating alliances with influential and helpful brokers both within and outside the workplace. These alliances are built around personal sharing, trust, and reciprocity. For them, the personal connection is an essential element within networking, since opportunities develop out of friendship networks. For Hispanics to recommend you, they have to like you. For them to like you they first have to develop *confianza* (trust) and a sense of connection. Consequently, Hispanics find that the best way to network for them is simply to create a social opportunity for people to get together.

ISOLATED   These are the Latina women who are very role driven and so overwhelmed with work that they don't have time to socialize. Nor do they have time to strategize about getting ahead, beyond showing loyalty to the boss, which is manifest as being ever present and available in service of his/her needs. For example, one Latina secretary didn't go to lunch until her boss went to lunch.

PEOPLE PLEASERS   These are the nurturing loyal caretakers who offer support to their colleagues—emotional and otherwise—often in anticipation of what they might need. Like those who are role driven in service of their boss, they never refuse a request to take on another task. Consequently, when a Latina woman leaves her job, as reported earlier, it is often the case that they have to hire two or three people to do all that she did.

NARCISSISTIC   These are the Latina women who are more demanding of consideration from others. They also command a great deal of attention by playing on the sympathy of others for how much they have sacrificed. The sacrifice and suffering of women in Latin America is often characterized as *marianismo*.[12] The Latina woman who sacrifices and suffers is also called *La Sufría*.

EVOLVED   These are women who are authentically caring and helpful without losing the ability to also be for themselves. What is interesting and noticeable from these comparisons of different types of women from different groups is that when women from each group reach an evolved state the cultural differences that matter so much early on in their development and create much of the conflict between women of different cultural groups at work begin to matter less.

Challenges and Opportunities

Some organizations we have worked with reported to us that they have women of color in their membership and assume that they are on track. In fact, when the industry is dramatically male dominant (e.g., manufacturing, engineering, or journalism), women of color often feel that they are also represented by women's issues vis-à-vis men. However, that doesn't mean they think the white women get behind issues of women of color. Sometimes women of color join the women's network to make the point that they are women, too, and then complain about how clueless the membership is about race. *Creating Women's Networks*—a book by Catalyst—describes one company's effort to include women of color in their women's network:[13]

> Two and a half years ago, we realized that our diversity was nonexistent. We have large Asian, African American, and Hispanic populations, but we didn't see those names popping up on our membership lists. So we did a benchmark study when we sent out the yearly renewal form to ask a few questions and then

we set goals. We made sure our programs and speakers were diverse and that the topics were of interest to all women. For example, we had a speaker from a local university talk about the research she had done on success strategies for Korean American women. That brought us a lot of members.

As I read the statement about Korean American women, I also noticed that Asian women were put ahead of African American women on the list even though "African American" comes first alphabetically. The question in my mind, as it would be in the minds of many African American women, "Is this group comfortable talking about racism, or are they only comfortable talking about ethnic group differences?" This taps into a nerve and identifies a real issue. CWW are often more comfortable with East Asian, Latina, Afro-Caribbean, or African women than they are with African American women. CWW who feel this way say, "Black women think it's all about them, and we have to think about Asian and Latina women, too" and often use white women values around the importance of being nice to everyone and making sure everybody is included to make their case. But the motivation to broaden the base of inclusion is, in part, due to CWW's discomfort with the more direct, confrontational style of African American women, who, more so than women from these other groups, are also more likely to voice their frustration if they don't feel adequately represented by the group's leadership team.

It is also true that Asian and Latina women often become invisible because their voices are less likely to be heard.[14] It would also be well if African American women and other women of color could network with each other even though it will create another set of challenges, because other women of color groups, like white women, don't realize how strongly racism still impacts African American women. There is also the danger that companies will create a surface landscape that appears to be diverse—our colleague Adrian Chan talks about the propensity of companies to hire first-generation immigrant Asians—or will define diversity in ways ("diversity of thought") so as not to have to deal with problems or issues that are more intractable, usually those having to do with the race and gender issues of ethnic minorities. But, as one black woman executive said, "Before we get *beyond* race and gender, we have to go *through* race and gender."

CHAPTER THIRTEEN

Ten Things That CWW Can Do to Befriend Women of Color at Work

CWW are assumed to be "clueless" about race and intrusive based on the nature of questions they ask to try to know someone better, so they are already climbing uphill in trying to establish comfort/fit with colleagues of color. However, there are ways to disarm this discomfort and open channels of communication.

1. "Reach Out"

Say hello! Ask work related questions and follow up when appropriate. Expand your lunch network by including women of color.

2. Offer Political Rather than Emotional Support

Credibility and sincerity is established by what you *do,* not by what you *say.* The most effective way to build relationships with women of color is to be helpful with their career. Speak up for others when they are not there; and, when they are, ask the question that might be difficult for them to ask, such as noticing when another woman/person of color is not present at the meeting or on the conference call who should be. Don't always leave it up to the person of color to have to look out for themselves or others of their group. Be alert to inconsistent treatment and intervene to correct it. Do it without regard to what may have been behind it.

3. Learn How to Build Trust

Take the initiative in showing consideration and help. Don't wait to be asked. Be open to developing relationships outside of work.

4. Don't Come across as a "Suzy Snowflake" Lightweight

Ask yourself what the risk is if you don't assume a cheery disposition. That's not to say you won't offer a warm greeting or will never kid around, but have a serious side, too. When trust is low, there is always a question about whether or not you have a hidden agenda, disguised by what is perceived as a fake smile. Be forthright. Say what you really mean respectfully and directly. Otherwise, women of color will suspect that you have a hidden agenda.

5. Think before You Inquire

People of color are individuals as well as members of a group. Don't automatically ask, "What [racial, ethnic group] are you?" because it is objectifying. Have a relationship before asking someone what it is like for them as a member of their cultural group at work. When asking a woman of color for advice with another member of her group, explain first what you have tried to do yourself that didn't seem to work. Be aware that African Americans are sensitive to the implication that they are "all alike." Consequently, be prepared to justify why you think her being black might bring with it some special insight that you couldn't figure out yourself. Show that you are concerned and be sure to get back to the person who advises you so you aren't viewed as just a user. Getting back to someone afterward is typically not an issue for whites—the fact that someone solicits their advice about another person is often enough. For people of color, however, a response or follow-up is expected as a sign of appreciation and respect for their insight and help.

6. Avoid Using First Names for Starters

When talking about a person, Asians and Hispanics tend to use their title plus last name as a sign of respect. When addressing African Americans, know that the use of first names is often reserved only for friends and never used with an older person. First names are marked for informality in mainstream U.S. culture and, while some African American women also follow that pattern, more traditional African American women often do not. Also, don't refer to African American women as "girls"; it denies women the respect owed to their adult status and also carries a servant connotation.

7. Protect the Privacy of Other People's Personal Information

After trust begins to be established and women of color start to share personal information with you, know that that information is just for your ears. Do not use it to help others know them better, too.

8. Learn What Topics Are Easy Openers

For African Americans, whatever is public is safe to talk about—dress, news, weather, or whatever is going on at the moment. Avoid probing questions that ask about the person's life outside of work such as, "Where do you live?" "Are you married?" or "Do you have any kids?" For Hispanics and Asians, learning about their personal life is appreciated. Relate to women of color as individuals before you speak to them as members of a group.

9. Beware of Compliments That Imply (or Might Be Heard as) Something Otherwise Negative about the Individual's Group

"You're not like other Asians" Or, "You're so articulate!"

10. Listen Empathically

Be aware of your relative social privilege around whiteness. This will help eliminate defensiveness. Listen to understand first; only share when asked. When someone approaches you about inconsistent treatment, show that you know race and ethnicity matter by not being stuck in either denial, defensiveness, or minimization. Also, don't change the subject by making your moral character the issue. Focus instead on the concern behind the question and treat it seriously.

CHAPTER FOURTEEN

The White Woman People Pleaser Tale of Woe

If white men within the social order symbolize the oppressor—"the man"—then white women symbolize "the man's wife." Some of the negative components of the image of white women include clueless, lightweight, little substance, spoiled, entitled, trying to help as long as it enhances their own image, backstabbing, and benefiting from the hard work of the civil rights movement without acknowledging they have benefited from affirmative action in corporate America more than people of color.

> White men think we nag, talk too much, and aren't real players.
>
> Black women think we're spoiled, clueless.
>
> Latina women think we're cold and untrustworthy.
>
> Asian women think we're selfish and don't fulfill role expectations.
>
> Other white women might be backstabbers and can't always be trusted.
>
> The real friends we do have are important; the problem is people pleaser friends have to agree with each other wholeheartedly, and we can't compete with each other.
>
> We don't think of ourselves as the subject of the workplace or, like white men, as the author of our lives.
>
> We try to figure out how to accommodate other people's wishes, while only indirectly pursuing our own ambitions or pretending we don't really have any—even to ourselves.
>
> Ambition is a dirty word.

The CWW Challenge

Women of color report that their closest allies at work are often CWW. They bond with CWW around issues of social and cultural oppression and shared frustrations with a common "enemy": the CWM power structure of the organization. Once all the layers of the diversity onion have been peeled away—cultural communication style, personality type, birth order, generation, sexual orientation, occupation, and so on—there is still the most insurmountable obstacle of all: the deep-seeded psychological legacy of racism, woman to woman. When CWW get close to the bone of truth about racism, a sharp pick of ice slides in under the ribs. "You white woman; you got your babies, but you let them take mine away; you let them put mine in jail, you let them send mine to war, you let them . . . you let them . . ." Just as CWW want CWM to hear about patriarchy before we can hear their personal stories, CWW have to demonstrate that they first respect race and ethnicity. CWW have to do this without making it about them; they have to respect the reality of the pain, without getting emotional in a way that becomes self-serving and is designed more to display empathy than to be truly compassionate. CWW quickly understand the profound depth of sexism, in a way that men can only imagine, just as women of color experience the conflation of sexism and racism in a way that white women can only imagine.

Kathy Weingarten writes, "If we are going to learn what truly suits us, and not just what the cultures we live in have convinced us we should desire, we are going to have to use more critical thinking about our cultural context, be more open to diverse others, and add a lively imagination to routine introspection. . . . Listening to each other is the heart of the matter."[1]

The psychological ramifications of the legacy of slavery pose the deepest challenge to reconciliation. There is tremendous fear on both sides. CWW, like CWM, are afraid of losing their social privilege, and women of color have little or no reason to deeply trust a white woman. Strong, evolving CWW who do recognize their privilege have an opportunity, and I would argue, a responsibility, to make a difference. To do so, however, requires a strong enough sense of self-esteem to stand up every time you are confronted with the pain you cause women of color because you don't know what you don't know and must endure the inevitable socially based transference wherein every mistake conjures up images of all the oppression the person of color in the interaction has heard or experienced vis-à-vis CWW. The journey requires humility, perseverance, and a healthy sense of humor. Yet it is also a journey rich in connection, relationship, and self-discovery. As Carlos Fuentes said, "My upbringing taught me that cultures are not isolated, and perish when deprived of contact with what is different and challenging. Reading, writing, teaching, learning are all activities aimed at introducing civilizations to each other. No culture, I believed unconsciously ever since then, and quite consciously today, retains its identity in isolation; identity is attained in contact, in contrast, in breakthrough."[2]

Afterword

The path of engagement—being open to diverse others and accepting the challenge of contact and contrast—is the path the two of us have taken most of our adult lives, following where it leads us and taking notes along the way. More often than not the greatest learning happened when we were out of our comfort zone on someone else's turf and out of sync with what others expected of us. Those experiences, disconcerting as they were, have been the catalyst to motivate us toward greater cross-cultural awareness as we tried to figure out what was going on for others that was different from what was going on for ourselves. This book reflects much of what we learned along the way.

This learning path is also what we try to create in the course of our training: moving people toward new levels of awareness—perhaps even toward reconciliation, which is built around a shared understanding of what happened by all the parties involved. That movement starts by members of diverse groups having different kinds of conversations with each other than they could have had before. That happens at the end of our training; the buzz and excitement that occurs when politeness gives way to informed, authentic, respectful exchanges on previously avoided "hot topics" is what leads to breakthrough.

Bill Clinton encouraged America to begin a dialogue on race. Barack Obama, in his campaign for the presidency, addressed the topic empathically and candidly. We hope that this book encourages others to do likewise. Conversations on race, ethnicity, and gender are necessary and important. We can't move forward as a multicultural society until those conversations happen.

Notes

Introduction

1. D. Tannen, *You Just Don't Understand: Women and Men in Conversation* (New York: Ballantine, 1990), pp. 76–77.

2. E. Liu, *The Accidental Asian* (New York: Random House, 1998), p. 11.

3. C. R. Chandler, "Traditionalism in a Modern Setting: A Comparison of Anglo and Mexican-American Value Orientations," *Human Organization* 38, no. 2 (1979): 153–59.

4. M. B. Sussman and J. C. Romeis, "Willingness to Assist Elderly Parents: Responses from United States and Japanese Families," *Human Organization* 41:256–59.

5. L. T. Doi, "*Amae:* A Key Concept for Understanding Japanese Personality Structure," in *Japanese Culture: Its Development and Characteristics,* Viking Fund Publications in Anthropology No. 34, ed. R. Smith and R. Beardsley (New York: Wenner-Gren Foundation for Anthropological Research, 1962).

6. "AARP Survey: Boomer Population Redefines 'Sandwich Generation,'" *seniorjournal.com,* July 3, 2007.

Chapter One

1. DiversityInc, "Women of Color Are Leaving Law Firms," *DiversityInc News,* August 27, 2006.

2. N. C. Aizenman and P. Constable, "'Every Korean Person Is So Very Sorry': From N. Virginia to Seoul, a Plea to Avoid Stereotypes," *Washington Post,* April 18, 2007, p. A10.

3. A. Hong, "Koreans Aren't to Blame," *Washington Post,* April 20, 2007, p. A31.

4. L. Visconti, "Ask the White Guy: Why Do You Have All the Answers?" *DiversityInc News,* December 7, 2006.

5. H. I. Hartmann, "Capitalism, Patriarchy and Job Segregation by Sex," *Signs: Journal of Women in Culture and Society* 1, no. 3, pt. 2 (Spring 1976): 137–70.

6. M. Reitman, "Uncovering the White Place: Whitewashing at Work," *Social and Cultural Geography* 7, no. 2 (April 2006): 267–82, pp. 274, 277.

7. R. Dyer, *The Matter of Whiteness: Theories of Race and Racism: A Reader* (London: Routledge, 2000), p. 539.

8. See P. McKintosh, "White Privilege: Unpacking the Invisible Knapsack," *Independent School,* Winter 1990, pp. 31–36.

9. J. Kroll, "Spiking a Fever: A Black-White Affair Is the Catalyst for Spike Lee's Panoramic View of a Culture in a Color Bind," *Newsweek,* June 10, 1991, p. 44; italics added.

10. T. Kochman, *Black and White Styles in Conflict* (Chicago: University of Chicago Press, 1981).

11. A. Murray, *The Omni-Americans* (New York: Discus, 1971), p. 143. See also K. Addison, *"We Hold These Truths to be Self-Evident": An Interdisciplinary Analysis of Racism and Slavery in America* (Lanham, MA: University Press of America, forthcoming).

12. H. Hill, "Race and Ethnicity in Organized Labor: The Historical Sources of Resistance to Affirmative Action," in *Ethnicity and the Work Force, Ethnicity and Public Policy,* ed. W. A. Van Horne and T. V. Tonnesen (Madison: University of Wisconsin System, 1985), p. 48.

13. N. Lemann, "Reversals," *New Yorker,* July 30, 2007, pp. 27–28. See also L. Greenhouse, "Judges Reject Diversity Plan in Two Districts," *New York Times,* June 28, 2007.

14. L. Guinier and S. L. Carter, 1995, *Tyranny of the Majority: Fundamental Fairness in a Representative Democracy* (New York: Free Press).

15. *Booknotes,* June 26, 1994; italics added.

16. *Boston Review,* June/September 1994.

17. *Booknotes,* June 26, 1994; italics added.

18. K. Blanchard and S. Johnson, *The One Minute Manager* (New York: William Morrow, 1982).

19. L. Newton, "Reverse Discrimination Is Unjustified," *Ethics* 83 (1973): 308–12. Reprinted in J. Olen and V. Barry, eds., *Applying Ethics* (Belmont, CA: Wadsworth, 1989), pp. 311–15.

20. *DiversityInc News,* "Church of England Apologizes for Slave Trade," *DiversityInc News,* February 11, 2006; Y. Cole, "Who Is Apologizing for Slavery?" *DiversityInc Newsletter,* November 30, 2006.

21. *DiversityInc News,* "Slavery Reparations Movement Getting Stronger," *DiversityInc News,* July 10, 2006.

22. B. Gross, "The Case against Reverse Discrimination," in *Morality in Practice,* 4th. ed., ed. James Sterba (Belmont, CA: Wadsworth, 1994), pp. 255–60.

23. *DiversityInc News,* "Whites-Only Scholarship Fuels Affirmative Action Debate," *DiversityInc News,* December 4, 2006.

24. A. Memmi, *The Colonizer and the Colonized* (Boston: Beacon Press, 1957), p. 52.

25. M. McLuhan, *The Medium Is the Massage: An Inventory of Effects* (New York: Random House, 1967).

26. A. Baker, "3 Detectives Are Indicted in 50-Shot Killing in Queens," *New York Times,* March 17, 2007.

27. D. O. Linder, "The Trials of the Los Angeles Police Officers in Connection with the Beating of Rodney King," in *Famous Trials,* ed. D. O. Linder (Kansas City: University of Missouri–Kansas City School of Law, 2001).

Chapter Two

1. A. B. Hart and H. R. Ferliger, eds., *Theodore Roosevelt Cyclopedia* (New York: Roosevelt Memorial Association, 1941). See also "Editorial: Keep Up the Fight for Americanism," *El Grito: A Journal of Contemporary Mexican American Thought* 1, no. 2 (1968): 1.

2. Quoted in O. Handlin, *The American People in the Twentieth Century* (Cambridge, MA: Harvard University Press, 1954), p.121. See also M. M. Gordon, *Assimilation in American Life: The Role of Race, Religion, and National Origins* (New York: Oxford University Press, 1964), p. 101n.

3. M. Lamont and V. Molnar, "The Study of Boundaries in the Social Sciences," *Annual Review of Sociology* 28(2002):167–95.

4. E. Liu, *The Accidental Asian* (New York: Random House, 1998), p. 116; H. Hill, "Anti-Oriental Agitation and the Rise of Working Class Racism," *Society,* January–February 1973, pp. 43–54.

5. C. N. Degler, *At Odds: Women and the Family in America from the Revolution to the Present* (Oxford: Oxford University Press), pp.395–417.

6. R. Blauner, "Colonized and Immigrant Minorities," in *From Different Shores,* 2d. ed., ed. Ronald Takaki, pp. 149–60 (Oxford: Oxford University Press, 1994).

7. W. E. Cross, Jr., "A Two-Factor Theory of Black Identity: Implications for the Study of Identity Development in Minority Children," in *Children's Ethnic Socialization: Pluralism and Development,* ed. J. S. Phinney and M. J. Rotheram, pp. 117–33 (Newbury Park, CA: Sage, 1987).

8. R. Alba and V. Nee, *Remaking the American Mainstream: Assimilation and Contemporary Immigration* (Cambridge, MA: Harvard University Press, 2003), p. 2.

9. Liu, *Accidental Asian,* p. 55.

Chapter Three

1. M. Walzer, *Spheres of Justice* (New York: Basic Books, 1983), pp. 143–54.

2. T. Sowell, *Preferential Policies: An International Perspective* (New York: William Morrow, 1990).

3. *Diversity Inc News,* "Did Motherhood Force Elizabeth Vargas Out of Anchor Chair?" *Diversity Inc News,* May 30, 2006; italics added.

4. Ian Ayers, *Pervasive Prejudice: Unconventional Evidence of Race and Gender Discrimination* (Chicago: University of Chicago Press, 2001); "True Colors," *ABC Primetime* live segment, September 26, 1991.

5. See Alex Ching, "The Edge," *Gazette* 91, no. 68 (January 29, 1998), for a position that supports Sprewell, albeit, with some misgivings.

6. See T. Kochman, "Truth and Consequences," in his *Black and White Styles in Conflict* (Chicago: University of Chicago Press, 1981).

7. G. W. Foote and A. D. McLaren "The Christian View of Death," in *Infidel Death Beds* (published for the Secular Society, Ltd.; London: Pioneer Press [G. W. Foot and Co.], 1886); available at http://www.infidels.org/library/historical/george_foote/infidel_deathbeds.html#2.2.

8. E. L. Lincoln, "Banning the 'N' Word: At Least Ann Coulter Is Upfront about Bigotry," *DiversityInc News,* March 8, 2007.

9. CNN-Interactive, "Kevorkian Trial Poses New Legal Questions," April 1, 1996.

10. See Elizabeth S. Anderson, "Bibliography on Race, Gender and Affirmative Action" (Department of Philosophy, University of Michigan, 2006); available at http://www-personal.umich.edu/~eandersn/biblio.htm.

11. *DiversityInc News,* April 24, 2006.

12. See also Joe Holley, "Who Was Burning the Black Churches," *Columbia Journalism Review* 35, no. 33 (September/October 1996): 16–19.

13. Carmen Cusido, *DiversityInc News,* January 9, 2006.

14. *DiversityInc News,* December 5, 2006; italics added.

15. DiversityInc management newsletter, "Jury Finds No Racial Bias against Overweight Air Passenger," DiversityInc.com, February 13, 2006; italics added.

16. J. Curry, "Sheffield, Still Ever the Talker, Stands behind His Accusations," *New York Times,* August 16, 2007, pp. C15, C17.

17. DiversityInc, "Halle Berry Takes on 'Big, Fat Black Guy,'" DiversityInc.com, May 20, 2006.

18. Y. Cole, "'Lynch Tiger Woods in a Back Alley' Gets Anchor Suspended," *DiversityInc News,* January 9, 2008; italics added.

19. All quotes found in Holley, "Who Was Burning Black Churches?"

20. T. Wheeler, "'Fires of Hate' Kindle National Fightback: Leaders Vow to End Racist Wave of Church Arson," *People's Weekly World,* July 20, 1996.

21. *Jet Magazine,* "At House Hearings Black Caucus Cites Urgency for End to Dixie Church Fires," *Jet Magazine,* June 10, 1996, p. 1.

22. Quoted in Holley, "Who Was Burning Black Churches?"

23. M. A. Fletcher, "No Linkage Found in Black Church Arsons," *Washington Post,* May 22, p. A08.

24. G. F. Casellas, "Biracial Employee Who Presented Himself as White Loses Race-Discrimination Case," *DiversityInc News,* October 16, 2007.

Chapter Four

1. "Ethics—Boeing to Navigate Capitol Hill Session," *Wall Street Journal,* July 29–30, 2006, p. A2.

2. R. Gutfeld, "Shades of Green: Eight of 10 Americans are Environmentalists, at Least So They Say," *Wall Street Journal,* 72(1991):204.

3. H. Higman, "Hypotheses on Conflict, Systemic Inertia, and Poverty" (paper presented at the Symposium on Poverty and Social Disorder, American Anthropological Association, Seattle, November 21–24, 1968), p. 8.

4. T. Kochman, "The Politics of Politeness: Social Warrants in Mainstream American Public Etiquette " in *GURT '84,* ed. Deborah Schiffren, pp. 200–209 (Washington, DC: Georgetown University Press, 1984).

5. P. Roth, *The Human Stain* (New York: Vintage, 2001).

Chapter Five

1. D. Finney, "Canadian Indian Land Grab," April 20, 2006, www.greatdreams.com/canada-land-grab.htm.

2. T. Kochman, "Black and White Cultural Styles in Pluralistic Perspective," in *Test Policy and Test Performance: Education, Language, and Culture,* ed. B. R. Gifford (Boston: Kluwer Academic Publishers, 1989).

3. B. McGhee, "Andrew Young Resigns from Walmart Post," *Associated Press,* August 18, 2006.

4. Ibid.; italics added.

5. S. Dewan and M. Barbaro, "Different Focus in Atlanta on Andrew Young's Remark," *New York Times,* August 19, 2006.

6. S. M. Hersh, "Annals of National Security: Last Stand," *New Yorker,* July 10–17, 2006, p. 42; italics added.

7. F. L. K. Hsu, *Americans and Chinese* (Honolulu: University Press of Hawaii, 1953), p. 378.

8. *Boeing Frontiers,* "Own Your Career," *Boeing Frontiers* 5, no. 1 (May 2006): 10–11; italics added.

9. M. R. Gottlieb, *Managing Group Process* (Westport, CT: Praeger, 2003), p. 19.

10. See J. Weisz, F. M. Rothbaum, and T. C. Blackburn, "Standing Out and

Standing In: The Psychology of Control in America and Japan," *American Psychologist* 39, no. 9 (1984): 955–69.

11. J. S. K. Lee, "Managerial Work in Chinese Organizations in Singapore," *Human Organization* 50, no. 2 (1991): 188–93; B. Wong, "The Role of Ethnicity in Enclave Enterprises: A Study of Chinese Garment Factories in New York City," *Human Organization* 46, no. 2 (1987): 120–30.

12. H. S. Kim, "We Talk, therefore We Think? A Cultural Analysis of the Effect of Talking on Thinking," *Journal of Personality and Social Psychology* 83, no. 4 (2002): 828–42.

13. K. Ueda, "Sixteen Ways to Avoid Saying 'NO' in Japan," in *Intercultural Encounters with Japan,* ed. J. C. Condon and M. Saito (Tokyo: Sumul Press, 1974), pp. 185–92. See also M. Zimmerman, *How to Do Business with Japan* (New York: Random House, 1985), pp. 104–17.

Chapter Six

1. G. Castile, "An Unethical Ethic: Self-Determination and the Anthropological Conscience," *Human Organization* 34(1975):35–40.

2. J. M. Walters and R. L. Sumwalt, III, *Aircraft Accident Analysis: Final Reports* (New York: McGraw Hill, 2000), pp. 187–210.

3. J. R. Weisz, F. M. Rothbaum, and T. C. Blackburn, "Standing Out and Standing In: The Psychology of Control in America and Japan," *American Psychologist* 39, no. 9 (1984): 955–69.

4. D. Reynolds, *The Quiet Therapies: Japanese Pathways to Personal Growth* (Honolulu: University of Hawaii Press, 1982).

5. J. Kabat-Zinn, *Full Catastrophe Living* (New York: Delta Trade Paperbacks, 1990).

6. H. Higman, "Hypotheses on Conflict, Systemic Inertia, and Poverty" (paper presented at the Symposium on Poverty and Social Disorder, American Anthropological Association, Seattle, November 21–24, 1968).

7. National Institute of Mental Health Web site, "Frequently Asked Questions about Suicide." See also "Epidemiology and the Methodology of Suicide" on the Wikipedia Web site.

8. See B. Lafayette De Mente's Asian Business Codewords: Etiquette in Asia, a monthly column from the Asia Pacific Management Forum (May 2002), excerpted from *Japan's Cultural Code Words* (Lincolnwood, IL: NTC Publishing Group, 1994).

9. *Time,* August 3, 1987. See also R. Atsumi, "Tsukiai—Obligatory Personal Relationships of Japanese White-Collar Employees," *Human Organization* 38(1979): 63–70.

10. See Castile, "An Unethical Ethnic."

11. C. Gilligan, *In a Different Voice* (Cambridge, MA: Harvard University Press, 1982/1993), pp. 42 ff.

12. Ibid., p. 42.

13. P. Slater, *The Pursuit of Loneliness: American Culture at the Breaking Point* (Boston: Beacon, 1970/1976), pp. 8 ff.

Chatper Seven

1. J. B. Miller, "The Development of Women's Sense of Self," in *Women's Growth in Connection,* ed. J. V. Jordan, A. G. Kaplan, J. B. Miller, I. P. Stiver, and J. L. Surrey, pp. 11–26 (New York and London: Guilford Press, 1991), p. 17; A. G. Kaplan, "The 'Self-in-Relation': Implications for Depression in Women," in *Women's Growth in Connection,* pp. 206–22, p. 209.

2. See P. R. Staff, "'Multi-Minding' Women and the Marketing Challenge," *Pink Magazine,* December–January 2007, http://www.pinkmagazine.com/resources/research.htm/.

3. A. Harris, *Future Girl* (New York and London: Routledge, 2004), p. 32.

4. M. Pipher, *Reviving Ophelia* (New York: G. P. Putnam's Sons, 1994).

5. P. Heim, "The Power Dead-Even Rule and Other Gender Differences in the Workplace," CorVision Media, video presentation.

6. L. Sax, *Why Gender Matters* (New York: Broadway Books, 2005), p. 75.

7. E. Goodman and P. O'Brien, *I Know Just What You Mean: The Power of Friendship in Women's Lives* (New York: Simon and Schuster, 2000); P. Chesler, *Woman's Inhumanity to Woman* (New York: Plume, 2001).

8. *Seventeen,* "Are You Too Competitive?" *Seventeen* (Fall 2004), p. 83.

9. See also R. Cohen-Sandler, *Stressed-Out Girls: Helping Them Thrive in the Age of Pressure* (New York: Viking, 2005).

10. G. Gilligan, *In a Different Voice* (Cambridge, MA: Harvard University Press, 1982/1993), p. 9; J. Lever, "Sex Differences in the Games Children Play," *Social Problems* 23(1976):478–87.

11. S. Martin, "Women Leaders: The Labyrinth to Leadership," *Monitor on Psychology* 38 (July/August): 7. See also A. Eagly and L. Carli, *Through the Labyrinth: The Truth about How Women Become Leaders,* (Watertown, MA: Harvard Business School Publishing, 2007).

12. Gilligan, *In a Different Voice.*

13. See D. Tannen, *You Just Don't Understand: Women and Men in Conversation* (New York: Ballantine, 1990), pp. 43 ff.

14. M. H. Goodwin, *He-Said-She-Said: Talk as Social Organization among Black Children* (Bloomington: Indiana University Press, 1991).

15. M. Leibovich, "Rights vs. Rights: An Improbable Collision Course," *New York Times* (January 13, 2008).

16. Chesler, *Woman's Inhumanity to Woman,* pp. 218, 219.

17. N. Mooney, *I Can't Believe She Did That! Why Women Betray Other Women at Work* (New York: St. Martin's Press, 2005), pp. 51 ff.

18. Gilligan, *In a Different Voice,* p. 42.

19. S. Hotchkiss, *Why Is It always about You?* (New York: Free Press, 2002), pp. 75–76.

20. Miller, "The Development of Women's Sense of Self," pp. 16 ff.

21. See, e.g., the discussion on "normative femininity" in school in A. Harris, *Future Girl* (New York and London: Routledge, 2004), pp. 103 ff.

22. "E" for evolved and "P" for people pleaser.

23. J. Benjamin, *Like Subjects, Love Objects: Essays on Recognition and Sexual Difference* (New Haven, CT: Yale University Press, 1995).

24. Hotchkiss, *Why Is It Always about You?* pp. 82–83.

Chapter Eight

1. D. Baumrind, "Effects of Authoritative Parental Control on Child Behavior," *Child Development* 37, no. 4 (1966): 887–907, "Child Care Practices Anteceding Three Patterns of Preschool Behavior," *Genetic Psychology Monographs* 75, no. 1 (1967): 43–88, "Current Patterns of Parental Authority," *Developmental Psychology Monograph Part 2* 4, no. 1 (1971): 1–103, and "Parenting Styles and Adolescent Development," in *Encyclopedia on Adolescence,* ed. J. Brooks-Gunn, R. Lerner, and A. C. Petersen, pp. 746–58 (New York: Garland, 1991).

2. D. Lewis, "The Black Family: Socialization and Sex Roles," *Phylon* 36, no. 3 (1975): 221–37. See also H. P. McAdoo, ed., *Black Families,* 2nd ed. (Newbury Park, CA: Sage, 1988), pp. 49, 234.

3. K. Jamison, "Sexism as Rank Language," *Social Change Ideas and Applications, NTL Institute for Applied Behavioral Sciences* 5(1975):2.

4. B. Spock, *Dr. Spock's Baby & Child Care,* 8th ed. (New York: Pocket, 2004); B. Spock and M. T. Stein, *Dr. Spock's The First Two Years: The Emotional and Physical Needs of Children from Birth to Age 2* (New York: Pocket, 2001); B. Spock, *Dr. Spock on Parenting: Sensible, Reassuring Advice for Today's Parent* (New York: Pocket, 1988).

5. AAUW, *Shortchanging Girls, Shortchanging America* (Washington, DC: AAUW, 1991); executive summary available at http://www.aauw.org/research/upload/SGSA-2.pdf. See also AAUW, *Growing Smart: What's Working for Girls in School* (Washington, DC: AAUW, 1995); more information available at http://www.aauw.org/research/growingSmart.cfm.

6. R. Diaz-Guerrero, *Psychology of the Mexican* (Austin: University of Texas Press, 1975), and "Historical Sociocultural Premises and Ethnic Socialization," in *Children's Ethnic Socialization: Pluralism and Development,* ed. J. S. Phinney and M. J. Rotheram (Newbury Park, CA: Sage, 1987).

7. S. C. Carothers, "Catching Sense: Learning from Our Mothers to be Black and Female," in *Uncertain Terms: Negotiating Gender in American Culture,* ed. F. Ginsburg and A. L. Tsing, pp. 232–47 (Boston: Beacon, 1990), pp. 240 ff.

8. T. Kochman, "The Politics of Politeness: Social Warrants in Mainstream American Public Etiquette," in *Meaning, Form, and Use in Context: Linguistic Applications, Georgetown University Round Table '84,* ed. D. Schiffrin (Washington, DC: Georgetown University Press, 1984).

9. P. R. Fenner, *Ghosts, Ghosts, Ghosts* (London: Franklin Watts, 1952).

10. M. H. Goodwin, *He-Said-She-Said: Talk as Social Organization among Black Children* (Bloomington: Indiana University Press, 1991).

11. P. L. Dunbar, *The Complete Poems of Paul Lawrence Dunbar* (New York: Dodd, Mead & Co., 1913).

12. T. Kochman, "Black and White Cultural Styles in Pluralistic Perspective," in *Test Policy and Test Performance: Education, Language, and Culture,* ed. B. R. Gifford (Boston: Kluwer Academic Publishers, 1989), pp. 267–68. See also C. Keil, "Motion and Feeling in Music," in *Rappin' and Styllin' Out: Communication in Urban Black America,* ed. T. Kochman (Urbana: University of Illinois Press, 1972).

Chapter Nine

1. I. C. Meijer and J. de Bruin, "Gender Gossip and Ethnic Ethics: A Comparative Approach towards Soap Opera Talk" (Amsterdam School of Communication Research, 2002), www.portalcommunication.com/ben2002/_eng/programme/prog_indpapers/c/pdf/c002_coste.pdf. See also R. F. Baumeister, L. Zhang, and K. D. Vohs, "Gossip as Cultural Learning," *Review of General Psychology* 8, no. 2 (2004): 111–21.

2. P. C. Harrison, *The Drama of Nommo* (New York: Grove, 1972).

3. T. Kochman, *Black and White Styles in Conflict* (Chicago: University of Chicago Press, 1981).

4. Ibid.

5. E. L. Rincon and C. B. Keys "The Latina Social Service Administrator: Developmental Tasks and Management Concerns," *Administration in Social Work* 6, no. 1 (Spring 1982): 47–58.

6. I. Adler and M. Garaitonandía, "Same Language, Different Meanings," in *Business Mexico* 8, no. 5 (May 1998): 36–38.

7. For more on ON, see T. S. Lebra, *Japanese Patterns of Behavior* (Honolulu: University Press of Hawaii, 1976). See also M. Zimmerman, *How to Do Business with Japan* (New York: Random House, 1985).

8. See the chapter "Information as Property" in Kochman, *Black and White Styles in Conflict,* pp. 97 ff.

Chapter Ten

1. N. Mooney, *I Can't Believe She Did That! Why Women Betray Other Women at Work* (New York: St. Martin's Press, 2005).

2. T. Kochman, *Black and White Styles in Conflict* (Chicago: University of Chicago Press, 1981), p. 23.

3. See ibid., pp. 18–19.

Chapter Eleven

1. E. L. Lincoln, "The N-Word Double Standard: Why Imus Burned Where Rappers Thrive," *DiversityInc Newsletter,* April 29, 2007.

2. J. Durando, "Al Sharpton Opens Up about Don Imus," *Newsletter,* April 14, 2007.

3. See S. Labaton, "Denny's Restaurant to Pay 54 Million in Race Bias Suits," *New York Times,* November 25, 1994; D. Dirks and S. K. Rice, "Dining while Black," *Cornell Hotel and Restaurant Administration Quarterly* 45(2004):30–47.

4. W. O. Beeman, "Status, Style and Strategy in Iranian Interaction," *Anthropological Linguistics* 18, no. 7 (1976): 305–22, p. 307.

Chapter Twelve

1. Catalyst, *Creating Women's Networks,* Jossey-Bass Business & Management Series (San Francisco: Jossey-Bass, 1999), p. 128.

2. See A. Enciso, "America's Guests: The Uninvited Speakers," in *Cora Uninvited,* American Collection Educator's Web site, http://www.ncteamericancollection.org/cora_uninvited.htm#Soj for the full text of Sojourner Truth's speech in which that declaration was made.

3. See M. Yamada, "Asian Pacific American Women and Feminism," in *This Bridge Called My Back: Writings by Radical Women of Color,* ed. C. Moraga and G. Anzaldúa (New York: Kitchen Table), p. 149.

4. E. L. J. E. Bell and S. M. Nkomo, *Our Separate Ways: Black and White Women and the Struggle for Professional Identity* (Boston: Harvard Business School Press, 2001), p. 149.

5. Yamada, "Asian Pacific American Women and Feminism," p. 149.

6. J. L. Chin and J. Sanchez-Hucles, "Diversity and Leadership," *American Psychologist,* September 2007, pp. 608–9.

7. E. Abel, B. Christian, and H. Moglen, eds., *Female Subjects in Black and White: Race, Psychoanalysis, Feminism* (Berkeley: University of California Press, 1997), pp. 6–7.

8. P. McKintosh, "White Privilege: Unpacking the Invisible Knapsack," *Independent School,* Winter 1990, pp. 31–36.

9. S. H. Tucker, "Black Women in Corporate America: The Inside Story," *Black Enterprise* 25, no. 1 (August 1994): 60–66

10. W. E. Cross, Jr., "A Two-Factor Theory of Black Identity: Implications for the Study of Identity Development in Minority Children," in *Children's Ethnic Socialization: Pluralism and Development,* ed. J. S. Phinney and M. J. Rotheram, pp. 117–33 (Newbury Park, CA: Sage, 1987).

11. T. S. Lebra, *Japanese Women: Constraint and Fulfillment* (Honolulu: University of Hawaii Press, 1984), pp. 46–47.

12. E. P. Stevens, "Marianismo: The Other Face of Machismo in Latin America," in *Female and Male in Latin America,* ed. A. Pescatelo (Pittsburgh: University of Pittsburgh Press, 1973).

13. Catalyst, *Creating Women's Networks,* p. 135.

14. Yamada, "Asian Pacific American Women and Feminism" (excerpt reprinted in M. Humm, ed., *Modern Feminisms: Political, Literary, Cultural* [New York: Columbia University Press, 1992], pp. 148–49).

Chapter Fourteen

1. K. Weingarten, *The Mother's Voice: Strengthening Intimacy in Families* (New York: Guilford Press, 1994), pp. 209–10.

2. C. Fuentes, "How I Started to Write," in *The Graywolf Annual: Multicultural Literacy,* vol. 5., ed. R. Simonson and S. Walker (St. Paul, MN: Graywolf Press, 1988), p. 47.

Bibliography

Abel, E., Christian, B., Moglen, H., eds. 1997. *Female Subjects in Black and White: Race, Psychoanalysis, Feminism.* Berkeley: University of California Press.

Addison, K. Forthcoming. *"We Hold These Truths to be Self-Evident": An Interdisciplinary Analysis of Racism and Slavery in America.* Lanham, MA: University Press of America.

Adler, I., Garaitonandía, M. 1998. "Same Language, Different Meanings." *Business Mexico* 8, no. 5 (May): 36–38.

Aizenman, N. C., Constable, P. 2007. "'Every Korean Person Is So Very Sorry': From N. Virginia to Seoul, a Plea to Avoid Stereotypes." *Washington Post,* April 18, p. A10.

Alba, R., Nee, V. 2003. *Remaking the American Mainstream: Assimilation and Contemporary Immigration.* Cambridge, MA: Harvard University Press.

Anzaldúa, G. 1987. "Borderlands/La Frontera: The New Mestiza," in *Women's Voices from the Borderlands.* Edited by Castillo-Speed, L., pp. 251–56. New York: Simon & Schuster.

Atsumi, R. 1979. "Tsukiai—Obligatory Personal Relationships of Japanese White-Collar Employees." *Human Organization* 38:63–70.

Ayers, I. 2001. *Pervasive Prejudice: Unconventional Evidence of Race and Gender Discrimination.* Chicago: University of Chicago Press.

Baker, A. 2007. "3 Detectives Are Indicted in 50-Shot Killing in Queens." *New York Times,* March 17.

Baumeister, R. F., Zhang, L., Vohs, K.D. 2004. "Gossip as Cultural Learning." *Review of General Psychology* 8(2):111–21.

Baumrind, D. 1966. "Effects of Authoritative Parental Control on Child Behavior." *Child Development* 37(4):887–907.

———. 1967. "Child Care Practices Anteceding Three Patterns of Preschool Behavior." *Genetic Psychology Monographs* 75(1):43–88.

———. 1971. "Current Patterns of Parental Authority." *Developmental Psychology Monograph Part 2* 4(1):1–103.

———. 1991. "Parenting Styles and Adolescent Development," in *Encyclopedia on Adolescence*. Edited by Brooks-Gunn, J., Lerner, R., Petersen, A. C., pp. 746–58. New York: Garland.

Beeman, W. O. 1976. "Status, Style and Strategy in Iranian Interaction." *Anthropological Linguistics* 18(7):305–22.

Belenky, M. F., Clinchy, B. M., Goldberger, N. R., Tarule, J. M. 1986. *Women's Ways of Knowing: The Development of Self, Voice and Mind*. New York: Basic Books.

Bell, E. L. J. E., Nkomo, S. M. 2001. *Our Separate Ways: Black and White Women and the Struggle for Professional Identity*. Boston: Harvard Business School Press.

Benjamin, J. 1995. *Like Subjects, Love Objects: Essays on Recognition and Sexual Difference*. New Haven, CT: Yale University Press.

Bergman, S. J. 1991. "Men's Psychological Development: A Relational Perspective." Stone Center Working Paper Series No. 48. Wellesley, MA.

Bergman, S. J., Surrey, J. L. 2004. "Couple Therapy: A Relational Approach," in *The Complexity of Connection*. Edited by Jordan, J. V., Walker, M., Hartling, L. M., pp. 167–93. New York and London: Guilford Press.

Blanchard, K., Johnson, S. 1982. *The One Minute Manager*. New York: William Morrow.

Blauner, R. 1994. "Colonized and Immigrant Minorities," in *From Different Shores*. Edited by Takaki, R., pp. 149–60. Oxford: Oxford University Press.

Boeing Frontiers. 2006. "Own Your Career." *Boeing Frontiers* 5, no. 1 (May): 10–11.

Carothers, S. C. 1990. "Catching Sense: Learning from Our Mothers to be Black and Female," in *Uncertain Terms: Negotiating Gender in American Culture*. Edited by Ginsburg, F., Tsing, A. L., pp. 232–47. Boston: Beacon.

Casellas, G. F. 2007. "Biracial Employee Who Presented Himself as White Loses Race-Discrimination Case." *DiversityInc News*, October 16.

Castile, G. 1975. "An Unethical Ethic: Self-Determination and the Anthropological Conscience." *Human Organization* 34:35–40.

Catalyst. 1999. *Creating Women's Networks*. Jossey-Bass Business & Management Series. San Francisco: Jossey-Bass.

Chancer, L. S., Watkins, B. X. 2006. *Gender, Race, and Class: An Overview*. Malden, MA: Blackwell.

Chandler, C. R. 1979. "Traditionalism in a Modern Setting: A Comparison of Anglo and Mexican-American Value Orientations." *Human Organization* 38:153–59.

Chesler, P. 2001. *Woman's Inhumanity to Woman*. New York: Plume.

Chin, J. L., Sanchez-Hucles, J. 2007. "Diversity and Leadership." *American Psychologist*, September, pp. 608–9.

Ching, A. 1998. "The Edge." *Gazette* 91, no. 68 (January 29).

CNN-Interactive. 1996. "Kevorkian Trial Poses New Legal Questions." April 1.

Cohen-Sandler, R. 2005. *Stressed-Out Girls: Helping Them Thrive in the Age of Pressure*. New York: Viking.

Cole, Y. 2006. "Who Is Apologizing for Slavery?" *DiversityInc News,* November 30.
———. 2007. "Shaquanda Cotton's Sentencing Exemplifies Rehabilitation Gone Bad." *DiversityInc News,* March 28.
———. 2008. "'Lynch Tiger Woods in a Back Alley' Gets Anchor Suspended." *DiversityInc News,* January 9.
Collins, P. H. 2000. *Black Feminist Thought: Knowledge, Consciousness, and the Politics of Empowerment,* 2nd ed. New York: Routledge.
Comas-Díaz, L., Greene, B., eds. 1994. *Women of Color: Integrating Ethnic and Gender Identities in Psychotherapy.* New York: Guilford Press.
Cross, W. E., Jr. 1987. "A Two-Factor Theory of Black Identity: Implications for the Study of Identity Development in Minority Children," in *Children's Ethnic Socialization: Pluralism and Development.* Edited by Phinney, J. S., Rotheram, M. J., pp. 117–33. Newbury Park, CA: Sage.
Curry, J. 2007. "Sheffield, Still Ever the Talker, Stands behind His Accusations." *New York Times,* August 16, pp. C15, C17.
Degler, C. N. 1980. *At Odds: Women and the Family in America from the Revolution to the Present.* Oxford: Oxford University Press.
Dewan, S., Barbaro, M. 2006. "Different Focus in Atlanta on Andrew Young's Remark." *New York Times,* August 19.
Diaz-Guerrero, R. 1975. *Psychology of the Mexican.* Austin: University of Texas Press.
———. 1987. "Historical Sociocultural Premises and Ethnic Socialization," in *Children's Ethnic Socialization: Pluralism and Development.* Edited by Phinney, J. S., Rotheram, M. J., pp. 239–50. Newbury Park, CA: Sage.
Dingfelder, S. F. 2006. "Whispers as Weapons." *Monitor on Psychology* 37 (April): 4.
Dirks, D., Rice, S. K. 2004. "Dining while Black." *Cornell Hotel and Restaurant Administration Quarterly* 45:30–47.
DiversityInc. 2006. "Church of England Apologizes for Slave Trade," *DiversityInc News,* February 11.
———. 2006. "Did Motherhood Force Elizabeth Vargas Out of Anchor Chair?" *Diversity Inc News,* May 30.
———. 2006. "Slavery Reparations Movement Getting Stronger." *DiversityInc News,* July 10.
———. 2006. "Whites-Only Scholarship Fuels Affirmative Action Debate." *DiversityInc News,* December 4.
———. 2006. "Women of Color Are Leaving Law Firms." *DiversityInc News,* August 7.
Doi, L. T. 1962. "*Amae:* A Key Concept for Understanding Japanese Personality Structure," in *Japanese Culture: Its Development and Characteristics.* Viking Fund Publications in Anthropology No. 34. Edited by Smith, R., Beardsley, R. New York: Wenner-Gren Foundation for Anthropological Research.

Dunbar, P. L. 1913. *The Complete Poems of Paul Lawrence Dunbar.* New York: Dodd, Mead & Co.

Durando, J. 2007. "Al Sharpton Opens Up about Don Imus." *DiversityInc News,* April 14.

Dyer, R. 2000. *The Matter of Whiteness: Theories of Race and Racism: A Reader.* London: Routledge.

Eagly, A., Carli, L. 2007. *Through the Labyrinth: The Truth about How Women Become Leaders.* Watertown, MA: Harvard Business School Publishing.

El Grito. 1968. "Editorial: Keep Up the Fight for Americanism." *El Grito: A Journal of Contemporary Mexican American Thought* 1(2):1.

Enciso, A. 2000. "America's Guests: The Uninvited Speakers," in *Cora Uninvited.* American Collection Educator's Web site, http://www.ncteamericancollection. org/cora_uninvited.htm#Soj.

Fels, A. 2004. *Necessary Dreams: Ambition in Women's Changing Lives.* New York: Random House.

Fenner, P. R. 1952. *Ghosts, Ghosts, Ghosts.* London: Franklin Watts.

Finney, D. April 20, 2006. "Canadian Indian Land Grab." www.greatdreams.com/ canada-land-grab.htm.

Fish, S. 2007. "But I Didn't Do It." *New York Times,* March 21.

Fletcher, M. A. 1996. "No Linkage Found in Black Church Arsons." *Washington Post,* May 22, p. A08.

Foote, G. W., McLaren, A. D. 1886. "The Christian View of Death." in *Infidel Death Beds.* Published for the Secular Society, Ltd.; London: Pioneer Press (G. W. Foot and Co.), 1886; available at http://www.infidels.org/library/historical/george_ foote/infidel_deathbeds.html#2.2.

Fuentes, C. 1988. "How I Started to Write," in *The Graywolf Annual: Multicultural Literacy,* vol. 5. Edited by Simonson, R., Walker, S. St. Paul, MN: Graywolf Press.

Gilligan, C. 1982/1993. *In a Different Voice.* Cambridge, MA: Harvard University Press.

———. 1990. "Joining the Resistance: Psychology, Politics, Girls and Women." *Michigan Quarterly Review* 29:501–36.

Goodman, E., O'Brien, P. 2000. *I Know Just What You Mean: The Power of Friendship in Women's Lives.* New York: Simon and Schuster.

Goodwin, M. H. 1991. *He-Said-She-Said: Talk as Social Organization among Black Children.* Bloomington: Indiana University Press.

———. 1993. "Tactical Uses of Stories: Participation Frameworks within Girls' and Boys' Disputes," in *Gender and Conversational Interaction.* Edited by Tannen, D., pp. 110–43. New York: Oxford University Press.

Gordon, M. M. 1964. *Assimilation in American Life: The Role Race, Religion and National Origins.* New York: Oxford University Press.

Gottlieb, M. R. 2003. *Managing Group Process.* Westport, CT: Praeger.

Greenhouse, L. 2007. "Judges Reject Diversity Plan in Two Districts." *New York Times,* June 28.

Gross, B. 1994. "The Case against Reverse Discrimination," in *Morality in Practice.* Edited by Sterba, J., pp. 255–60. Belmont, CA: Wadsworth.

Guinier, L., Carter, S. L. 1995. *Tyranny of the Majority: Fundamental Fairness in a Representative Democracy.* New York: Free Press.

Gutfeld, R. 1991. "Shades of Green: Eight of 10 Americans Are Environmentalists, at Least So They Say." *Wall Street Journal* 72:204.

Gutierrez, L. M., Lewis, E. A. 1999. *Empowering Women of Color.* New York: Columbia University Press.

Hamilton Robinson, B. 1995. *Where Is My Leading Man? A Black Woman's Guide to Man-Love and Self-Love.* Chicago: Hamilton Robinson Consultations.

Handlin, O. 1954. *The American People in the Twentieth Century.* Cambridge, MA: Harvard University Press.

Harper, G. M., ed. 1918. *President Wilson's Addresses.* New York: Henry Holt and Co.

Harris, A. 2004. *Future Girl.* New York and London: Routledge.

Harrison, P. C. 1972. *The Drama of Nommo.* New York: Grove.

Hart, A. B., Ferliger, H. R., eds. 1941. *Theodore Roosevelt Cyclopedia.* New York: Roosevelt Memorial Association.

Hartmann, H. I. 1976. Capitalism, Patriarchy and Job Segregation by Sex. *Signs: Journal of Women in Culture and Society* 1, no. 3, pt. 2 (Spring): 137–70.

Heim, P. "The Power Dead-Even Rule and Other Gender Differences in the Workplace." CorVision Media, video presentation.

Hersh, S. M. 2006. "Annals of National Security: Last Stand." *New Yorker,* July 10–17, pp. 42–49.

Higman, H. 1968. "Hypotheses on Conflict, Systemic Inertia, and Poverty." Paper presented at the Symposium on Poverty and Social Disorder, American Anthropological Association, Seattle, November 21–24, 1968.

Hill, H. 1973. "Anti-Oriental Agitation and the Rise of Working Class Racism." *Society,* January–February, pp. 43–54.

———. 1985. "Race and Ethnicity in Organized Labor: The Historical Sources of Resistance to Affirmative Action," in *Ethnicity and the Work Force, Ethnicity and Public Policy.* Edited by Van Horne, W. A., Tonnesen, T. V. Madison: University of Wisconsin System.

Holley, J. 1996. "Who Was Burning Black Churches." *Columbia Journalism Review* 35, no. 33 (September/October): 16–19.

Hong, A. 2007. "Koreans Aren't to Blame." *Washington Post,* April 20, p. A31.

Hotchkiss, S. 2002. *Why Is It Always about You?* New York: Free Press.

House, J., Robbins, C., Metzner, H. L. 1982. "The Association of Social Relationships and Activities with Mortality: Prospective evidence from the Tecumseh Community Health Study." *American Journal of Epidemiology* 116(1):123–40.

Hsu, F. L. K. 1953. *Americans & Chinese: Passage to Differences.* Honolulu: University Press of Hawaii.

Humm, M., ed. 1992. *Modern Feminisms: Political, Literary, Cultural.* New York: Columbia University Press.

Jamison, K. 1975. "Sexism as Rank Language." *Social Change Ideas and Applications, NTL Institute for Applied Behavioral Sciences* 5:2.

Jet Magazine. 1996. "At House Hearings Black Caucus Cites Urgency for End to Dixie Church Fires." *Jet Magazine,* June 10, pp. 1–2.

Jones, W. M., McKenna, J. 2002. "Women and Work-Home Conflict: A Dual Paradigm Approach." *Health Education* 102:249–59.

Jordan, J. V., ed. 1997. *Women's Growth in Diversity.* New York: Guilford Press.

———. 2004. "Relational Resilience," in *The Complexity of Connection.* Edited by Jordan, J. V., Walker, M., Hartling, L. M. New York and London: Guilford Press.

Jordan, J. V., Kaplan, A. G., Miller, J. B., Stiver, I. P., Surrey, J. L., eds. 1991. *Women's Growth in Connection.* New York: Guilford Press.

Jordan, J. V., Walker, M., Hartling, L. M, eds. 2004. *The Complexity of Connection.* New York: Guilford Press.

Kabat-Zinn, J. 1990. *Full Catastrophe Living.* New York: Delta Trade Publishing.

Kaplan, A. G. 1991. "The 'Self-in-Relation': Implications for Depression in Women," in *Women's Growth in Connection.* Edited by Jordan, J. V., Kaplan, A. G., Miller, J. B., Stiver, I. P., Surrey, J. L., pp. 206–22. New York and London: Guilford Press.

Keil, C. 1972. "Motion and Feeling in Music," in *Rappin' and Styllin' Out: Communication in Urban Black America.* Edited by Kochman, T. Urbana: University of Illinois Press.

Kim, H. S. 2002. "We Talk, therefore We Think? A Cultural Analysis of the Effect of Talking on Thinking." *Journal of Personality and Social Psychology* 83, no. 4 (October): 828–42.

Kochman, T. 1981. *Black and White Styles in Conflict.* Chicago: University of Chicago Press.

———. 1984. "The Politics of Politeness: Social Warrants in Mainstream American Public Etiquette," in *Meaning, Form, and Use in Context: Linguistic Applications, Georgetown University Round Table '84.* Edited by Schiffrin, D. Washington, DC: Georgetown University Press.

———. 1989. "Black and White Cultural Styles in Pluralistic Perspective," in *Test Policy and Test Performance: Education, Language, and Culture.* Edited by Gifford, B. R. Boston: Kluwer Academic Publishers.

Kroll, J. 1991. "Spiking a Fever: A Black-White Affair Is the Catalyst for Spike Lee's Panoramic View of a Culture in a Color Bind." *Newsweek,* June 10, p. 44.

Labaton, S. 1994. "Denny's Restaurant to Pay 54 Million in Race Bias Suits." *New York Times,* November 25.

Lamont, M., Molnar, V. 2002. "The Study of Boundaries in the Social Sciences." *Annual Review of Sociology* 28:167–95.

Lebra, T. S. 1972. "Acculturation Dilemma: The Function of Japanese Moral Values for Americanization." *Council on Anthropology and Education Newsletter* 3(1):6–13.

———. 1976. *Japanese Patterns of Behavior.* Honolulu: University Press of Hawaii.

———. 1984. *Japanese Women: Constraint and Fulfillment.* Honolulu: University of Hawaii Press.

Lee, J. S. K. 1991. "Managerial Work in Chinese Organizations in Singapore." *Human Organization* 50:188–93.

Leibovich, M. 2008. "Rights vs. Rights: An Improbable Collision Course." *New York Times,* January 13.

Lemann, N. 2007. "Reversals." *New Yorker,* July 30, pp. 27–28.

Lever, J. 1976. "Sex Differences in the Games Children Play." *Social Problems* 23:478–87.

Lewis, D. 1975. "The Black Family: Socialization and Sex Roles." *Phylon* 36(3):221–37.

Liebes, T., Katz, E. 1990. *The Export of Meaning: Cross-Cultural Readings of Dallas.* New York: Oxford University Press.

Lincoln, E. L. 2007. "Banning the 'N' Word: At Least Ann Coulter Is Upfront about Bigotry," in *DiversityInc News,* March 8.

———. 2007. "The N-Word Double Standard: Why Imus Burned Where Rappers Thrive." *DiversityInc News,* April 29.

Linder, D. O. 2001. "The Trials of the Los Angeles Police Officers in Connection with the Beating of Rodney King," in *Famous Trials.* Edited by Linder, D. O. Kansas City: University of Missouri–Kansas City School of Law.

Liu, E. 1998. *The Accidental Asian.* New York: Random House.

Martin, S. 2007. "Women Leaders: The Labyrinth to Leadership." *Monitor on Psychology* 38 (July/August): 7.

McAdoo, H. P., ed. 1988. *Black Families,* 2nd ed. Newbury Park, CA: Sage.

McGhee, B. 2006. "Andrew Young Resigns from Walmart Post." *Associated Press,* August 18.

McGoldrick, M., ed. 1998. *Re-Visioning Family Therapy.* New York: Guilford Press.

McKintosh, P. 1990. "White Privilege: Unpacking the Invisible Knapsack." *Independent School,* Winter, pp. 31–36.

McLuhan, M. 1967. *The Medium Is the Massage: An Inventory of Effects.* New York: Random House.

Meijer, I. C., de Bruin, J. 2002. "Gender Gossip and Ethnic Ethics: A Comparative Approach towards Soap Opera Talk." Amsterdam School of Communication Research, www.portalcommunication.com/ben2002/_eng/programme/prog_indpapers/c/pdf/c002_coste.pdf.

Memmi, A. 1957. *The Colonizer and the Colonized.* Boston: Beacon Press.

Miller, J. B. 1988. "Connections, Disconnections, and Violations," in Stone Center Working Paper Series No. 33. Wellesley, MA.

———. 1991. "The Development of Women's Sense of Self," in *Women's Growth in Connection.* Edited by Jordan, J. V., Kaplan, A. G., Miller, J. B., Stiver, I. P., Surrey, J. L., pp. 11–33. New York and London: Guilford Press.

———. 1991. "Women and Power," in *Women's Growth in Connection.* Edited by Jordan, J. V., Kaplan, A. G., Miller, J. B., Stiver, I. P., Surrey, J. L., pp. 197–205. New York and London: Guilford Press.

Mooney, N. 2005. *I Can't Believe She Did That! Why Women Betray Other Women at Work.* New York: St. Martin's Press.

Murray, A. 1971. *The Omni-Americans.* New York: Discus.

Newton, L. 1973. "Reverse Discrimination Is Unjustified." *Ethics* 83:308–12.

Olen, J., Barry, V., ed. 1989. *Applying Ethics.* Belmont, CA: Wadsworth.

Pipher, M. 1994. *Reviving Ophelia.* New York: G. P. Putnam's Sons.

Reisman, K. 1974. "Noise and Order," in *Language in Its Social Setting.* Edited by Gage, W. Washington DC: Anthropology Society of Washington.

Reitman, M. 2006. "Uncovering the White Place: Whitewashing at Work." *Social and Cultural Geography* 7, no. 2 (April):267–82.

Reynolds, D. 1982. *The Quiet Therapies: Japanese Pathways to Personal Growth.* Honolulu: University of Hawaii Press.

Rich, A. 1983. "Compulsory Heterosexuality and Lesbian Existence," in *The Signs Reader: Women, Gender and Scholarship.* Edited by Abel, E., Abel, E. K. Chicago: University of Chicago Press.

Rincon, E. L., Keys, C. B. 1982. "The Latina Social Service Administrator: Developmental Tasks and Management Concerns." *Administration in Social Work* 6, no. 1 (Spring): 47–58.

Roth, P. 2001. *The Human Stain.* New York: Vintage.

Santiago-Rivera, A. L., Arredondo, P., Gallardo-Cooper, M. 2002. *Counseling Latinos and La Familia: A Practical Guide,* vol. 17, *Multicultural Aspects of Counseling.* Thousand Oaks, CA: Sage.

Sax, L. 2005. *Why Gender Matters.* New York: Broadway Books.

seniorjournal.com. 2007. "AARP Survey: Boomer Population Redefines 'Sandwich Generation.'" July 3.

Seventeen. 2004. "Are You Too Competitive?" Fall, p. 83.

Slater, P. 1970/1976. *Pursuit of Loneliness.* Boston: Beacon.

Sowell, T. 1990. *Preferential Policies: An International Perspective.* New York: William Morrow.

Spock, B. 1988. *Dr. Spock on Parenting: Sensible, Reassuring Advice for Today's Parent.* New York: Pocket.

———. 2004. *Dr. Spock's Baby & Child Care,* 8th ed. New York: Pocket.

Spock, B., Stein, M. T. 2001. *Dr. Spock's The First Two Years: The Emotional and Physical Needs of Children from Birth to Age 2.* New York: Pocket.

Staff, P. R. 2007. "'Multi-Minding' Women and the Marketing Challenge." *Pink Magazine,* December/January.

Stevens, E. P. 1973. "Marianismo: The Other Face of Machismo in Latin America," in *Female and Male in Latin America.* Edited by Pescatelo, A. Pittsburgh: University of Pittsburgh Press.

Surrey, J. L. 1991. "Eating Patterns as a Reflection of Women's Development," in *Women's Growth in Connection.* Edited by Jordan, J. V., Kaplan, A. G., Miller, J. B., Stiver, I. P., Surrey, J. L., pp. 237–49. New York and London: Guilford Press.

Sussman, M. B., Romeis, J. C. 1982. "Willingness to Assist Elderly Parents: Responses from United States and Japanese Families." *Human Organization* 41:256–59.

Tannen, D. 1990. *You Just Don't Understand: Women and Men in Conversation.* New York: Ballantine.

———, ed. 1993. *Gender and Conversational Interaction.* New York: Oxford University Press.

Tucker, S. H. 1994. "Black Women in Corporate America: The Inside Story," in *Black Enterprise,* August, pp. 1–8.

Ueda, K. 1974. "Sixteen Ways to Avoid Saying 'NO' in Japan," in *Intercultural Encounters with Japan.* Edited by Condon, J. C., Saito, M. Tokyo: Simul Press.

Visconti, L. 2006. "Ask the White Guy: Why Do You Have All the Answers?" *DiversityInc News,* December 7.

Walters, J. M., Sumwalt, R. L., III. 2000. *Aircraft Accident Analysis: Final Reports.* New York: McGraw Hill.

Walzer, M. 1983. *Spheres of Justice.* New York: Basic Books.

Weingarten, K. 1994. *The Mother's Voice: Strengthening Intimacy in Families.* New York: Guilford Press.

Weisz, J., Rothbaum, F. M., Blackburn, T. C. 1984. "Standing Out and Standing In: The Psychology of Control in America and Japan." *American Psychologist* 39:955–69.

Wheeler, T. 1996. "'Fires of Hate' Kindle National Fightback: Leaders Vow to End Racist Wave of Church Arson." *People's Weekly World,* July 20.

Wong, B. 1987. "The Role of Ethnicity in Enclave Enterprises: A Study of Chinese Garment Factories in New York City." *Human Organization* 46:120–30.

Yamada, M. 1983. "Asian Pacific American Women and Feminism," in *This Bridge Called My Back: Writings by Radical Women of Color.* Edited by Moraga, C., Anzaldúa, G. New York: Kitchen Table.

Zimmerman, M. 1985. *How to Do Business with Japan.* New York: Random House.

Index